MATTIE JO COWSERT

GOD, SEX, and RICH PEOPLE

A Recovering Evangelical Testimony

First Edition

THE HOLY BIBLE, NEW INTERNATIONAL VERSION®, NIV® Copyright © 1973, 1978, 1984, 2011 by Biblica, Inc.® Used by permission. All rights reserved worldwide.

Cover design by Matthew J. Distefano
Cover image by Claire Forrest
Interior Layout by Matthew J. Distefano

Print ISBN 978-1-964252-05-6
Electronic ISBN 978-1-964252-06-3

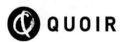 QUOIR

Published by Quoir
Chico, California
www.quoir.com

CONTENTS

For my "seester," Ashley

ACKNOWLEDGMENTS

As you can see from the length of this book, brevity is not my forte. Not to mention, I have a lot of anxiety about leaving people out in general. So just know, I have so much more to thank each and every person for than there is space in my typesetting budget. So, if I left you out or I left out a reason to thank you here, I'll just tell you in person, K?

Thank you to ...

Mark and Val, my parents, for always emboldening me to think and speak for myself, even if you disagree with what I'm thinking and speaking. To Dad, for laughing the loudest at all of my jokes, giving me the false confidence that got me to this very moment of releasing a book with all my own jokes. And to Mom, for giving me the funny gene that makes Dad laugh. Thanks for having premarital sex at Bible college, thus beginning an amazing legacy in the form of your religiously rebellious (revolutionary!) offspring.

Brodder Derek, for giving me wisdom I carry beyond this book. To "seester" Ashley for being a hot mess (jk, jk). Actually, thanks for joining the Kanakult. And then unjoining the Kanakult, consequently inspiring my oversharing. To "bigster" Krischanda for having zero reason to have your shit together, but somehow you still do enough to have really awesome, insightful, teaching-full conversations when I need them. Thank you all for being examples to your baby sister in your own beautiful, hilariously specific ways.

Bree, my eight-month super-shy subletter turned seven-year roommate and beloved best friend. From hearing me scream at my computer during grueling writing sessions, to organizing my Amazon returns post–*God, Sex, and Rich People* pilot production, to being a beta reader, to being *the reason* life in New York was livable when it really should not have been. I could not have asked for a better emergency contact until I met Ken (who arguably is less capable of this position, if you want the role back). I know you don't believe in God, but I'm grateful every day for the divine design that brought us two unlikely characters together.

My beta readers, for your time and feedback. I do not take the fact that you read a 420-page manuscript lightly! To every author friend I miraculously made in this process, for answering all my questions, from typesetting to turning down publishers. Thank you for your patience.

Every single blog reader who has shared and followed and sent me sweet messages about how much you love my writing, your encouragement is the reason I found this love for storytelling via words (and curse words).

Nikól Rogers, the creative career coach who helped me start paving this creative path for myself in 2018, you are the best investment I've made in my life to date.

My book team! Editor Liz, *you are a godsend*. Thank you for making this book so much better than I ever could. For the little encouraging comments alongside edits, like when you said you would stitch a quote of mine on a pillow and sell it on Etsy. Matthew J. Distefano, for the book cover art; Claire Forrest, for the amazing photography; and Teresa and Jessica—my publicists—who helped get this book into the hands of anyone who needs it! To Heather Hamilton, for introducing me to Keith and Matthew at Quoir, who ultimately finished out my publishing journey! All the magic of these incredible people that brought this vision together.

Every friend I made in my early twenties in New York City, who were once just in Brooklyn but now spread out all over the globe—Olivia, Chris, Tia, Kim, Heather, Jenna, Alex—thank you for loving me through my Mattie-Jo-in-Manhattan mess.

Ken, the love of my life I found while continuing to love my life, thank you for making a space for me in your home office where I could complete this book, three months after we met. For always encouraging me, and constantly telling me what a great butt I have. I love looking back at all the ridiculous dating stories and personal development woes that led me into your exceptionally muscular arms. Thank you for having zero religious knowledge, so when I tell you stories about how I grew up, you confirm it's as weird as I suspect. I love you so very much but I'll never forgive you for being funnier than me.

My therapist, Patrick. You are 10,000 percent the reason I am the woman I am today, and I can't wait to write my next book about our time together. Hopefully, with some of your commentary and fancy words.

Andrew, for making me one of the very few non-rich kids to live in an actual rent-controlled apartment. (Not rent stabilized; I know the difference!) And continuing to connect me with owners of buildings you know throughout the city so I can live in great apartments without broker fees to this day.

Liz and James, for funding my dreams for the last two years so I could actually make this book a reality. For letting me use your home for PR meetings, editing sessions, and zone 2 cardio while working on more book stuff. Your generosity is unmatched, and I remain in awe of it even as I write this (from your guest home on Martha's Vineyard, lol).

Every rich-ass family who let me utilize my maternal midwestern skills to take care of their kids so I could pay my rent. Who let me eat their fancy private-chef-cooked organic food to offset the cost of paying for my own groceries. Who took me to Broadway shows, concerts, introduced me to celebrity icons, former presidents, and private-jet travel. Who allowed me to enjoy life of luxury by proxy even though I am a humble artistic plebe.

And finally, Jesus. Without you causing so much fucking drama in your short lifetime, my story would not exist. I am releasing this book, ironically, at the same age you died (thirty-three), and I can't think of a better way to celebrate my Jesus year than making this dream you inspired come true! But for real, I am really sorry that, for all you went through, history has landed you in a place where American nationalists think you like them (we know you love them blah-blah, but you don't like *like* them). And I want you to know I still love you, because I realize all the bullshit associated with your name isn't exactly your fault. I hope in Heaven everyone is very okay with you not being white (and knows Mary Magdalene was totally your gf).

PREFACE

BEFORE TERMS LIKE "EXVANGELICAL," "deconstruction," or "purity culture" were a thing, I started sharing the stories of my religious and overall identity implosion in 2015 in my very first public blog entitled *God and the Gays*. Before "Evangelical" was a household term thanks to Donald Trump and his supporters. Before large numbers of millennials started speaking out about the trauma from our Evangelical purity-culture years that permeated every aspect of our lives. Before I recognized or even truly saw the extent of my own trauma. Before I understood the extent to which Evangelical purity culture saturates every bit of American culture via the poison of the patriarchy.

Before all o' that, I shared my Recovering Evangelical stories.

Stories make us feel less alone. On my "Recovering Evangelical Journey"—finishing bottles of wine by myself before a 5 a.m. audition for the nonunion tour of *Fiddler* in Midtown; washing down Plan B with French fries for the too many–eth time because *What even is birth control? They didn't teach us that in my abstinence-only education*—I would have loved to feel less alone.

So, if I don't say it enough after this: You are not alone. You are part of the niche-but-actually-rather-large group of emotionally, sexually, and spiritually confused grown-ups trying to unconfuse ourselves. We are the Recovering Evangelicals. Huzzah!

What does "Recovering Evangelical" even mean? The funny thing about being a Recovering Evangelical is, if you are one, you hear the term, laugh, and immediately say, "Yup." We know what it means without really having to define it.

If you're *not* a Recovering Evangelical, I hope this introduction gives you context for what that means and also demonstrates that this book can be a helpful tool to unfuck yourself from all the patriarchy garbage that has been dumped on you and seeped into you (how's that for a visual!).

Though there is an actual academic definition, in this book I use the term "Evangelical" as a catchall term for the culture in which Jesus is not just some dude above the baptismal on a stained-glass window or crucifix; Jesus is someone, a *real being*, with whom you share or once shared a deep, intimate relationship.

Other important markers of the Evangelical experience are:

1. Obsession with sexual purity

2. Adherence to strict traditional gender roles

3. (Mostly) Literal translation of the New Testament and whichever parts of the Old Testament support their particular view of God

4. Converting non-Christians to Christianity, because Jesus as the savior of the world is absolute, infallible truth

Given this definition, even if you identify as Catholic, Orthodox, or any of the innumerable Protestant denominations—if Jesus was a figure who consciously and unconsciously stuck his lil' holy nose in every part of your life—you are included in my definition of Evangelical.

Because this masterful manipulation system seeps into every part of the Evangelical, the "getting out" requires the dismantling and reconstructing of self. Escaping certain ideals, beliefs, and behaviors cannot be accomplished by simply "getting out" of a community, church, or condescending small group.

Even if you leave your church, town, and/or your relationship with a worship pastor who you later found out is "addicted to porn" ... you're still there. With a mess of beliefs and behaviors to sift through and decide what are truly yours and which were feared upon you.

This effort is nuanced and messy, and it requires:

- A deep, unwavering commitment to prioritizing and listening to yourself after years of hearing you must be selfless.

- Trusting your brain, logic, and feelings to work together in guiding you, when you were taught to "lead with faith alone."

- Being able to accept you don't actually know the answers after a lifetime of believing you possessed "absolute truth."

- Giving yourself the radical grace you learned only God could provide.

- Understanding that your wants and desires are not bad. *You* are not bad.

- Realizing that you can replace a love outside of you—God and/or a husband—with love for yourself.

- Accepting the professional help of a *real-life therapist*. (Not a Christian counselor. You cannot heal from an abuser if the abuser is your healer.)

Maybe you're thinking, *WTF, Mattie Jo?! I don't know how to do any of that!*

Fair. That's a lot to ask of a person who has been taught original sin and self-abandonment as a lifestyle choice. So, let's just start with the most important practice throughout all this: prioritizing and trusting yourself.

Regardless of what they taught us in church, there is a difference between being a heartlessly selfish asshat who completely disregards everyone else's feelings and being a self-prioritizing person, honoring your own feelings and needs so you can stop living in constant suffering.

It will feel icky. And, at times, your friends and family will probably make you feel like you're a heartless bag of dicks for listening to your deeper knowing over cultural and societal expectations. But you must keep listening. You are not a bag of dicks.

Furthermore, it turns out we Recovering Evangelical ladies, who wore purity rings, wrote letters to our future husbands at middle school sleepovers, and kept lists of our sexual activity to report to our Bible study leader, priest, future fiancé ... we are not alone in this unfucking ourselves in grown-up times.

On my storytelling journey, I've found that regardless of gender expression, current religious affiliation, previous religious affiliation, income, or relationship status—whether you were raised by a single mom or two great dads; attended private liberal high school in Portland, Oregon; or dated LAX bros in Portland, Maine—if you are a woman, I guarantee you have some internalized shit to work out in regards to your identity as a woman, your sexual expression, and the very nuanced ways we center our existence around straight men.

I also acknowledge that women are not the only ones affected by the cellular and cultural poison of the patriarchy.

I know some of y'all think the patriarchy is a group of white men who buzz-cut-headed, bra-burning, fuming feminists are out to kill. It's one of those culture war trigger words whose meaning is unjustifiably reduced and then weaponized across generations and political affiliations.

So let me clarify: A patriarchal society, in short, is a system of government and society in which men hold the power and women are largely excluded from it. Some people would argue that America is not literally patriarchal, since we have come a long way in our political and professional inclusivity of women. Which is true!

But the patriarchy is like the wind. Even if it's not visible, it's everywhere. We *feel* it. We feel it differently in different seasons, and its severity varies based on your geographical location. Being aware of its realness helps us predict disasters. Is this metaphor working?

The point is, our country's cultural and historical roots in white male power influences all of us in sometimes blatant and sometimes very, *very* subtle ways.

America, at its core, is still hyper-male and -masculine focused. From how we conduct medical research (which is focused mostly on male bodies) to what we prioritize—devaluing rest, our emotions, and any kind of softness—we uphold men and masculinity while diminishing women and femininity.

We are all—including straight, cis men—negatively affected and robbed of our personhood in a world that insists we fit into certain roles in order to keep only certain people in power. Yes fellas, you're welcome here too.

That being said, I do refer to God as "He" a lot in this book, because familiarity. However, let it be known, I do not believe God to have a specific gender identity, and I think the popular view of God as man is just further encouraging the dominance of power by male/men/masculinity in the world.

And now, for the Evangelical skeptic who thinks this book will be full of God-smearing terms and atheist tantrums, I will explain what this book isn't: This book is not a universal, tyrannical, angry effort to make everyone reject Christianity. No, no. I pinky promise you; I have zero investment in your religious affiliation.

What I do have an investment in, however, is your religious experience. I am deeply concerned with freeing you of the noise that Jesus culture—a culture where everything is influenced by the Evangelical representation of Jesus—has buried you in over the years. I am interested in pulling you out of the shame-rubble and into living, truly, your most abundant life.

Basically, I am here to help you Marie Kondo your relationship with God.

I would also like to state that I am not an expert on religious- or sexual-trauma therapy. I am simply a thirty-year-old woman who spent the first twenty-two years of life as an Evangelical in rural Missouri and the past eight years as an actor in New York City unfucking myself from the layered trauma bestowed upon me by the first twenty-two years. And I want to share a little bit of that unfucking process.

That being said, though I don't go into detail about my experience with rape-and-sexual-trauma therapy in this book because I believe that's another book entirely, I am a huge proponent and advocate for anyone who has lived through Evangelicalism and Purity Culture to get professional help in the form of a sexual trauma therapist.

As you read, reflect, wreck, and reconstruct (an almost alliteration!), remember:

Do not abandon yourself.

You are recovering beautifully.

You are not a heartless bag of dicks.

P.S. — I've included fun little Jesus-culture terms in the back of the book, like a little Christianese glossary, à la *Revolve Bible for Teen Girls* (remember those?) for us Recovering Evangelicals to laugh at and to further explain certain Evangelical-specific terms to the non-Evangelicals.

PART ONE

My Testimony

1

SUNDAYS

I AM TWENTY-TWO YEARS old, visiting New York City for the last time before I'll officially move here. In a few short months I will be able to call myself a real New Yorker! But for now, I am still Mattie Jo from Missouri, and I've just done the ultimate no-no as a self-proclaimed woman of God who has a sincere and personal relationship with Jesus Christ.

I just *P-in-the-V sexed* before marriage.

I peek over the giant body pillow placed between me and a basically stranger with whom I'd just had sex for the very first time while wearing the purity ring my pastor father had gifted me on my fifteenth birthday. It's 4 a.m. on a Sunday. I should be too hungover from my debauchery the night before to get out of bed this early, but I am not. Because I am twenty-two.

Time to get the eff outta here.

I slip on the shoes purchased from my hometown Walmart and quietly walk out of a Lower East Side apartment (that costs more per month than a semester's tuition at my state school) into the uncharacteristically quiet New York City streets. *Only commuting construction workers and harlots like me get to experience this New York.*

I quickly Google "can you get pregnant if you use a condom?" My screen populates no concrete information, but there are ads for Plan B.

I walk to the only twenty-four-hour pharmacy I know of—the Times Square Duane Reade—and hope whoever unlocks the Plan B isn't, like, visibly Muslim or Jewish or some other "Abrahamic and just as judgy to premarital sex having" person.

3

I internally fume at the price of Plan B, buy it anyway, then wash it down with some twenty-four-hour Times Square McDonalds fries and Diet Coke.

This is not how I am used to spending my Sundays.

Every Sunday for as long as I can remember before coming to New York was spent in church.

My earliest memories involve reluctantly peeling my eyes open from my little-girl deep-dreaming crusty crusts only to spend a morning scurrying around my three older siblings, trying to dodge my mom combing relentless knots out of the hair I refused to cut, looking for a dress she approved of that didn't make me look like a "ragamuffin," and hand-me-down tights that actually fit.

Eventually, after I lied about brushing my teeth and worried a little bit that I'd go to Hell for lying (so I'd ask for forgiveness at the altar call later), we'd all pile in the station wagon or minivan (whichever was working properly), hungry (because we were waiting for the donuts that would be served during fellowship hour, duh) and smelly-breathed, waiting on my dad—the most non-punctual pastor there ever was—to drive us to a building filled with Jesus and old people.

A few months before my virginity-losing ceremony on the Lower East Side, I'd been fervently praying for God to help provide me the resources to move to New York, and spending all my free brain space memorizing as much encouraging scripture I could and all my free time on the elliptical reading a book written by a nun about how to battle depression via the Holy Spirit.

So ... *How did I get here?* On a bench saturated with pigeon shit and *sin*, enjoying my Plan B–French fry–Diet Coke breakfast?

So glad you asked.

2

IN THE BEGINNING

MY ROOTS IN EVANGELICAL culture are as deep as my roots in America. (My dad says, "Well, your roots are more steeped in revivalist Baptist culture than Evangelical culture but that's a different book so just go with it! LOL.")

My maternal great-grandfather was a first generation American who became a Baptist preacher. My paternal great-grandfather was also a Baptist preacher, and both of my grandfathers became Baptist preachers. My dad ended up also becoming a Baptist preacher which made my mom a preacher's kid who became a preacher's wife, thus giving birth to four preacher's kids whose existences will involuntarily be influenced by the Baptists forever and ever amen.

This shit is literally in my DNA.

I was born the youngest of four children in southern Indiana, where we lived until I was five. My father worked at a General Baptist (which is a real denomination—different from First or Second Baptists—not like, "basically Baptist") college where both of my parents—and both of my grandfathers—received their degrees. I'm still a little confused about what the General Baptists believe, but I know we weren't allowed to drink alcohol or dance.

I didn't care much about the drinking, because I was five. But *dancing*? Where is your expression of joy, people?! Not sneaking VH1 music videos in the morning before school, clearly. Even then I knew they were a bunch of wet blankets, those General Baptists.

My father eventually left the college in Indiana to become a pastor at a church in Missouri because of its proximity to our favorite vacation spot—Branson, Missouri. Who doesn't want to spread the word of the Lord while basically on vacation year-round?

Branson is an easy vacation spot to sell to Evangelicals. If Nashville and Vegas made a baby who, instead of loving gambling, strippers, and bachelorette parties, loved Jesus, veterans, and all-you-can-eat pizza buffets, you'd have Branson.

Branson is the definition of "good clean fun." In fact, at our favorite Branson theme park, set in an 1800s mining town—Silver Dollar City—there is a saloon show. At the top of the show, the "floozies" (don't worry, they are not actual sex workers! They're just dressed in 1800s cave town sexy clothes) sing a song entitled "Good Clean Fun" to reassure the audience this is not an actual 1800s strip club, and the bar only serves root beer floats.

The point is, people who love Jesus and have lots of kids but can't afford Disney World *love* Branson. My family was one of those "Branson fan" families.

But we didn't actually live *in* Branson. We lived in the poorer, less-theme-park-having next-door neighbor of Branson, Hollister. Yes, Hollister like the store. But think, less overwhelming fragrances and puka-shell necklaces, more meth and overwhelming poverty.

When my father left his job at the no-dancing-or-drinking college, and entered THE MINISTRY, this promptly gave me and my siblings the fraught role of "preacher's kids" and my mom the even more fraught role of "preacher's wife."

While being in a preacher's family is typically brimming with all kinds of escalated pressures about morality and acceptable behavior (see: *Footloose*), in my family much of that pressure was mitigated by the fact that my father is a stand-up man whose faith is genuinely founded on keeping goodness in the world, not being a power-hungry misogynist. And my mother was an unapologetic introvert who had no interest in being a preacher's wife.

Mom loved Dad but did not love church people. Her years spent around them as a preacher's kid created a strong distaste for the judgment and shame she felt from a community that was supposed to be supportive. Dad didn't become a preacher's kid until later in life, after his father's transformation to sobriety, so he didn't experience that same distaste.

So when Dad answered The Call[1] (he began college as a business major), Mom broke off their engagement.

Mic drop, Mom!

"I grew up a preacher's kid and I didn't want to relive that life or bestow it upon my kids. But ..." she goes on, "In time, I realized I loved your dad for the man he was, not for his job title. I knew your dad's character and how much he loved me. He'd listen to me if I told him I wouldn't do the preacher's wife rigamarole."

They got back together and promptly got pregnant—'cause break up sex—at their super conservative Bible college.

Purity panic!

As you can imagine, being pregnant before their wedding caused both of them to experience their fair share of spiritual side-eye from fellow Christian friends and family.

I think because my parents experienced the "struggle" of sexual purity, combined with enduring shame and judgment from Christians, they doubled down on shame and judgment not being the voice of God in our family. They felt they knew a God of love and grace, so that's what we learned at home. Those qualities, above all else, were the qualities of Christians they taught us to be.

That being said, Mom and Dad were not perfect in their execution of sexual education—after all, they still very much upheld marriage as the only relationship where true, healthy romantic love and intimacy can be experienced. Mom sprinkled personally unsettled, projected slut-shaming onto her daughters by saying things to us like "Just don't be a slut like I was in high school!" *but* they did their due diligence in making sure their children felt empowered as individuals to ask questions, think for ourselves, know a God who loved all of us exactly as "He" created us.

Despite their commendable efforts, I was still a preacher's kid and being a preacher's kid meant I spent *a lot* of my development hours, days, years ... in church, on the playground of the church, attempting to take baths in the baptismal of that church, at a retreat the church was hosting; which meant I was bound to absorb some of the fucked-up Evangelical rhetoric.

I became a Christian, verbally, when I was eight years old. I asked my father from the back of our minivan if I could get *saved*. My grandmother had just passed away, so I was suddenly very aware that death could occur at any time. I didn't want to be sent to hell should I choke on a gummy bear or whatever other risky things eight-year-olds do. I needed to be prepared!

We had a brief conversation about what "getting saved" meant. From my kiddie brain understanding, I accepted Jesus into my heart, which meant He was now with me forever. No getting anything around this guy! If I was mean to a kid at recess, He'd know. If I was dishonest about eating toppings off my fro-yo before we weighed it, He'd know. If I sneakily ripped out all the photos of Taylor Hanson from the J-14 magazine my sister just bought, He'd know. This lack of privacy seemed like a total bummer. But hell sounded worse, so I complied.

After getting saved in the minivan (the title of my next memoir), we held a baptism ceremony for me in the pool at a health club, because our church at the time didn't have a baptismal and the eternal paradise show must go on (and on, and on ...), where one of my granddad pastors did the honors of welcoming me officially into the family. *Of Christ!*

Other than a fear of eternal damnation before I could even spell "eternal" or "damnation," I can't remember actively having an opinion about church/God until around fifth grade. The Evangelical community was slowly making its way toward establishing a fun church, with modern music and children's programs advanced beyond Noah and the Ark on a felt board. Christian music that wasn't entirely terrible, such as DC Talk, Stacie Orrico, and Lecrae, started to appear. Being an Evangelical Christian was, at least in my world, becoming the cool-kid thing to do.

My father moved through multiple ministry jobs throughout my elementary years. As my mom predicted, Dad had zero job security in ministry, as his role was basically to make bored people feel more excited about the life they might have when they die and protect them from people and ideas that make them uncomfortable while they're alive. I don't think Dad was very good at either of those things. He was more about challenging congregations to be better people on earth, welcoming those who make us a little—or a lottle—uncomfortable. Sort of like this guy named Jesus. Maybe you've heard of him?

Anyway, by the time I hit junior high, Dad took a break from ministry and, with no experience whatsoever, got a job at an advertising firm.

While dad was there, we started attending a new, cool, nondenominational church, The Stream.

Nondenominational didn't mean we were super open to all religions. No, no, we weren't Universalists! We just didn't follow the beliefs of any specific *Christian* denomination. I think nondenom churches were founded mostly as an effort to continually modernize the church experience without having to have a vote every time they wanted to hire a pastor with tattoos or something. We didn't need church hierarchy to follow Jesus. We had the Bible!

Nondenom churches claim to be "Bible-based." Even though saying your church is "Bible-based" is cryptic and means different things to different people, in the case of The Stream, it meant the Bible was our sole authority. Looking to any other person or book as authority from God was unacceptable. In fact, it was downright un-Christian.

If nondenoms had a creed, it would be "We don't need a creed!" and then they would say (but not in tandem) "We do not concern ourselves with nonsensical organized church stuff like liturgy." *Please.*

I learned that rules and religion were useless when it came to pleasing God. God cared most about our personal relationship with Jesus Christ, so we should spend all of our energy on developing that relationship, not "following rules of religion." And people who did just "follow the rules"—like Catholics or any sort of "dogmatic" religion—weren't "real Christians."

Not having to follow strict rules sounded very appealing and way more fun than the no dancing no drinking churches of my yesteryear, so I was pretty sold on this brand of Christian.

Also, nondenoms were *cool.*

This super-cool church building wasn't embellished with art and stained glass like other churches. It was meant to be functional because it was there to build the Kingdom of God, not be "flashy."

The sanctuary doubled/tripled as a gymnasium and rock-climbing facility. We had a sick worship band, complete with a sound and lighting system that was better than that of my college theater department. The irony that my "not flashy" church didn't invest in embroidered robes for priests, iconic Mary art, or precious-metal chalices but instead rock-climbing walls, basketball courts, and computer-operated spinny stage lights is not lost on me.

We hosted concerts by Christian rock bands and had an in-house sketch writing team. Every Christmas we held an event called Coffee House that was basically a jingle-ball for Jesus. This was our biggest "outreach event" of the year.

Outreach events are designed to coerce potential converts by means of relatability, not exclusivity (like those denomination-having churches). Free food, "good" music, fun activities, palatable/nonaggressive sermons, and no memorized prayers (because we didn't want to make newcomers feel out of place by not knowing the church script) are just a few of the tactics. Oh, and as a Christian, being really, *really* nice to anyone you don't recognize. Afterall, being #JustLikeJesus means smiling a lot for no reason.

Anyway, at my *nondenom-super-cool-church* building you could chant cultish worship reprises, convert people with Panera pastries, *and* belay on! I mean, the efficiency! My church was so cool, my parents didn't have to force teenage me to go. I *wanted* to be there.

After a few years of falling absolutely in love with a church that seemed nothing like the previous churches we'd experienced as a family, my dad was offered the job as community pastor (made the church feel like a community, not just a place people show up to on Sundays, got people "plugged into" groups in the same age group, etc. ... to meet weekly for a Christian book or Bible study, time to hang out, be friends in Christ, ya know. Build community). He was on staff at that church for fifteen years.

My family loved our new church. It was our home.

By high school, I told people my favorite place in the world was my church. I looked forward to Wednesday night small group,[2] Friday morning school small group, leading Tuesday morning junior high girls' small group, and Sunday morning service to end a long week of managing being a hormonal teenager and devout follower of Christ via so many small groups.

Church was where I went through my first twelve-step program for my eating disorder. It's where I learned to prioritize a quiet, meditative time with the divine before I started my day. It's where I learned to always look out for the person who is being excluded and make sure they feel welcome. It's where I learned the responsibility of service to our community as nonnegotiable Christlike behavior.

Church is where I decided to develop my personal relationship with God by spending time with him everyday in prayer, reading scripture, and by leading a countercultural life.[3]

Instead of partying, I spent weekends clearing people's yards in rural Oklahoma after a major ice storm or watching High School Musical for the umpteenth time while baking cupcakes.

My senior year, instead of going on a trip to Daytona Beach like a normal Midwestern high schooler, I went to Honduras and laid the foundation for an orphanage.

When a sweet baseball-player boy who had a big crush on me showed up at my house unannounced to apologize for drunk-calling me the night before, I told him he couldn't come in. "My parents aren't home and I have created a boundary for myself of no boys if my parents aren't home." This young man agreed to go on a walk with me where I told him I didn't think we were compatible because someone who would get drunk at a party they threw while their parents were gone did not have the kind of character I was looking for in a husband. We were fifteen.

Super-cool church is where I became a *real* Christian.

Ultimately, I am grateful for church being the place where I developed a respect for something beyond me that was a foundation of my existence. Instead of the typical teenage girl experience of an *emotionally-un-*

hinged-slinging-hormones-at-football-players traipse through puberty, I learned to acknowledge the mystery and deeper meaning of the divine, utilize collective support, and honor personal purpose relatively early on in life.

Though committing to being counter cultural did come with doing some commendable stuff like pointing out to my health teacher that maybe it's a little fucked-up we make pregnant girls sit through abstinence class—*Can't they take a parenting course instead?*—or sitting at a different lunch table every day so as not to seem "cliquey," it also came with all the stuff that would ultimately lead to trauma processing in my adult years, including but not limited to:

- Proud purity ring wearer: I committed to no sex before marriage and *meant it.*

- Date to Marry: No dating unless the men are serious potential husband prospects.

- Strict Boundaries: I made pacts with my friends that we wouldn't go past kissing with any boys, wouldn't kiss anyone unless he was our boyfriend, and we would never date someone who wasn't *leading us spiritually.*[4]

- No Masturbating: Because even thoughts about having sex with someone outside of marriage was sinful.

- Exclusively consume Christian media: No TV, music, or books that elevated a sexual or secular lifestyle. *Fill my thoughts with things of the Lord that are worthy of praise, dear Jesus God.*

- Modest is Hottest:[5] I would not dress in a way that could cause a fellow Christian man to stumble. That meant no spaghetti straps, no shorts that weren't at least three sizes too big, and definitely no two-piece bathing suits around men of God.

As an Evangelical, all these rules were part of my faith package. If I believed Jesus died on the cross for my sins, I had to try very, very hard not to sin. I couldn't simply be a Christian *and* rock a crop top and/or date without intent to marry. I had to glorify Him in all of my life.

In my most formative years, my identity coalesced around and within all the things it meant to be a "real" Christian. My faith was not part of my life; it was my life. It was not part of me; it was me.

3

EVERYONE IS GOING TO HELL

Hello, sinner/non-Believer of sorts. I have something to share with you. Have you heard of the Bridge Analogy? Here, let me show you.

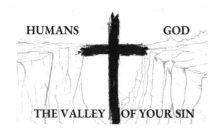

This shows you how humans are separated from God because of our sin. But not to worry (I know you were definitely worried about the valley of your sins before I unsolicitedly decided to interrupt your Blimpie lunch break to tell you about it), I have the Good News!

Jesus came to forever and finally heal the divide between God and humans by dying on the cross for our sins so we can be united with God on earth and ultimately forever in Heaven! All you have to do to be united with God is accept that Jesus is the one who forgives your sins.

Why is it called the Good News, you ask? Because in the Old Testament, there are a lot of really rigorous rules to be kept about how to get forgiveness for those sins and remain clean. Things like not eating shellfish, animal sacrificing, and putting women in isolated tents while they menstruate. Well, I guess people got tired of that, because how time consuming (and messy), so they decided to look for a Messiah who would save them from their sins once and for all. Enter: Jesus!

Now, as long as humans *actually believe* Jesus is the Messiah, son of God, and can forgive their sins, they're good to go with Big G! No more animal sacrifice and "tedious rule following" to get into heaven. Just be a Christian! That's all!

Why am I telling you this? Well:

1. Evangelicals believe it's our Christlike duty to butt into others' lives for no reason.

2. Despite sort of claiming repeatedly that Jesus would make a cosmic grand reentrance back to earth to deliver this message himself, He never did make it back. Whoopsie, Jesus.

So that's my job! To tell people Jesus's sin-forgiving, God-human-uniting Good News.

Anyway, wanna get saved?

By the time I got to junior high, I started to notice I didn't quite fit in with the other "Christ-like" girls at church. I tried to play the part of being a quiet and gentle spirit (1 Peter 3:4), but I wasn't very successful.

According to my parents, my filter just never developed. The journey between my thoughts and words was lightning fast and left many of the adults around me either laughing or face-palming.

I was curious and loud, always asking the questions I shouldn't but *Come on, everyone is thinking it, right?* Such as, "Is masturbation a sin if I'm picturing myself having sex in my wedding dress?" We love a work-around.

I was "animated," taking up a lot of space by physically entering every story I told, playing all the roles.

I won every talent show and put on plays for my family constantly. Corralling my cousins at Thanksgiving—any family gathering, really—to sing and dance as a girl band. We used craft pipe cleaners to make handless microphones à la Britney Spears. True innovation.

I was outspoken or straight up disruptive, depending on who you asked. Basically, I was a born theater kid.

Unfortunately, I was not born in the liberal Northeast where artistic types abound and flourish because they have cultured (usually rich) parents. I was born in the rural Midwest, where everyone saw me as "something else," and I saw everyone as "dreadfully boring." Since we didn't have a great theater department at my school and I wanted to do theater, I did what I do best—got creative.

My brother was accepted to USC for film writing, so I thought he might have some theater-people knowledge. Thanks to his uber-rich, Upper East Side–hailing girlfriend, Lisa (she's important; stay tuned), I learned of the top theater camps in America: French Woods Festival of the Performing Arts and Stagedoor Manor. Stagedoor had more famous alumni, but French Woods had horseback riding. I couldn't think of a better way to live out my *Bug Juice* dreams than a summer of horseback riding and musical theater, so I chose French Woods.

I spent the next six months raising $4,000 to attend one session of that theater camp.

At fifteen years old I called local businesses in my hometown and asked them for either monetary donations or physical donations I could use for a raffle. I held a car wash at Walmart, babysat, and walked dogs.

I ended up raising all the money (and more!) because God is so good and all that.

So that summer, instead of going to church camp like every other summer of my life, I spent three weeks as a preacher's kid from Taney County, Missouri, at theater camp with the coastal elite's offspring, and my life was forever changed.

Of course, I didn't know this theater camp was only for exceptionally privileged kids. I just figured it was hella expensive because any camp where we were doing activities besides prayer and being traumatized with *Left Behind*[1] screenings had to cost a lot.

It was in Upstate New York with the rich kids where I discovered there are lots of "something elses" of this world. I was in Heaven. These theater weirdos were my creative comrades!

Theater camp didn't just bring about the awareness that I was not actually *that* different and, therefore, not alone. It brought about a slew of new experiences that changed my entire life's trajectory.

I ate veggie burgers for the first time and met people from countries like Nigeria, China, and Russia who weren't adopted by Christians as a mission effort. I began my journey of healing from a terrible bout of teenage anorexia caused by incessant pressure to be desired by boys and, therefore, small. It's where I learned my passion and joy was worth battling this eating disorder for. I experienced a world bigger than Missouri, and I was going to live in that world. I was going to take up space in *that* world.

Theater camp is where I met devout Jewish people for the first time. And, after enough almost crushes, discovered most of my favorite people were (are) gay.

Wait.

Gay?

Jew ... ish?

I was in second grade when I consciously encountered my first non-Christian person. A girl in my class wore a Star of David necklace her mother had gifted her. I told this girl she needed to take it off, that it was a "witch's star." I'd recently watched *The Craft* with my older cousins and was now an expert on all things witch stuff, including the pentagram.

She explained that the pentagram and the Star of David are not the same; they don't even have the same number of points! I pushed back: "Well if it's Jewish, it's not for Jesus, and that's just as bad as being a witch! It's all Satan, so you're basically just asking to go to hell!"

By second grade, I knew absolutely nothing about Jewish people except that they don't think Jesus is the Messiah. They are still waiting, *all* these years later, for a king on earth to come save them. What idiots! Didn't they read the NeW tEsTaMeNt?!?

Later my mom did tell me it is not okay to tell Jewish people they're the same as Satan (even though that is what I had learned in church).

I was even younger when I, unbeknownst to me, encountered my first gay person; My great-uncle Phil. I'd heard utterances about Uncle Phil's sexuality from my grandmother (his sister) and other extended family. Nothing crazy. Just the usual he was "living in sin" and "going to hell." That they were praying really hard for him to stop choosing sin, because they wanted the family to be together in Heaven one day.

Sermons, youth group discussions, Evangelical literature, and members of my family all taught that being gay was very, very wrong.

Once on a church retreat, a worship pastor gave a sermon saying that America's social acceptance of gay people by legalizing gay marriage was the last step before accepting bestiality.

There's more.

God punishes this social acceptance of gayness in the form of natural disasters. Yes, according to some (probably closeted) pastors, the LGBTQ+ community—not global warming—are the cause of divine punishment. Kinda like Noah, but now God just spreads out the tragedy year after year instead of a one-time universal genocide. We trust these (probably closeted) pastors about science because they have an associate's degree from a community college and attended the Kanakuk Institute.[2]

But, it's okay! All these gay people are still worthy of God's love! You can be friends with them, and you should! But please always remember, we "love the sinner, not the sin."

"Love the sinner not the sin" is the way Evangelicals justify demonizing individuals and discriminate against entire groups under the guise of love. The belief is that you can love a person without supporting their "lifestyle choice" or agreeing with any of their fundamental beliefs. They're worthy of God's love, sure, but God is still sending them to hell unless they change.

This "love the sinner not the sin" thing doesn't just end with LGBTQ+ people. It applies to non-Christian people too. As followers of Christ, it is our job to impart the wisdom of God's love to our homosexual and/or non-Christian friends by letting them know, lovingly, that if they don't stop this nonsense, they'll burn in hell.

So here I am having the time of my life at theater camp, while simultaneously truly distressed over the eternal address of my new friends.

Do they know they're going to hell? I should tell them. Where's a piece of paper? I'll draw them the bridge analogy!

When I got back to Missouri, I asked my church's lead pastor about this "the gays and anyone other than Christians are going to hell" thing. I told him I loved my theater friends a whole lot. I know I'm supposed to want to ungay and save them, but suggesting for someone to change so much of who they are and what they believe, especially when it isn't really harming anyone else, didn't seem super loving. "How can I call it love if I'm only loving them in order to change them?"

His response was that gay people *are* harmful. By acting on their gay impulses, they're making earth even less Godly than it already is; they are perpetuating an unholy standard on earth! Since it is our job as Believers to create the Kingdom of God on earth, we must do our part to stop this unholiness Manifest Destiny.

He then told me a story about a gay friend of his who started coming to church and then, after a while, inexplicably, just wasn't gay anymore. Voila!

If I were witty enough back then, I would have asked if God does this magic trick in reverse. Like, if a bunch of straight guys start going to church, will they eventually become gay? Does that explain the priests?

In regards to the Jewish-people thing, he said we just have to go on loving them, plant that Jesus seed, and eventually they will come around to conversion. "There are plenty of Jews for Jesus!" he claimed anecdotally and yet so confidently. "And if they don't convert"—he breathed a deep belly full of bullshit breath—"that's their personal choice to reject the truth and they will have to suffer the consequences. That is no longer your responsibility."

By college, where I received my BFA in Musical theater and was therefore in theater camp for always, I encountered even more weirdo compadres who, turns out, were LGBTQ+. In time I learned that, regardless of my fervent prayers, my gay friends were staying gay. In fact, most of them tried to ungay themselves at some point, to no avail. "If it was a choice, do you really think I'd choose *this*?" one friend asked.

I heard story after story of my exceptionally wonderful friends experiencing deep sadness and depression over coming to terms with their sexuality. One of my closest friends cried to me after working a particularly triggering scene. "I have prayed so hard to not be gay." He shared, "If I want so badly to not be gay, why can't God do this for me? Haven't I been obedient? My heart wants to change, it does!" *Why wasn't it working?*

My friends were expressing what I know now to be trauma caused by simply wanting to *be*. Of wanting to date someone during puberty without having the hurricane blood of New Orleans residents on their hands. Of wanting to experience relationships and love without blowing up their families. Of wanting to be themselves without fear that God will hate them.

When my great-grandmother passed, Great-Uncle Phil took in his severely schizophrenic brother, who had been living with her, my uncle Terry. No one else in the family—despite being devout church attenders and some of them even pastors—was interested in the gig. No one stepped up to take Uncle Terry in except for non-church-attending gay Uncle Phil.

Uncle Terry changed after he moved in with Phil. Terry developed hobbies, had a social life, and actually *talked* to us. (Last time I visited him he told me, "Your dad, my nephew, is remarkable. *Remarkable Mark*." I wanted to cry.) Uncle Phil brought Terry back to life.

Why weren't people like my Uncle Phil good enough for God? According to this all-loving God, Phil needed to first nix the butt sex and then he could experience divinity's fullest love?

Getting to know and develop friendships with members of the LGBTQ+ community made me realize the church's inveterate sinful label of "gay" was being used to dehumanize and therefore effectively vilify a whole bunch of actual human beings. My friends are not a conversion project, but people with stories that matter, whom I deeply love. Many of them far better people than the so-called Christ followers in my life.

Admittedly, it would be a few more years before, in the name of libido and a love of Zabar's, I was surrounded by (and accidentally always interested in) Jewish men who further challenged my discriminative/Christian-centric worldview. But still. The wheels were spinning.

I started to doubt if my pastors really knew what they were talking about. My personal experience was proving one thing to be undeniably true, despite hearing repeated sermons saying the opposite was "absolute truth."

If I loved my new friends this much, how could the God who created them not love them that much more? If God can create a solar system and we call it "majestic creation," why can't He find it in His big galactic-making-heart to love and accept all iterations of goodness? If someone is a genuinely good-perpetuating person in the world, why does their sexuality or religion even matter?

If God is infinitely good and powerful, why are the margins for accessing His love so narrow?

4

BIBLICAL MARRIAGE

HERE I AM, A college freshman. I've gotten into the BFA Musical Theatre program at Missouri State University, because I went to theater
camp and knew I was destined for the *theater forever!*

I made it to college holding on to my virginity, strong and proud.
In fact, I even held an *actual* V-Card; a solid-gold card given to us in
abstinence class, signed in front of a witness, meant to be given to our
future spouse on our wedding night along with the real-deal slit swipe.
I carried this in my wallet instead of an actual credit card because I was
raised by parents who loved Jesus and Dave Ramsey.

While I was excited that majoring in musical theater would finally put
me in theater camp for always and I would no longer have to hang out
with boring people, I was more excited for the pinnacle of life college
would for sure bring: my husband.

Which I knew God would bless me with because I had agreed to the
whole purity thing and succeeded. So far ...

But after some little make-out marathons with a few football players
(and maybe soccer players? Who can know? Sports are hard) in my first
semester of sweet college life freedom, I was feeling really bad. I worried
if I kept on this path of sexual immorality, God would not give me
my desired husband by graduation. So I got together with my Bible
study leader, and we made a list of all the sexual sins I'd ever committed.
Together, we ripped up this list, prayed over it, and I started anew.

Not too long after my purity séance, I saw him—my future husband.
He was singing in the men's a cappella group on campus, and I was

immediately enamored. What can knock off puritanical lady knickers quicker than a group of college dudes singing Boyz II Men covers?

Of course, I didn't say a word to him. I just got his name from a few guys I knew in his fraternity and then crept his Facebook for all of winter break. His name was Brandon.

Let the husband background check commence!

Husband background checks are very important. I couldn't even think about unguarding my lil' Proverbs 31[1] wifey heart if I didn't know some critical information about this guy first.

1. Can he lead me spiritually?

2. Does he have a personal relationship with Jesus?

3. Is he also saving himself until marriage?

4. How many times do we think he's read Hebrews?

I would be able to tell all this from his father-son-hiking-trip Facebook photo albums, obviously.

After four long weeks of Facebook-studying this guy, I had decided we were perfect for each other. He was a junior (an older, more sophisticated man!), pre-med, athletic, liked musicals, and was religious. Also hot. So very swoony hot.

As soon as I returned from winter break, we serendipitously met at a musical theater audition. *What is he doing here?* I thought. *He's a cell and molecular biology major!* Which I knew, of course, from his Facebook.

Omg, MJ! He is here because you did that purity seance so the Lord is blessing you with the perfect opportunity to strike up a conversation!

I had managed to get myself within three feet of the guy when the audition monitor interrupted my marriage mission, announcing they were running behind. "So please keep your cuts to 16 bars!" (that's musical theater speak for make it snappy and hit your best note within 30 seconds). I saw Brandon start to panic. *This is your in, MJ!*

"Is your cut too long?" I asked.

"I ... don't really know."

"Want me to take a look?"

"Oh, umm, sure."

Then he handed me his audition book, I confirmed his song was perfectly cut, and off we went.

I did it! Thanks for this amazing opportunity, God!

I was mostly relaxed in that first conversation, but also hypervigilant in making sure I didn't reveal too many details I already knew about him:

"Cell and molecular biology huh? Oh, you went to Catholic High and you're two years older than me? My friend Charlie went to Catholic High and graduated in '07! You're in Zelda Tao Omega-Twelve?! Do you know [insert a million names]? A cappella? So, you're like a celebrity on campus. Wow, you're so interesting I didn't know any of this."

Then I invited him to breakfast at the dining hall, and he politely declined because he had to go to Mass.

Mass. What is ... Mass? Oh, Catholic church. Right.

Wait. This guy's CATHOLIC?!

Fuck.

Maybe you're thinking, "What's so bad about that? Catholics are Christian too, right?"

The answer is, yes, by definition Catholics ARE Christians, because they believe Jesus died on the cross for our sins, blah blah. Where it gets a little dicey for the Evangelicals—who are definitely in charge of judging who is a legit Christian and who is not—is that Catholics don't usually have a "personal relationship with God."

Catholics epitomized that kind of Christians nondenoms despised. The dogma obsessed, liturgy possessed, think they can just get to Heaven by "going through the motions" Christians. All the stuff we nondenom Evangelicals don't have so that we can focus on what really matters—an intimate relationship with Jesus—and feel superior to everyone else's efforts at religion. A Catholic, I assumed, just went to church, said the prayers, and called it good.

How could a person who doesn't truly practice faith, outside of Sunday Mass, lead me spiritually? Would we be equally yoked[2]? Should I have even invited him to dining hall breakfast?

So of course I said, "Oh, that's okay. Enjoy that!"

And then he asked, "But, maybe we can hang out another time? Are you on Facebook?"

EL. OH. EL.

He added me on Facebook that night, we chatted for hours, and just like after I met Jewish people and LGBTQ+ people IRL, I decided God probably didn't care *that much* if we were different brands of Christian, because this guy was smart, hot, and could sing a cappella! I put aside the Catholic-Protestant marriage anxiety for the time being, for the sake of not letting this total ten go. Brandon, I guess, also decided my being the Montague of Christians to his Catholic Capulet was not a dealbreaker. At least, for now.

Two weeks later we were bf/gf.

This happened so rapidly, I assume, because when he tried to kiss me the first time, I told him I only kiss boyfriends. Except for the football players and soccer players who I had no intention of marrying, so I didn't need to prove desirability with my leveled-up chastity boundaries. I saved my purity magnetism for the men of God.

Unlike women, who are directed to Proverbs 31, dudes don't have specific scripture telling them what they must be in order to be loved by God and by women. As far as I could tell, however, Men of God were all very committed to participating in daily Bible reading, purity culture, and a secret addiction to porn. Their presentation varied, however. A few different man of God brands:

- The screamo-loving, hardcore lead singers of Christian rock bands who will one day open for Chris Tomlin[3] if they played their cards right

- The outdoorsy, bear-fighting slack liners who are really into public service and will inevitably grow up to be stoners/advocates for ayahuasca retreats

- The Polo-outlet-wearing, really-good-at-sportsing preppy destined to be a college Republican and/or church planter (see "Missionary Positions" chapter for further explanation on this term) in areas of "crucial need" like rural Texas—and Nicaragua

Anyway, Brandon was none of these varieties, but he was still a quality MOG, which made him, like, *so super interesting.*

From the time Brandon became my boyfriend I was all in, because I knew he was My Husband. I knew God had sent him to me as a gift of the desires of my heart. According to Psalms 37:4, if you do what God asks of you, He will give you the things you want in the deepest depths of your soul, i.e., if you save yourself until marriage, He'll give you a Jesus-loving husband who is smart, likes musicals, and can sing pretty (/insert any dream-guy fantasy).

Although this was not explicitly stated in my Evangelical upbringing, it was strongly suggested that if you follow God's commands, he will bless you with all the blessings. So, naturally, I thought this whole "do good behavior, get blessedness" thing was the Human-God arrangement.

I mean, if you read the Bible (except for Job,[4] which is very confusing to the Evangelical message of "do good, get good"), that's pretty much the deal. God tells the Bible characters what to do, and if they do it, they get rewarded with winning wars (Jericho, or any of the Old Testament, really), becoming kings (David), or get entire planets to repopulate post-apocalyptic flood (Noah).

Well, I didn't want to win any wars, become king/queen, or repopulate a planet. (Honestly, this is just further proof that the Bible is painfully patriarchal. Like, *of course* the ultimate gift from God to men is repopulating a planet with their seed. All they have to do is have an orgasm to make that happen. Women, on the other hand, have to gestate, feed, and raise all those offspring. Anyway, even back then I was not interested in *that*.) I just wanted a husband so I could have sex by my mid-twenties without fear of going to hell.

I was a woman of God, getting my Biblical Marriage. This whole living-like-Christ thing didn't suck.

5

THE MOMENT YOU THOUGHT YOU WERE WAITING FOR NEW YORK, NEW YORK WAS WAITING FOR YOU

I'VE GOT MY ADORABLE going-to-turn-husband-soon-enough boyfriend. He's Catholic, and that's sort of a bummer, but he is otherwise perfect. Everything is going just as (God) planned.

That is, until a few weeks later in Voice and Movement class, when I made a declaration that would forever disrupt that Godly woman vision of my life.

Voice and Movement is a BFA class meant to help you hum, breathe, and pelvic thrust your way out of Western conditioning, so you can deeply connect with your body. At nineteen, however, it just seemed like a very eccentric "now project this rainbow onto the wall and squat deep into your solar plexus so you can become a great actor!" yoga class. I was confused, but where else could me and my purity ring get in a quality pelvic thrust? So, I went with it.

We opened every class with "Today I feel ..."

This practice was meant to give us space to connect with our feelings and speak on impulse without filtering through our brains, while simultaneously "clearing the space" for new exploration. We were learning to honor what we felt in the moment without letting it hinder creation. What'd you learn in college?

Anyway, I will take any chance to tell someone how I feel, so I loved this opening practice. One very special day, I shocked myself and shared, "Today I feel ... like going to New York City."

Like a good Midwestern musical theater lover, I'd only really been exposed to the musicals *Grease, Annie,* and *Wicked.* My parents had been telling me for years that they'd take me to see *Wicked*—since it was the only one of those three not adapted to screen—and just never got around to aligning their intentions with regional tour dates, so I decided to take myself. I was twenty years old now, after all, and basically engaged. I was a grown-ass woman, as far as my Voice and Movement feelings were concerned.

After finishing the solar-plexus-squatting, rainbow-pelvic-projection session, I left class and promptly bought a round-trip ticket to New York City for the upcoming spring break. I received an A+ in following my impulses.

I knew exactly one person in New York City. Her name was Jane, and we'd met at a theater intensive I attended in California right before my senior year of high school. She and I connected over being brooding teenagers with eating disorders and a love for bone-chillingly cold Diet Coke in a can.

Jane and I were also total opposites. She was raised by a single mom in Las Vegas and had a lesbian sister. She went to a performing arts high school and loved to say "fuck." She was also learning German, because she had a beautiful German boyfriend. Teenage Evangelical Mattie Jo lowkey wanted to be Jane.

She was studying acting at a conservatory in New York, so I asked if I could save some money by staying with her for a week. She obliged, and yet again, a fellow theater weirdo helped get me truly #saved.

We did all the New York things.

Brooklyn Bridge photos, dim sum in Chinatown, buying fake Coach purses in Little Italy, seeing concerts by cool indie bands on the Lower East Side. I saw allllll the Broadway shows. Although the shows were amazing, my weekly highlight was meeting Corbin Bleu after seeing *Billy Elliot.* He was not in *Billy Elliot*; he was in *In the Heights*, and I just shamelessly asked for a photo with him after not seeing his show.

I knew it wasn't classy, but WTF else was I gonna do? *It was Corbin Bleu*. Anway, I got a photo with Corbin Bleu, which means I basically made out with Zac Efron.

I ate hot dogs and pretzels from a cart (they're gross; save your dollars), meandered Central Park, and filmed my first sighting of Times Square, because I'm obnoxious and also, I truly wanted to capture that moment for forever.

I know it sounds horrifically cliché, but seeing Times Square was the moment I knew New York was my home. First of all, I had never in my life seen buildings that tall! Except for random giant objects sticking out of buildings in Branson, I don't think I'd seen *anything* that tall!

Who is the architect mastermind behind this?

As I looked up at those massive structures, the lights, and more humans than I'd ever seen in one place, I felt so insignificant and yet—special? Because the God of the universe had placed me exactly where I was created to be in that moment.

For most of my life, I always took up the most space. I made the most noise and unintentionally (okay, sometimes intentionally) demanded everyone's attention. In New York, I could be unintentionally or intentionally boisterous and no one would give a fuck, because I'd be competing with the naked eighty-three-year-old baton twirler asking for tips two feet from me.

It was nice to feel anonymous but still important. Tiny, but still doing big things. Ironically, in the most crowded city in America, in its most crowded location, I felt I had room to breathe. Room to grow. Expand to my potential. I could not wait to one day be part of the exciting, eclectic microcosm that is New York City.

The City was a place that had everything I didn't know my heart desired. Up until that point, I thought all I wanted in life was to be called someone's wife, glorify God by being a Proverbs 31 woman, and have lots of not-sinful married sex. Turns out, I had lots of desires in this big ol' heart that had nothing to do with a husband or Proverbs 31. But yes, definitely still lots of sex please.

I love seeing live shows whenever I want, and trying new food, even if it's shitty cart pretzels. I love being able to engage with people who are wildly different from me and actually becoming friends. I also learned I really love men in suits, shiny shoes, and fun socks—not the Midwestern styleless "college basketball Ts and cargos will do" look—of which New York City had a-plenty. And because I hate cars, I love public transportation.

I know maybe you want this to be a sudden and glamorous *Sex and the City* style sexual awakening, but that's not this chapter. During this first trip, the only titillating infidelity was my emotional affair with New York City over my love for Brandon. Every night, as I regaled him with my stories of the city, I could feel his concern. One evening he even said, in an almost jealous tone, "You really love it there, huh?"

I really did love it there.

I didn't know how to articulate it for myself at the time, but what I was experiencing was an undefined closeness to God that was specific to my Mattie Jo design. In all my worship-song sessions at retreat centers or Bible studies at Starbucks, I'd never felt like *this*. I'd never felt this alive, fully expressed, free.

Maybe I didn't need a morning devotional, to be surrounded exclusively by Christians, or to constantly consume scripture in order to feel close to God. Maybe I just needed to be in New York City with fellow theater weirdos, soaking up all the excitement and adventure the City offered by the minute.

By the end of the week, I was certain of this: Someday I would be one with this incredible city. New York was not just a desire of my heart; it was the pulse of my heart. If I was going to live a life of my highest purpose, I had to be here, my home. Nearest to my greatest love.

I didn't know how the heck this was going to align with my engaged-by-graduation plans, but I guessed I'd figure that out another time.

For the rest of college, I spent every single day of the year awaiting my annual trip to New York. Perhaps more exhausting, I spent each year leading up to the trip convincing myself I liked singing worship songs more than I liked saying the fuck word, that I liked Wendy's more than lox on an everything bagel, that I loved my Man of God boyfriend more than I loved my own dreams.

I'd found ultimate love, standing atop pavement and rat piss in the city that never sleeps and never stops sleeping around. Where was that in the Bible?

6

PURE LOVE

I RETURNED TO MISSOURI in a subtle-but-prevailing love affair with Brandon and New York City. But Brandon held the promise of God-approved sex and was in my physical presence every day, so he consumed more of my attention for the next three years.

Brandon really was the best first go at love.

Since we were both falling in love for the first time, it was the kind of reckless excitement you can never replicate again in life. We were love without walls, because we did not yet have any idea what true heartbreak felt like. We were every mushy-gushy couple cliché, and it was FUN.

Brandon did little romantic college things, like sneak food out of the dining hall for me when I didn't have a long enough break to get lunch. He'd plan our "study" breaks together just so we'd have time to see each other between my running Chekhov lines and him learning how to identify squamous cells. I say "study" because he knew the only way he'd actually study with me around is if I was asleep. So, he'd snag us a couch in the library, I'd take a nap, and he'd actually do work.

One year for Christmas he gave me a shopping spree for new audition dresses. (RIP jewel tones.) Brandon knew how hard it was for me to justify spending money on clothes when I felt I had so many other financial priorities. Since he was on full scholarship and actually got a "living stipend" to attend college, he had more expendable income. So off to JCPenney I went, heart aswoon.

I got super nauseous with lack of sleep, so he'd surprise me with saltines and Sprite after long travel days or intense academic all-nighters.

His fraternity held a Rent a Zelda Tao Omega-Twelve fundraising event. I told him I wouldn't bid on him, because that would be cheating and also, I'd leave it to the rich sorority girls to fund his frat's shenanigans. I showed up to the event, where he sang a Michael Bublé song *to* me. I was embarrassed/not-so-secretly reveled in every minute of his public declaration of infatuation. After another girl "won" him, he walked back through the audience and gave me a huge kiss. My foot popped! Just like Mia in *The Princess Diaries*! Which leads me to ...

I was obsessed with the *Princess Diaries* book series throughout adolescence and well into adulthood. In the books, Michael Moscovitz, Mia's (princess) best friend's brother and Mia's boyfriend, uses Ivory soap. When I made an extensive list of nonnegotiable boyfriend qualities in middle school, "Must use Ivory soap or some other really simple, clean fragrance" made the cut. #priorities

After one of our first make-out sessions, I gave Brandon's neck a big whiff, like a total creep. "What soap do you use?" I asked. "Oh, I just use the Ivory soap stuff. It's the cheapest at Kroger." Fiscally responsible and a middle school dream come true. How could I not fall for this man?

Brandon was also a fierce introvert, which seemed, at least initially, to balance well with my extreme extroversion. He and his friends commented on how I brought out the best in him. "You get him out of his studying, stressed shell," they'd say. "He needs that." I loved that I was part of making another human better through love. We balanced each other well.

Though Brandon was incredibly handsome (and shockingly fit—underneath those thick, long-sleeved Catholic Campus Ministries shirts he definitely got for free were a set of abs only a college football player should have possessed, but somehow my nerdy science-guy boyfriend had them), above all I was viciously attracted to his intellect. He was the smartest person I knew, and I felt beyond flattered that someone with such a big brain thought I was also smart. I loved that he was so ambitious and hardworking, he valued integrity, respected his parents, and took all his commitments very seriously.

I had respect and awe for this guy. I felt sincerely lucky to call him *mine*. Maybe more: I felt incredibly lucky to be called *his*.

The point is, we were in love and well on our way to postgraduation matrimony.

Right? *Right?*

Well, that is if we could figure out how to get through three more years of college without having sex. Otherwise, it was no "buried in college debt to wedding debt" bliss for us.

So, we did the work. We created *boundaries*.

I'm not talking Brené Brown, personal-development boundaries. I'm talking rules-that-make-sex -an-impossible-option boundaries. In purity culture, it wasn't just about *not* doing sex. It was about ensuring that you never get to the point where sex could even be possible. Our boundaries were preventative.

Many fellow purity ringers succeeded grandly at this preventative-boundary thing by simply (unknowingly) not being at all attracted to their significant other. This was not an option for me. Unlike the girls who were, I guess, purer than I, I was not willing to date someone I wasn't attracted to for the sake of my purity efforts. In my mind, if your purity efforts were going super well, that was probably a very bad sign. If there wasn't a struggle, you weren't horny for each other (see: my parents), and that would make for a very boring marriage.

Just like Evangelicals, Catholic's religious practices vary vastly from person to person. Some Catholics think being Catholic is stupid, but they go to Mass until they're old enough to decide Sundays are for hangovers/aren't under their parents' jurisdiction. Some Catholics find beauty in the church's mysticism but don't get too caught up in the legalism. And some Catholics—Brandon Catholics—will tell you a year into your relationship they're considering joining the Jesuit priesthood, and you'll be mad but also slightly okay because "at least it's the Jesuits?"[1]

Brandon was not anything like the casual Catholics I'd heard about growing up in Protestantland. This motherfucker was serious about his faith, including following the Catholic Church's teachings on premarital sex. It's part of why I liked him so much and considered him a viable "spiritual leader" option, despite our different brands of Jesus worshiping.

One date, over milkshakes at Steak 'n Shake, he informed me of the catechism's teaching of premarital ejaculation. Apparently, without intent to reproduce, blowing a load is a sin.

"So, every time you jerk off, it's a sin?" I asked. "What about like, wet dreams?" I told you. I know a work-around!

Quick aside: One step in my slow evolution out of purity culture was talking to my mom about masturbation. At some point, I noticed not masturbating was becoming more distracting to me than just masturbating, so I sought her insight to see if maybe she had some knowledge my Bible study leaders and pastors didn't. Our convo went something like this:

"Mom, can I ask you something weird?"

"Sure."

"Is it a sin to masturbate?"

"Who told you that?"

"Um, like every Christian dating book and small group leader ever."

"No, Mattie. Masturbating is not a sin. Also, stop reading those books."

"Are you sure? What about lusting? Isn't even thinking about it just 'fueling the fire'?!"

The "fire," here, is my desire to have sex before marriage, to be clear. Christian dating literature is expansive, and the information in those books is mostly anecdotal. Since I have always been interested in humanity, sexuality, and religion, I buried my head in way too many of these books from my adolescent to college years.

My parents, however, thought these dating books were "extreme." Though my parents supported dating with intent to marry and sex within marriage only as being God-honoring, they found the extraneous advice in these books to cause undue stress, e.g., telling me not to masturbate because it would make me an uncontrollable sex addict.

Anyway, my mom carried on.

"Yes, I'm sure. I guess masturbating *could* fuel the fire, but I think it actually is more effective in calming the fire down."

"What do you mean?"

"Masturbating is a way better option than having sex with a bunch of dumb high school boys who can't keep it up for longer than seven seconds. Your sex life at this age will be better experienced with yourself right now, trust me. More importantly, you need to know your body and be comfortable with it, or how else will you ever tell your husband what you like?"

Back to Brandon and my date where we're discussing the moral conundrum of wet dreams.

I honestly can't remember what he said. Probably something about confession. Which probably spurred me to ask if you have to keep track of all your sins *and* potential sins to take to confession? Isn't that like, a lot of work? Which probably prompted a conversation about the Catholic Church's teaching on mortal sins vs. venial sins. Which probably then prompted me to inform him of the Protestant theology that all sins are the same in God's eyes. Which probably got us into an argument, because obviously "all sins are not equal, Mattie Jo. Killing someone is not the same as a wet dream." I digress ...

All I know is I was dating someone to whom I was deeply attracted, and he was my sexually repressed equal. We were in this "preventative boundary making against our wild attraction to each other" effort together.

Which meant ...

If lying horizontally together could eventually lead to sex, then no lying down. If watching *Finding Nemo* alone in the dark could eventually lead to sex, no *Finding Nemo* in the dark. If closing the door to either of our bedrooms could lead to sex, no door closing.

Our boundaries included but were definitely not limited to:

- No sleepovers. Even if we were dead tired from studying until 1 a.m. at one of our places, we had to sleep in our own beds. I would try to get around this rule by suggesting naps. (Another quality work-around. I am honestly shocked I was not one of those "backdoor virgins."[2]) I thought I was pretty clever, but Brandon saw right past my attempt at bending the rules and nixed the nap-taking too. Tough crowd.

- No second base until we'd been together for at least four months. And then, I suppose, like a performance evaluation at work, we would see if we'd earned a boob fondle.

- No third base until the "I do's." In hindsight, this was the worst/least effective boundary. If Brandon had been going down on me for all of college, I wouldn't have even cared that we weren't having penetrative sex. What a missed opportunity!

You get the picture. We mostly adhered to these rules successfully, except for a few times when I did accidentally suck his dick. Just kidding!

In all seriousness, Brandon and I were not super successful at keeping our boundaries. What can I say? We were hot for each other! And yes, I did give him the occasional BJ. I never felt bad about this, because I *just knew* we'd get married eventually so "what was the harm?"

Brandon, however, always felt really guilty after, which made our sexual relationship very stressful. There were definitely times when I thought *What is even the point of having a boyfriend if we have to have a couples meeting every time we get a little handsy (and/or mouthy)?*

Then I remembered to count my blessings. At least I wasn't with a dude who had committed to no kissing until his wedding day. Of which, on my college campus, there were many. Yes, those homeschooled hill-people from TLC shows, I knew them personally.

Not surprisingly, a little over a year into our relationship we transgressed the "Oh shit" of almost doing *it*. One night, after a beautiful day spent together, we went back to his place, shut the door, and definitely lay horizontally.

This was the first time I'd ever been naked with a man. It was the most vulnerable I'd ever felt, and I was incredibly nervous. But I was also ... excited? I wanted Brandon, and I felt completely safe knowing he wanted me too. There was no one else with whom I could imagine sharing this vulnerable, nerve-recking, exciting experience.

His clothes came off. He was on top of me, kissing my neck. Brandon, thanks to me reading a lot of articles about making-out skills in *Seventeen* magazine and then teaching him, was actually a phenomenal kisser. This was it! This was the pinnacle of existence as an Evangelical woman. *WE ARE GOING TO HAVE SEX. My parents did it before marriage, and they turned out great! Oh, except for the baby thing. Do we need a condom? Does he even know how to use one? Anyway, I'll deal with the purity ring later.*

The passion halted abruptly as he stood up and started to have a purity panic attack right before my naked body.

"This is wrong. I ... we shouldn't be doing this. I think you should go."

"What?" *Oh no. What did I do?*

"We shouldn't be doing ... this. You shouldn't be here. You should leave."

"Brandon, it's one a.m."

"Yeah ... Umm ... Maybe you can sleep in my roommate's room? He's gone for the weekend."

It felt like my heart fell into my butt.

I fought back tears as I silently put on my clothes and shuffled quietly out of his covers into his roommate's crusty bed.

I stayed up most of the night weeping tears of a hurt I didn't understand. My head and heart were a cacophony of conflict and confusion. *What is this feeling? Sadness? Embarrassment? Slutty-ness? Is slutty a feeling?*

Shame. I definitely felt shame.

But I didn't feel shame for wanting to have sex with Brandon, which made me feel even more ashamed. *Is my shame button broken? Why don't I feel bad for wanting sex with someone who isn't my husband?*

Instead, I feared the shame and disgust Brandon felt *at* me.

I learned that based on the night's goings on, Brandon would never see me the same as he had before that night. I was no longer a viable-wife option in his eyes.

This wasn't a feeling on the inside of me; it was all coming from the outside of me. I was experiencing all the bad feels bestowed upon me by my pastors, small-group leaders, peers, an entire community, and, now, by the very first man I'd ever loved. At the time, I didn't know the difference. I was told feeling gross, dirty, and bad after an act is "conviction sent by the Holy Spirit."

In normal-people world, conviction is simply a strong belief/opinion. Or it's a formal declaration of someone committing a crime. In my Evangelical upbringing, however, this term was used to describe that feeling you get when you do something you were (taught) not to do. This "feeling" was the Holy Spirit informing you that you are sinning and you should stop. If what you were doing was okay, why would you feel badly about it?

It couldn't possibly be the socialized guilt and shame I'd been experiencing about my sexuality since my belly button stopped being a body part and became a stumbling block.[3] It couldn't possibly be that I'd been told certain behaviors were "bad" and therefore defined them as bad for myself. Nope! It was definitely the Holy Spirit telling me to "stop!"

Anyway, I was feeling very bad, and I believed it was conviction. I'd done something terribly wrong, and Brandon no longer seeing me as a potential wife was my punishment.

The next morning Brandon came and lay down (horizontally!) next to me.

He held me in silence, and after a while, my subtle but slowly cultivating intuition told me something was up. "What's wrong?" I asked. And because truly good men cannot tell a lie, he didn't even try to hide it.

"After you left the room last night. I ... I came."

"Good for you." I rolled my eyes. How could he even think about sex while I was in the other room sobbing about our imminent "stumbling block" breakup?

"No but ... I came because I ... I looked at a woman. On my computer."

Oh God. The heart-in-my-butt feeling again.

I clenched my throat as tears worked their way out of wherever tears are stored and into my eyes. Afraid to move my mouth, because it might make the tears fall, I still had to ask for clarification, so I muttered, "What?"

"I'm sorry. It won't happen again. I just ... I was you know ... aroused and ... and it just happened."

My throat couldn't hold the tension any longer. I rolled over, making sure my face was hidden from him. I clenched my fists and held my chest, trying with every possible muscle in my body to make sure he couldn't see me sobbing. *You will not experience this vulnerable moment with me. You do not deserve it.*

He held me tighter and offered what I think was supposed to be encouragement. "We just have to work harder to stick to these boundaries." *LET. ME. GO.*

A newfound feminist fumed on my insides.

"We? We? What did *I* do? Except be physically and emotionally the most vulnerable I've ever been at this point in my life, and then get sent into another bedroom for the night *by my boyfriend.* Just so you could get off to some other girl—a stranger on a screen—instead of your real-life girlfriend!? Where was my error here?! *Fuck you, Brandon! Fu—Actually, I hope you never get fucked you!"*

But that's not what I said.

Instead, I involuntarily released my efforts at a cry cover-up and erupted into a full-on huff-and-puff meltdown in my boyfriend of two years' roommate's bed the morning after not having sex.

Even steeped in patriarchal religiosity, I knew this whole situation was just ... *wrong.* And I was furious at Brandon.

How could this happen?

After many years (and lots of therapy) spent unpacking how the layers of fucked-up-ed-ness of purity culture played out perfectly in this evening, I now know exactly how this could happen.

First of all, of course I was experiencing simultaneous sadness, shame, and outrage. I was sad and hurt but couldn't even fully lean into my sadness about how hurt I felt by Brandon's actions, and that made me angry.

In purity culture, and American patriarchal culture at large, women are conditioned to bypass any hurt or sadness associated with being mistreated by a man when sex is involved. We are taught to immediately go to self-blame. From one-night stands you thought would turn into something more to full-on abuse or rape, the not-ideal result is usually *our* fault. Something we "asked for."

So was it really Brandon's fault I was sad? Did I really have a right to be angry with him? No, it was my own fault. I was excited about sex; I *wanted* it. That's why this all turned out so poorly. My "unhinged" sexual desire. I "asked for it."

For years I remained angry with Brandon over that night. But now I know we were both operating within a culture that perpetuates the idea that women exist as either wife or whore. Honorable or harlot. Saint or slut. Women are not granted the privilege of complexity; we are compartmentalized.

I could remain a respectable figure in Brandon's life only insofar as I could avoid crossing the threshold of a "sexually enjoyable figure." If he was enjoying me sexually outside of marriage, that meant he didn't respect me. He was using me as a body for his own pleasure. Which put me in the harlot/whore/slut camp.

Given all this, and Brandon's commitment to honoring-Jesus-with-no-sex-until-marriage purity, it was better and godlier for him to just get off to a woman with whom he had no emotional attachment than to have sex with me, and therefore defile the vision of "wife" I was in his mind. It was better for Brandon to perpetuate the belief that within her sexual expression a woman becomes an object, a *thing* to be enjoyed apart from her humanity—an experience of isolation instead of full integration—instead of experiencing what we had: an expression of *pure love.*

Brandon was living out what he had been taught, just as I was.

But before I knew anything about internalized, projected, and learned shame, in that moment, as an Evangelical young woman in love, I felt a very strong ... something. Somewhere beyond my lungs, whisper scream-ing in my soul-arteries, was an undeniable, not-yet-definable truth: *This isn't how it's supposed to be.*

I did not listen to that whisper.

Instead, I covered it up with familiar Evangelical narratives.

You just need to get closer to God, Mattie Jo. You and Brandon can still have a godly marriage! Seek His will in all you do and He will direct your path.

I chalked that night up to a normal part of traversing temptation as a godly couple. We were learning to show God we loved Him more than we loved our sexual attraction to each other.

I wanted to show God I was serious about being committed to Him, being as close to Him as possible, and not falling short of the glory of the Lord because of my "lust." Furthermore, subconsciously anyway, I believed we needed to get married to make what happened that night okay, so we had to stay together. If I ended up with someone who wasn't Brandon, they'd never want to marry me knowing I'd been naked with intention of intercourse with another man.

So, I threw myself into this God-seeking closeness with unrelenting commitment.

And ended up in Indonesia.

7

CURFEWS, CHASTITY, AND THE GREAT COMMISSION

By SOPHOMORE YEAR OF college, I couldn't be as active in my home church, because it was farther away and also I was working multiple jobs, saving to move to New York City, performing A+ pelvis rainbow projections, and trying to do ballet without looking like a field hockey player on my tiptoes. I was very busy.

But I needed to be part of a community, for more accountability in my pursuit of closeness to Christ, so I joined a mission-focused group on my campus: Jesus Beacon Light. Jesus Beacon Light's "About Us" can be summed up in one statement: "With every action in your life, live out THE GREAT COMMISSION."

The Great Commission, based on Matthew 29:16–20, is the foundation and, theologically speaking, the most important distinguisher of being an Evangelical. To be an Evangelical is to live a life driven by "spreading the Gospel." To go and "make disciples of all nations." What makes an Evangelical an Evangelical is that they possess the "Good News" of Jesus Christ, and boy howdy, are we gonna share it.

As an Evangelical, if you are not committed to bringing as many people as possible to believe in Jesus Christ as the Son of God, sent to die for our sins, you cannot call yourself a Christian. This is a command, not a suggestion. End of Story.

Growing up, I learned to share the Gospel through actions first, and then words. By living out compassion, service and empathy and wearing a purity ring (duh), I would be exemplifying Christ in my everyday life. Since this kind of living is so exceptional and foreign to most people, nonbelieving Secular Joes should be very moved by my Evangelical qualities and might want to know why I am just so exceptional.

"What makes you so kind, compassionate, and a wearer of purity?" Secular Joe will ask.

This, as a good Evangelical, is your chance to make a new Christian!

At this point, I should/could share the Gospel effortlessly and in a not-preachy/off-putting way. I will make a grand speech explaining to Secular Joe that "the love of the Lord" is why I live out certain morals. Secular Joe will want to know more about this Lord and may even want to come to church. Eventually, Secular Joe will become Saved Joe, and voila! The Great Commission fulfilled.

In Jesus Beacon Light's model for Great Commission–focused living, the organization purchased properties around college campuses. These properties were then rented by Jesus-loving tenants like me, and the rental profits would go toward funding mission work in other countries. JBL funded things like pastoral housing in Africa and sewing classes in small villages in Southeast Asia to stimulate job growth. Additionally, as a member of the organization, I would spend the year fundraising to take a short-term mission trip abroad.

In the Great Commission world, there is long-term mission work and short-term mission work. The long-termers are the real deal. They uproot their entire lives, learn a new language, and fund their entire lives through donations in USD transferred to a much weaker currency.

The short-term missionaries are the less devoted, or perhaps just not yet ready to answer God's (cruel) call to full-time mission work. So, although they probably won't see any successfully saved folks during their week in a "third-world country," they will fuel their egos knowing they've "planted seeds" in potential Christ followers. And maybe get a tan.

I had an experience in short-term mission work in high school with the motto, "blessed to be a blessing." We were given much, and therefore we should give much. So I spent weeks laying concrete for tilapia farmers in Honduras, weekends clearing debris in local homes after an ice storm, and Friday nights shopping for meals to leave anonymously on people's porches. JBL's structure perfectly aligned with my "blessed to be a blessing" Christlike-living motto! Send rent abroad to help those in need instead of to greedy landlords? Spend the year studying musical theater *and* preparing to go serve in places of need?! Hot dog, let's go! Saving the world, college MJ was.

After joining, however, I quickly discovered Jesus Beacon Light was not about living out the Great Commission in the way I had learned and loved. The organization was less focused on compassion and service, more focused on making sure all their members followed God exactly the way JBL said we should, and keeping a tally of all successful converts by the week. Compared to my already-pretty-narrow worldview and pursuit of "living like Christ," JBL was other-level.

Each JBL campus had a few houses and a leader. These leaders were expected to live out the Jesus Beacon Light brand of Christian perfectly, so that we JBL minions would not be confused on what was expected of us. They were not volunteers, but actual employees of Jesus Beacon Light, who raised their annual salary by soliciting donations/had rich parents.

My campus leader was a quiet, subtly bitchy white woman named Laurel, who wore a low side-pony and owned way too many gauchos for anyone not in a Limited Too catalog. She also never wore makeup because beauty is fleeting.[1]

Laurel's miraculous testimony included feeling really bad about getting drunk at football games too much during her freshman year of college, so she eventually became a Christian and now knew everything about overcoming sin and hardship through the Lord. She was in her mid-twenties, engaged to a man she met at Bible certificate school (remember the Kanakuk Institute? That's the one), and was committed to not kissing until their wedding day. My point is, this woman had so much life experience, I could clearly trust her as my leader in all things spirituality, sexuality, and general life discipleship amen.

In order to ensure I was living the JBL lifestyle, I had to sign written vows of purity and abide by really strict rules in the house. Brandon couldn't be over after 10 p.m., and we weren't allowed to close the door while in my room. I had to be home by 11 p.m. on weeknights, I suppose to make sure we weren't out drinking? Or laying horizontally with our boyfriends.

Since I was the only one in the house with a boyfriend and also decided to rush a sorority that year, I was the only one to whom these rules seemed to apply. I could have not followed them in protest, but they were enforced through accountability with an elected roommate: My personal Purity Prefect.

That's right, we had a representative *in the house* who had the right to call us out on missing curfew or demand I open the door when Brandon was over. Fun fact, two of my (female) roommates were hooking up and went on to date after their own personal deconstruction journeys. Which means, as the straight girl in the holy house, I was the only one not getting any action!

A quick aside about Christian communities and their obsession with "accountability." This word is thrown around in the name of moral discipline but is actually just an excuse for nosy, codependent know-it-alls to feel like their personality flaws are justified through Jesus.

I only ever saw accountability heavily enforced in regard to sexual relations. For example, in high school, a small-group leader wanted to help me break my habit of flirting with men who weren't pursuing the Lord. So, she suggested I tell her anytime I texted a non–Man of God. Or text her instead!

For Christian dudes, they needed to tell someone how many times they jerked off that week and then ask for forgiveness. A group of teen-to-mid-twenties dudes recounting their personal handy Js to each other in the name of the Lord with a male leader present ... that is someone's preferred porn genre. Or an episode of *Dateline*.

So anyway, a note about "accountability" in your process, Recovering Evangelicals: You don't owe anyone shit. You do not have to give a person every detail of your life because they are a "brother/sister in Christ." And if they try to guilt-trip you by saying, "Well you probably aren't sharing because you feel conviction about the things you're doing," tell them to live a more exciting life and go to therapy for their codependent tendencies. And mind their own beeswax.

I also had to attend weekly "obligations" that would help refine my Christlike-ness.

One of these obligations was one-on-one Bible study time with Laurel. This, for me, was particularly painful, as Laurel spent most of the time telling me how I needed to break up with Brandon because we were unequally yoked. She once showed up with a printout of all the reasons Catholics aren't real Christians and earnestly implored me to break things off. Marrying Brandon would, apparently, land me right in hell with Mother Teresa.

We also had to attend weekly group Bible studies with the house. These group studies included learning Bible lesson acronyms like we were in kindergarten and answering questions such as "How many people have you led to The Lord recently?" Idk, *Laurel.* How many times have you had an orgasm recently? Probably that many.

When I told Laurel I was going to have to leave group study early every week for musical rehearsal, she reminded me of my commitment to Jesus Beacon Light. If I didn't uphold that commitment, I was ultimately only hurting myself and, ya know, the entire mission of Jesus. I think I told her I wasn't paying my own college tuition to go to her Bible study. If she would like to pay for my degree (since I knew she didn't pay for hers) I'd happily stay longer.

The obligations didn't end there.

There were mandatory house dinners where Laurel would ask forced questions between awkward silences over Hamburger Helper in the name of fellowship—the churchy word for hanging out with other Believers. This is very important to do as a seriously committed follower of Christ, as "bad company corrupts good character" (1 Corinthians 15:33), so you better be fellowshipping with way more Christian people than non-Christian people or you might become one of those non-Christians! Also, everyone needs a safe space to use words like "fellowship" where no one looks at you funny.

We were to regularly host "outreach" nights, which entailed inviting foreign exchange students over for a game night and Doritos, then attempting to inconspicuously share the Gospel. I mean, are you even an Evangelical if you didn't attempt conversion over language barriers, Doritos, and Uno at some point in your college career?

We were required to spend our year fundraising *thousands of dollars* to go to the 10/40 Window for mission work. If you were raised anywhere near Kanakuk Kamps, you probably know this "10/40 Window" term. If not, allow me to enlighten (frighten) you by summarizing varied definitions of this region.

The 10/40 Window is a rectangular area encompassing North Africa, the Middle East, and Asia between 10- and 40-degrees north latitude. Most of the people in this area of the world identify as Muslim, Hindu, or Buddhist. The 10/40 window has the largest "unreached people" population. Unreached people are groups who have not yet even been exposed to the Gospel. These are not people like your liberal relatives in California who have heard the Gospel many times and still reject it. These are places in the world where there are so few Christians, these people have not even once heard the story of Jesus. Which is why mission work there is so important! We need to share the Gospel so they can all go to Heaven!

Except for the fact that—theologically speaking—people who haven't heard the Gospel, unborn babies for example, are actually spared from the whole "must be saved to go to Heaven" rule. Which poses the question, weren't these unreached people already going to Heaven? And aren't missionaries sort of fucking them over by sharing the Gospel? By this rule, the second those Muslims, Buddhists, Hindus, etc. hear the story of Jesus and don't immediately convert, we've bound them to hell.

In other words, missionaries in the 10/40 Window are sending more people to hell than were going before they got there.

I had to ask a bunch of people for money so I could go to a Muslim country and try to convert the Muslims to Christianity. This, I was told, was my role as a Believer. If I didn't do it, then the blood of those Muslims would be on my hands.

According to Jesus Beacon Light, being a truly committed Christian meant having no other interests besides The Word, only hanging out with other Christians, *not marrying a Catholic*, and converting literally anyone I could with my Jedi-mind-trick-Gospel-spreading powers. And other people's money.

The scariest part about all this is that Jesus Beacon Light's model for Christ-following was not viewed as "weird" in my world. It was normal to be that kind of Christian. Trendy, even. If I could manage to follow all these rules and maybe even learn to enjoy it, I'd be a popular girl in the Kingdom of Heaven on earth. #goals.

But *ugh*. I didn't realize getting closer to God was going to involve all of ... this. I didn't want to spend my year asking people to help me convert the Muslims. I didn't want to go to these stupid Bible studies, house dinners, or outreach nights! Mostly because I found it all to be wildly boring, but also because I thought, if the goal here is to make more Christians, the JBL model of Great Commission living was ineffective.

Since I had secular theater friends now, I was at least a little hip to how Evangelicals appeared to non-Evangelicals. And it wasn't ... great. People are not stupid. They know when you see them as a social experiment, only hanging out with them in order to "achieve" something. Interactions seem scripted (and often were! See: Bridge Analogy, Secular Joe talk, etc.) and disingenuous.

However, I am a woman of character, so I kept my commitments to JBL. I attended the Bible studies, fellowship dinners, and adhered to the curfews (for the most part ...). I refused to attend the outreach nights with the foreign exchange students though. That part, to me, was just too icky.

That being said, I was very afraid that if I didn't uphold some version of the whole attempt-to-convert-the-foreigners thing, Laurel would personally burn me alive with her sexual repression fury. So, I got creative, once again, implementing a solid "this is okay, right?" work-around.

8

MATTIE JO MEETS A MUSLIM

THROUGH SOME RESEARCH, I found that my university had a program for native English speakers to meet once a week with a student learning English, who would be able to practice their conversation skills and maybe make a friend. The English Conversation Partner program was a volunteer role with the only requirement being *to talk*. This I could definitely do.

I was partnered with a Muslim woman from Saudi Arabia named Arma.

Arma was, on paper, the perfect practice convert. After all, I was preparing to go to the 10/40 Window and evangelize to the Muslims, and she was, well, from the 10/40 window and a Muslim. This detail alone, I hoped, would keep Laurel off my back about missing the Dorito Uno outreach nights.

Spoiler: I did not successfully convert Arma.

Once a week Arma and I met, conversed, and she unknowingly busted open my ignorance of foreign, non-Christian people.

She shared her studying struggles with me. Although it was forcing her to learn English very quickly, studying required so much more time for her than it did for American kids, because she wasn't just trying to absorb the information; she was translating as she went through all the material.

Between trying to translate her business textbooks, actually studying, and navigating the isolation of American anti-Muslim culture, Arma found it basically impossible to make friends. "I live here, but I don't really *live* here, you see?" So, most of Arma's time was spent only with her husband, Mehmet.

Based on zero knowledge or factual information but instead "studies" of Southeast Asian culture during some of my JBL fellowship nights and, like, post- 9/11 news, I had learned Muslim men were brutal and abusive. Muslim women basically had no rights. All the marriages were arranged and therefore not happy, and women were murdered if they were seen without their heads covered by anyone other than their husbands. This was a culture of extremism and woman-hating in the name of God. Nothing at all like Evangelicals, oh no.

But Arma and Mehmet were nothing like this brutality in marriage I'd heard about. In fact, their story was so romantic, it sounded like a Saudi Arabian Nicholas Sparks story. And they were obsessed with each other!

Arma and Mehmet grew up together. As Arma explained it, she and Mehmet always had a crush on each other but of course could never act on it. So as soon as he was old enough to ask for her hand in marriage, he did.

When Mehmet graduated high school, he asked Arma's father for permission to marry her. Arma's father said, "No way! You have to get an education first." So, Mehmet enrolled in university.

When Mehmet arrived a year later to say, "Hey, Arma's father, I'm getting an education, can I marry your daughter now?" Arma's dad still said no. "You have to get an *American* education before you can marry my daughter!" So, Mehmet, speaking no English and never having been to the States, applied to universities all over the US. He would go on to leave Arma for two years while getting his degree in *Missouri* (of all fucking places in America to have to live, alone, as a Saudi man for your true love—*the sacrifice*) only to return before his senior year and ask once again for Arma's hand in marriage.

Third time and a second language's the charm I guess, because Mehmet finally got to propose to Arma! They were married, she applied to university, and together they received a great education and made up for the years apart by spending a lot of time with each other, plus an undercover Muslim-converting Evangelical (me).

From time to time, Mehmet and Arma invited me over for dinner, where I got to see Arma without her hijab and with makeup. Between bites of delicious Saudi food and language barriers, I reluctantly asked about her faith. I didn't want to be the white missionary in the room, but Laurel kept asking "how it was going with my friend," and I needed something to report back. What I learned was...a lot.

1. The word "Islam" translates to "submit (to God) for peace/safety."

The way Arma explained it, most Muslims are just trying to live the way Allah suggests they live, because He knows better than they do about this whole life thing. Seems pretty commendable, and not at all unlike what I was taught about following Jesus.

2. There are Five Pillars of Islam that every Muslim is to implement in their lives.

These pillars are profession of faith (only one God), prayer, charity, fasting, and pilgrimage to Mecca. Similar to the Ten Commandments and visiting the Vatican if you're Catholic, or a Hillsong United concert if you're nondenom.

3. Islam has some ideas about gender roles and modesty, just as Christians do.

Women who wear hijabs want to save their physical beauty for their husbands only, not unlike Pentecostals with their long hair and ankle-length denim skirts or the teachings of modesty/purity in my Evangelical upbringing. As a Western Christian woman, it's just more scandalous to show my shoulders in a spaghetti strap or my upper thigh in non-Bermuda shorts than showing my hair. Tomato *toe-mah-toe*.

Islam also does not necessarily teach that women are inferior to men, just "different." This was not any dissimilar to how I'd been raised!

I heard this sermon countless times in the form of "Wives, submit to your husbands, and, husbands, love your wives as Christ loves the church—sacrificially. So you see, wives submit, but if the husband is truly giving his life for his wife, it's all good!" It was all the same oppression wrapped in a bullshit separate-but-equal narrative.

4. Muslim people know Jesus.

They call him "Isa ibn Maryam" which is very fun to say and translates to "Jesus, son of Mary." There are stories of him in the Quran very similar to those in the Bible. Isa was born of a virgin, from the earth, just like Adam, and he performed many miracles in the name of God. He is revered highly in the Muslim tradition, given the term "spirit" and "word" of God. No other prophet, not even Muhammad, receives that particular honor.

However, in the Islamic tradition, Jesus was not crucified and resurrected.

Screech! Say what now about the son of God sent to earth *to die for our sins on the cross*, Arma?

Correct, Muslims do not believe in the crucifixion or resurrection of Jesus. The belief of what exactly happened to Jesus in his death varies among Muslim-identifying people. Arma believed God helped Jesus escape before he was crucified, while some other guy who the Romans thought was Jesus got killed.

Turns out, that guy was Judas Iscariot. Yeah! That is the Judas who betrayed Jesus to the Romans and who Christians believe hung himself in guilt over the whole ordeal. Not in Islam. In Islam Judas gets brutal, earthly justice handed to him.

5. Islam teaches the existence of one, big-G God.

There are no other Gods ... *ever*. This is why Muslims can't get down with the Christians; they deem the Trinity polytheistic. When I first heard this information, I wanted to be all "No, no, Arma. Our God is three-in-one, like an egg!" But then I was like "Actually, the Trinity concept is pretty wacko."

Take Jesus's baptism for example. God is up in Heaven, while also flying down to earth as a dove, in order to bless himself as a ... human? First of all, that's pretty self-indulgent, God. Second of all, is this *Inception* or theology?

Other than Arma not believing Jesus is God incarnate, her religion seemed very similar to mine and like it was working out just fine for her. I mean damn. She had a husband in college! That's, like, every Evangelical woman's dream.

Needless to say, I dropped the converting effort rather quickly.

My Evangelical culture taught and assumed that all non-Christian people, even if they don't know it, can't wait to hear the Good News because their lives suck so bad. They have a God-shaped hole that only Jesus can fill the sermons say. "Until they accept Jesus into that God-shaped hole, they will keep trying to fill it unsuccessfully with things of the world—money, sex, achievement—or maybe even other religions." But until these dummies accept Jesus into that God-shaped heart hole, they will remain miserable.

But this didn't seem to be the case with Arma. Arma wasn't interested in being like me at all. Arma enjoyed being Muslim and didn't want to be a Christian, enjoyed Saudi food more than Doritos, preferred her marital customs over Western marital customs. She wasn't even bothered by the whole hair-covering thing. "I don't do my hair much. It's so easy." Fantastic point, Arma. Who is more victim of the patriarchy? Those styling our hair for the male gaze or those simplifying their daily routine to detour it?

Much like with my LGBTQ+ friends, I didn't want to change Arma. I liked that we had varied life experiences, perspectives, and comfort foods. She added so much to my life just as she was! She added to my life *because* of who she was.

If I had listened to Jesus Beacon Light's approach to my time with Arma, I would not have developed a genuine friendship with her. I would not have opened myself up to the possibility that she had more to teach me than I had to teach her. That *maybe* all these "Christ-followers" need to revisit the Gospels, review Jesus's massive emphasis on practicing humility, and stop being so fucking self-important.

JBL offered a version of Christianity that was super confusing for me to navigate as a well-intentioned, "wanna please God because He's so good" Believer. I wanted to please God, and I wanted to love others well. JBL claimed their entire mission was motivated by Christ's love, but ... was that true?

How is it loving to constantly look for an opportunity to tell people their fundamental identity is wrong and if they don't change immediately, they'll go to Hell?

How is it loving to say you're someone's friend when really, they're just another tally mark on your Heaven treasure scorecard?

How is it loving (or realistic to the human experience, like, at all) to say that a person is only truly living a Christlike lifestyle if they pursue a relationship with God in one specific way?

How is it loving to take the beautifully diverse creation of God and try relentlessly to homogenize it?

I didn't like this JBL Jesus. I was pretty trash at following this Jesus. And yet, I still had to go on a mission trip across the globe to pitch this Jesus to strangers and hope to make the sale.

Goddammit!

9

MISSIONARY POSITION

By THE END OF the year with Jesus Beacon Light, I was so ready to get back to my previous life: attending *Cabaret* rehearsals without being condemned and dry-humping my Catholic boyfriend in peace. Sweet freedom awaits! *As soon as I get this dumb mission trip over with ...*

Our destination country was Indonesia, which I was actually way excited about. Well, I was excited about the potential to live out a very PG version of *Eat, Pray, Love* on the beach in a one-piece swimsuit. Not the converting the Muslims part.

As soon as I stepped off the plane, I was greeted by a couple of American Texans, Karen and Larry. They had moved to Indonesia ten years prior to become full-time missionaries and secret house church planters.

House church planting in other countries is really just colonialism in Chacos (under Christ). Here's how it works:

These missionaries aim to model early-Christian churches—when followers of Christ were being literally persecuted—by meeting in secret. The congregation is usually a small group of locals in someone's home, led by a white American male missionary who increases the church numbers and determines the service structure, then leaves to go start another church and hopes that church doesn't split a few months later over varying opinions on the translation of a single verse in Acts. The Great Commission fulfilled!

In our weekly Bible studies leading up to the trip, we were told the Muslims of Indonesia were so hostile to Christians, we would be thrown in jail and maybe even killed by local governments if we were found out. They also told us the government and police are "very corrupt." So don't expect police to defend us should we get in some serious Christian abduction disaster.

In my research for this book, however, I found there are no laws in Indonesia that ban being a Christian or converting others to Christianity. Apparently, Indonesia is actually, comparative to other Muslim dominated countries, pretty religiously tolerant to their Abrahamic cousins. While it's true there have been fringe terrorist groups who attacked Christian churches over the years in Indonesia, this was never the norm. And, at least from my perspective, how is that any different from the random attacks on Muslims, LGBTQ+ communities, or other minorities in America by Christians with guns?

The point is, while Indonesia is by no means "progressive" by Western standards, no one was legally permitted to imprison or kill us for being Christians. While we did have reason to be careful, I think this rhetoric was mostly racism, religious demonizing, and ethnocentrism at play.

Oh, *and* we had to sign a release before taking this trip stating that if we got kidnapped while abroad, Jesus Beacon Light was not liable and would not be responsible for our ransom. Our parents were not required to see or sign this document, because we were over eighteen. Since we were required to go on this mission trip as part of our commitment to JBL, we were also required to sign this document. They didn't really offer us a choice.

And yet, given *all* that, as soon as we landed in Bali, Karen sent me to publicly proclaim the Gospel by "beach evangelizing" while she acted as translator. Apparently, she and Larry could do their Kingdom building in the privacy of house churches, but the college kids could be volunteered as tribute.

Well, here go my PG Eat, Pray, Love *plans! I am probably going to die at the hands of the Christian-hating Indonesian government! What a way to go.*

I saw a young girl wearing a Playboy bunny logo pin on her shirt. Karen told me to ask if she knew what it meant. She didn't, so I told her. Well, sort of. I think it went something like this:

"So, Playboy is not cool in America. Well, it is cool, but we don't wear the bunny on our clothes, because it means ... it means uh ..." *How do you say, "It means you're a proud slut" in Indonesian?*

"It means you think it's okay to have se—"

Ugh, this girl is like eleven years old. I'm not going to talk to her about sex! Why am I here? Why did I agree to this?! Why did I ask people for money to do this? I just want to drink water from a coconut in my one-piece!

"... to show your body to a lot of men who are not your husband. But I don't believe that! See, I wear a ring—like the opposite of your pin—to show I don't think that's okay. And the reason I don't think it's okay is because I have a relationship with Jesus Christ ..."

Well, that leap didn't really make sense. Clarify, MJ!

"You see, I'm a Christian and as Christians we believe it's best to only show your body to your husband. Because Jesus died on the cross for our sins and I'm so grateful He did that so I want to live my life the way He tells me to live and that includes not showing my body to anyone other than my husband and also wearing this ring okay *bye!*"

Looking back, this was a terrible sales pitch for Jesus. But more importantly, why did Karen think I had the authority to talk to this *child* about all the ways her wearing a Playboy pin is problematic not just through the lens of Christian purity teachings but through that lens and in another language?! Also, had she been a little older, it's likely none of this would have been news to her. The Balinese are Hindus surrounded by a country of Muslims. I'm sure all of this messaging is very familiar to them.

I wasn't concerned with the adequacy of my beach sermon. I was more concerned about dying for breaking the law halfway across the world.

As I finished my panic preaching, my heart was beating so fast.

Will my mom and dad be proud of me for finally being a true Evangelical or sue JBL for my death? Wait. I can't die yet. I am a virgin!

After my mild blackout, I asked Laurel how this was okay. "Do our parents know we are being put in danger of dying while our leaders and hosts—Karen and Larry—are doing their mission in secret?" Or some version of that where I was a little more afraid of Laurel but still pointing out JBL's terrible optics on this one.

Her answer was that this is the call of being a true Believer. Karen and Larry, and so many other brave missionaries before us, risk their lives for the sake of spreading the Gospel every day. This is but a little taste of what they face. Every. Day.

"Modern martyrdom," she said, "is not something Western Christians understand or value."

After all, the disciples of the Bible died horrible deaths proclaiming the truth of Jesus Christ. Martyrdom was what made early-days Christianity so profound, popular, and reputable.* If I was not willing to do the same, could I really call myself a disciple of Christ?

I would find out nearly a decade later that all my housemates got similar responses from Laurel any time they or their parents expressed concern for our safety while in Indonesia.

---

*One time I was babysitting this twelve-year-old daughter of billionaires on 5th Avenue in Manhattan and had to help her study for her world religions class. One of the questions on the study guide was, "What made Christianity spread so quickly and effectively?" And one of the answers was "Martyrdom." The following convo ensued:

Me: What does that mean?

Tween Billionaire: If people are willing to die for a cause, it must be the real deal, right? All these people saying they'd be willing to die for the truth that Jesus died and resurrected gave their stories clout.

Me: Right. Their testimonies.

Tween Billionaire: Huh?

Me: Nothing. How do you know the word "clout"?

Tween Billionaire: How do you not know something on a sixth-grade study guide?

Me: Public school and No Child Left Behind.

Tween Billionaire: What?

Me: Let's talk about the Buddhists!

When the mom of one of my housemates shared articles about Christian girls being beheaded and Christian churches being burned in Indonesia with Laurel via email and asked how this could be safe, Laurel's response was basically "We risk our lives even when going to Target or a getting in a car. Bottom line is, God is sovereign and we have faith that His best plan will be done. So excited to see what He has in store for your daughter while in East Asia!"

That housemate did not end up going on the trip. I wish I would have had the girl gonads to do the same.

Laurel's response was not exactly my first introduction to modern martyrdom. I was in elementary school when the mass shooting at Columbine occurred. After this horrific event, "intruder drills" became a regular thing, 'cause America. I also remember hearing that if an intruder does come in, he's probably coming for the Christians first. At which point, if he holds a gun to my little third grade head, then asks if I'm a Christian, what will my answer be? Was I willing to die for Jesus?

So as a nine-year-old, I am being asked to make a game plan for the potential and likely scenario that an angry man will come into my classroom while I'm learning *6 x 7 is 42 Columbus sailed the ocean blue* and ask me if I believe in Jesus. If I say yes, I go to Heaven. If I say no because I want to live and he shoots me anyway, I'm going to hell.

Modern martyrdom.

If I just unlocked this memory for you, just like the rest of us Recovering Evangelicals, I kindly suggest seeking professional help.

However, between the fucked-up childhood lessons I learned during intruder drills and my time in Indonesia, I think I'd repressed the martyrdom part of being a Christian. I was already not having sex for the Gospel! Now I have to *die*? No thank you please.

The remainder of my time in Indonesia was entirely focused on literal evangelism. We spent a few days in Bali and then island-hopped, spending time with locals in their homes, churches, and restaurants. The goal was to build "quality relationships" so that, in just ten days, we could find at least one moment to share the Gospel with our new "friends" and hope they didn't report us to the authorities, because we are "friends."

We spent some of the trip visiting schools, under the guise that we were college students completing a sort of travel internship that required us to teach "natural disaster relief." Our "relief" training was a total joke, including instructions for tsunamis and earthquakes like "Climb on the roof!" and "Cover your head!"

Of course, the disaster-relief sham was just an effort to exploit the admiration the kids would have for us because we were white, American (some of us even *blond*!), and "Have you met Justin Bieber?" and then get to spend quality time with them.

In addition to the school visits, Karen and Larry took us to meet a rice farmer they had converted. We sat on his floor and listened to his testimony, which I was supposed to be very excited to hear. But I honestly don't remember a thing he said; I was too interested in learning about his farm.

I was mesmerized by the simplicity of this man's life. He lived in a handmade hut. I could not even tell you what it was made out of but he and his family built it straight from their surrounding resources! He had a whole farm full of food and lots of chickens I knew would be part of our dinner. He even had a breadfruit tree in his yard. Have you seen breadfruit? It's gigantic without any genetic modifications! Miraculous!

For dinner we had rice from his field, chickens from his backyard, and rambutan from ... I don't even know! The jungle bushes? How cool that he had everything he needed right there and didn't have to go to Walmart.

I wasn't sure how living in America was better than Rice Farmer Convert's life. I mean, sure, he didn't have water pressure or plumbing or mascara, but he had *enough*. And, at least from what I could tell, way more happiness and contentment than most, if not all, Americans I'd ever met. What exactly did he need from us? *Jesus. Right.*

I also learned that, despite it sort of being a no-no within Islam, Indonesians often visit witch doctors for immediate "supernatural" healing because health care is largely inaccessible and, in Larry's words, "The nearest hospital I'd trust is in Singapore." Apparently, this Indonesian rice farmer Christian possessed similar supernatural healing powers to the disciples of the Bible! But to everyone else within Indonesian cultural context, he just looked like a witch doctor, not Jesus's miracle-working minions. Swing and miss.

We got a real treat when someone showed up the night we were there for dinner asking to get their eye infection healed by Mr. Rice Farmer Convert. "Well, that's freaking cool!" I said audibly after the whole situation was translated. I was gonna see a Bible-story-level miracle!

Apparently, it was not freaking cool.

"I've told them they have to start turning people away," Larry explained. "It makes the mission of the Gospel completely irrelevant if fellow villagers think the Christians are witches."

First of all, LOL. What a *not*-first-world problem.

Second of all, I'm in my thirties and living in America. My left shoulder, right knee, uterus, and small intestine are all victims of our shit healthcare system. I'd love a witch doctor neighbor!

Third of all, *Wait a second. So these Indonesian Christians are getting shit done by literally healing folks, and it's discouraged because it nixes the chance to potentially fulfill a Kingdom of God Manifest Destiny?*

All year long I was told that my time Abroad4God was going to radically change my heart and bolster my faith. I was going to come back as an entirely transformed individual, ready to move to the 10/40 Window and beach evangelize all of my days.

But that's not what was happening within me. Instead, I kept thinking what a colossal waste of time and resources all this was. I was angry at JBL. And Laurel! And Karen and Larry!

Before we went to Indonesia, Laurel spoke to our house group about the country's "facts," but I truly don't remember anything beyond "It has a very high percentage of Muslims." We didn't learn about the history of Indonesia, how it came to be the world's third-largest democracy, why Bali is randomly Hindu when the rest of the country is Muslim, and actually that it is far more progressive than many other Islamic countries. We didn't learn about the place we were going, outside of the fact that it was Muslim and any information related to that.

Karen shared at one point that female mutilation is still practiced in Indonesia. (I looked this up during the writing of this book, and turns out, she isn't wrong. Among Indonesian girls under the age of nineteen, 51 percent have been subjected to some form of FGM, according to the UNFPA's *Demographic Perspectives on Female Genital Mutilation*. But this is not an Islamic mandated law; it is a deep-seated cultural practice that many advocates in Indonesia are speaking out against and educating on.) I asked how this could be legal (turns out, it isn't), but Karen's response was "Indonesian government law is directly linked to Islamic law. Indonesian culture has no concept of church and state." Lol, as if America is absolutely killing it by compartmentalizing its citizen's religious views from enforced policy …

She also shared that it's very common in Muslim communities for the men to do whatever they want—sleep with sex workers, look at porn, beat their wives and children—meanwhile adultery in women is cause for time in prison. Again, I did some research, and she's also not exactly wrong here either. As recently as 2022, Indonesia made a law that women who have sex outside of marriage could be arrested and face up to a year in prison.[1]

Let me be clear, this is horrifying data. But just how different is this Muslim-influenced culture from pastors who get to repeatedly cheat on their wives with younger women and keep their jobs, while if a woman did the same, she'd be ostracized forever? Furthermore, the victims of said pastor's manipulation and grooming are seen as the cause of his "stumbling" instead of what they are—victims!

OR if a pastor gets caught jerking off to porn at his church office, he'll get sent away to a sex-addict-recovery center, aka an isolated retreat resort, for three months where his biggest struggle is having wet dreams as a grown man while his wife has to stay back home with the kids and deal with the fact that her husband did something really fucking weird and she'll get blamed for it because she didn't put out or wasn't desirable enough. None of these are from personal experience or anything!

Log in your own eye,[2] motherfuckers.

As far as I could tell, there were educated and tactical ways we could have been utilizing our time in Indonesia and in support of the communities there during our year in JBL. Couldn't we have spent the year investing in women's advocacy movements on the ground in Jakarta, etc. ... ? Instead of sitting around learning Bible lesson acronyms, hosting outreach Uno Dorito nights, then taking people's money to tell eleven-year-olds what a Playboy logo means. We could have, like the witch doctor–disciple–rice farmer, gotten shit done.

I brought this up to Laurel as well. "Are we going to do any *actual* work while we are here?" Aghast, because, *am I insinuating that telling people about Jesus in a Muslim country isn't actual work?* she informed me, "The Gospel is the ultimate healer, Mattie Jo. If we can just share it with enough people, the pain and injustice within this country will be eradicated."

On an individual spiritual level, the "if your heart changes, your actions will change" thing could apply. Ideally anyway. But on a national/cultural level? Not so much.

For example, when Hitler was burning people in ovens, were we supposed to just wait for "The Lord to change his heart" or go fuck shit up? There is a time for spiritual healing and there is a time for literal healing. These two things are often conflated in Evangelical communities.

P.S., Remember my Evangelical propaganda Columbine trauma? I was told that mass shooting happened because Bibles and prayer were no longer allowed in American Public schools. And Marilyn Manson.

Never once did I hear an adult in my life talk about preventing devastating mass shootings by *actively* voting or lobbying for more restrictive gun laws. That maybe our children wouldn't have to experience tornado, fire, and *intruder* drills at school if heavy weaponry weren't sold next to electronics at your local supercenter. Nope! Just pray and send a child martyr: The Evangelical way.

Maybe you're thinking, "But didn't your JBL rent go toward funding some things like education support, protecting those in need, building homes, etc.?" Yes, you're right. Our rent did supposedly go to projects *like* this. But, if you look at the current JBL website, a lot of our money also goes to fund "pastoral homes" all over the 10/40 Window.

Well, I got to see Karen and Larry's—two people whose entire lives were supported by USD donors—pastoral home while we were there. And let me tell you, they were not living in a hut.

They lived in a gorgeous, expansive house, complete with a house-keeper and *landscapers*. These missionaries were living a privileged life by anyone's standards, but for Indonesia? They were living like absolute royalty! They earned this exceptionally privileged life by

Making.

More.

Christians.

Most of this trip had my insides screaming in conflict.

Why were we not doing actual service things to help? Isn't, like, all of this completely missing the point? Is waiting to share the Gospel, flee, and then hope those little Christian seeds we planted grow big enough to get some souls into Heaven one day really the "just like Jesus" thing to do (Proverbs 3:5-6)?

But because I was not yet confident in my opinions or personal experience, and was constantly up against being taught *not* to be confident in them, I was also scared of my thoughts.

Why was I so averse to sharing Jesus's story publicly? If I loved Jesus, shouldn't I desire to live the way He calls me to live? Why were His desires not my desires? Why did I want to move to New York more than Indonesia? Why did I not care about converting the Muslims? Why on that trip did I miss my boyfriend more than I wanted to get better at beach Evangelism? Why was I more fascinated by rambutan for dessert and Christian witch doctoring than the details of a testimony?

Instead of leaving that trip fully absolved of my JBL duties, I left further convinced that I was doing it all wrong; sincerely convinced that maybe all these conflicting thoughts and feelings were arising within me because I still had too much sin in my life. *Why are my desires still not God's desires?*

If I made it back to America alive, I promised God I would be willing to make the ultimate sacrifice for our relationship.

10

SPIRITUALLY GASLIT

I WAS ELATED TO arrive in the US unharmed by Muslim vigilantes, but very very sad that I now had to uphold my end of my bargain with God. He'd spared my life over there in Indonesia; now I had to sacrifice my boyfriend.

It was time to break up with Brandon.

If you were raised Evangelical, you know the greatest sacrifice you can make for your relationship with God is to "be single like the Apostle Paul."

If you're not a Recovering Evangelical, that's an unexpected curveball and what does that have to do with God? Great question! The answer is it doesn't actually.

It's based on 1 Corinthians 7, where Paul—a convert who used to kill Jesus followers and then became a Jesus follower. He is their golden boy/poster child and they are obsessed with everything the guy wrote—speaks to the people of Corinth about their relationship statuses and what to do within them. He says to the single people:

> *Now to the unmarried and the widows I say: It is good for them to stay unmarried, as I do. But if they cannot control themselves, they should marry, for it is better to marry than to burn with passion.*

I read this verse and thought, "This is proof I will for sure get married! I am way too horny; Paul said so! I burn with too much passion."

But church told us this verse means, if you're "still single," it's all good! Singlehood is a gift. Use all this single time to focus more on The Lord like the Apostle Paul!

If you were not single and a little too focused on your boyfriend/girlfriend instead of Jesus, they'd use this passage to tell you to break up with your bf/gf so you can love Jesus more. If all of our energy is going to be poured successfully into upleveling your relationship with Christ, you shan't be distracted by things like love and libido.

I was really distracted by things like love and libido.

I remember writing in my journal on the flight back that I didn't have enough space in my heart for Jesus *and* Brandon. As it stood, Brandon took up way more space than Jesus. I mean, look at how ready I was to get back to the States to see him instead of telling more Muslims about Jesus. Clearly, my desires were all out of whack!

So, despite being devastated and not wanting to follow through with it at all, I broke up with Brandon upon my stateside return.

We sobbed Like, a lot.

"This is what sacrifice feels like," I told Brandon through ugly cries.

This part of my story makes me so mad, because I put myself and Brandon through so much unnecessary emotional pain, as if that carried the same gravity as Jesus's brutal death on the cross for the sin of humanity. I was just like Jesus in the Garden of Gethsemane![1] Following God wasn't about me and what I wanted. It was about doing whatever He required to further His Kingdom. I was being a *real* Christian.

I'd done the #breakup4Jesus. Now I had to give up my grandest love—New York City.

This one really stumped me. The whole letting go of love and libido for God was so heavily touted in Evangelical culture, I understood removing that "distraction." But I was absolutely devastated to think that the passion for acting I'd had my entire life was being divinely snuffed out. Hadn't God helped me raise the money to find my calling at rich-kid theater camp? Hadn't my love for acting helped heal my eating disorder and put me on a path of deep joy? Didn't I feel closer to God in the artistic mecca of New York City than I felt anywhere else?

I signed up for another year of Jesus Beacon Light, mentally changed my post-graduation plans to full-time mission work, and cried every day for months.

My heart sank deeper and deeper into my stomach as I thought about my life if I continued on the JBL trajectory. The discomfort and absolute misery I felt around the call to full-time mission work should have been enough to keep me from going through with it. But there is the whole elevation of self-sacrifice for the Lord norm in the Evangelical world that kept me thinking these bad feelings were a *good* sign: The more I sacrificed my personal wants and desires for God, the more I was living in accordance with His will.

At the same time, there was a nagging voice in the back of my heart wondering if I was making the wrong choice here. Was it really God's will that I abandon things that I loved and was passionate about—acting, my relationship with Brandon—for something that gave me a deep icky feeling down to my toenails?

I spoke with my dad about this whole Great Commission life transformation I was undergoing. He was a pastor, so I could trust him to give me that Gospel-following good-good and not sugarcoat "the truth." I asked if he thought I needed to sacrifice my love for Brandon, for performing, and my dreams of moving to New York if I wanted to live out God's will.

He laughed at me, acknowledged my distress, and then said, "Matts, you have been full of this actor/performing/wildly-in-love sparkle since you were born. To not live out your passions would be going against what God has intended for you from your start. If you don't follow *your* dreams, you will be doing the world a disservice."

"But isn't leaning into my dreams and passions being 'fleshly'?"

"Fleshly" is probably a male masturbation toy made in Japan, and also a word Evangelicals use to describe anything that is a personal desire and not in alignment with God, i.e., "of the flesh." Based on Romans 8:5–6, "the flesh" is all your human wants, desires, stuff; "the Spirit" is anything that is of God/Jesus/holy.

As the teaching goes, the flesh and the Spirit are constantly in conflict with each other. The flesh is your sin, and the Spirit within you fights the sin. Of course, what each sect and subset of Christians deem "fleshly" varies. But across the board, as a Christ follower with the Holy Spirit within you, you're experiencing an ongoing internal civil war. Super fun stuff!

Dad shook his head. "Following the flesh is not the same as following your personally and divinely designed purpose. Not everyone's pursuit of the Lord is meant to look the same."

Thank God for a pastor dad who is more like Mel Robbins than a pastor. That was exactly what I needed to hear.

The leaders of JBL went to huge lengths to make me feel like I was going to Hell if I didn't live out their mission, that I was hugely harming the message of Jesus on earth if I didn't maintain their unrealistic morality measures accompanied by modern martyrdom.

This organization—and many others like it—set up environments that took vulnerable, not-yet-fully-formed adult people and spiritually gaslit them into chambers of high manipulation. All in the name of spreading the love of Jesus.

I was made to feel like I, the lazy, not-enough Christian, was the problem. When actually, JBL members were the problem. They were lazy motherfuckers!

It is so much easier to sit around in a Bible study echo chamber all year, hanging out only with other Christians, looking down on people who don't follow the exact faith you do, than it is to actually engage in the messy, complicated world in which we exist.

It is so much easier to go to other countries and *do absolutely nothing but look like ethnocentric American assholes*—how is that not all incredibly harmful to Jesus' message of love and service?—than it is to actually meet an immediate need and get shit done.

I get really heated about this, mostly because I totally bought into it.

By the end of the summer, I gave a big, empowered, and metaphorical middle finger to JBL. I got back together with Brandon and told them I was not signing on for another year. They gave me a scolding in hopes of changing my mind, but it didn't work. I still get their emails. I should probably unsubscribe.

I had traversed a massive part of my Jesus culture deconstruction that summer.

I didn't have to follow someone else's version of Christ following in order to truly follow Christ.

I didn't have to fall into the "Christian enough" shame spiral.

Morphing myself into something I hate will never be in alignment with God's purpose for me.

God's purpose for me will always be in alignment with feeling fully me.

I didn't know it then, but I would revisit these truths countless times in my deconstruction, as my faith looked less and less recognizable:

- My desires are not in conflict with Jesus's desires.

- Being fully me is not a sin.

- I am enough.

11

BIBLICAL MARRIAGE, PART 2

I'VE RECLAIMED THAT MY personal dreams are valid and I don't have to move to Indonesia to prove my commitment to Jesus, I've still got two more years before I can fully immerse myself in the life I'm dreaming up with every dance class and voice lesson, and I've gotten back together with my hot Catholic boyfriend I'll need to marry soon so I can get laid.

Moving into my junior year, even though I'd only just become old enough to drink alcohol legally, shit started to get "serious." Brandon had graduated the year prior and was now teaching high school physics during his gap year before medical school. We were doing long distance, and although we still cared deeply for each other, the reality that our future ambitions were more than likely going to implode due to our conflicting visions was setting in.

My future included moving to New York City upon graduation, and then who knew where my acting would lead me? Brandon's future was a little more ... predictable. Or as predictable as life can really be. He still had a year of teaching, four years of medical school in Missouri, and three more years of residency literally anywhere before his career would begin. We discussed every possibility for "making this work."

"Well, we can get engaged next year," I proposed (lol, proposed proposing). "We'll get married the year after I graduate, I'll move in with you at medical school for four years, do some regional theater, and then you can get your residency in or near New York City! Voila!"

"MJ, no."

Okay, I thought that was fantastic problem-solving, Brandon. Tell me your genius ideas.

"Medical school is going to be all-consuming," Brandon explained. "I don't think I will be able to juggle being a good husband to you and the pressures of medical school. Furthermore, I don't have a choice of where I get my residency. What if I don't get it anywhere near New York City? What then? You just put your dreams on hold for an entire decade waiting for me to become a doctor?"

My pre-feminist self was internally saying, *Um, yes, obviously I will put my dreams on hold while you become a doctor, because doctors are very rich.* And: *Yes, because at least I will be getting laid without fear of going to Hell.*

Also: *What is my other choice? Not get married in my early twenties?? I am not prepared for that, Brandon!*

We went back and forth on this issue for the entire year. I'd start to feel more secure in our relationship when he let his love for me lead the way. Then pragmatism would kick in, and he'd get all anxious and distant again.

I was so frustrated because, like, *of course* I'd hold off on my New York–actor-life plans to marry Brandon! Couldn't he see that my love for him simply overfloweth?!

But the truth was, I wasn't willing to endure this self-sacrifice because of "love." I was willing to endure self-sacrifice because of fear.

I honestly had never even considered a life where I made it past twenty-three years old unmarried and therefore, a "virgin." (And by *virgin*, of course I was using the narrow definition of penis-in-vagina penetration that I'd received from the church.)

Life as an Evangelical woman had not given me a road map for potentially being single and sexless well into adulthood. If two years in a serious relationship had taught me anything, it was that I was not meant to be single like the Apostle Paul. My libido and I needed to become one flesh[1] sooner than later.

Which leads me to a not-so-popular opinion especially in the eyes of my friends who did get married right out of college: Most young Evangelical couples are getting married to have divinely approved sex. They will try to deny this, but they are lying. I mean, sure, there are other reasons, like they love each other like Christ loves the church, blah

blah. But at the root of their Christlike connection is the lure of (wildly disappointing) wedding-night sex.

Anyway ... my inner Evangelical panic attack over potentially not being a postgraduation bride:

If I don't marry Brandon, how can I go on being a woman of God? How do you pursue Jesus without a husband and divine permission to bump uglies?

I know it sounds like I just wanted to marry Brandon for his dick, because I did, but it was also for something much deeper. (See what I did there?)

As a young woman in the church, my entire existence and value would be validated by being chosen by a man. If Brandon and I ended things, I thought I could deal with the no-sex thing—well, I'd figure that out eventually. What I didn't know if I could handle, however, was that I would no longer be *chosen*.

It's not news to women in American culture at large that most of us, even non-Christian women, are brought up being taught by media, our peers, and sometimes even our parents that the most important quality to possess as a woman is desirability by a man. We see it in the Disney movies, rom-coms, literature. At a certain point in a woman's life, there's an underlying story that if you're single, it's because there's something you're doing wrong.

Evangelical culture compounds and expedites these bogus beliefs by attaching them to God and a woman's sexual history—which is why the age for getting the "what's wrong with her?" singleness side-eye is closer to teens than the secular standard of like, your forties.

Though not explicitly stated (so maybe this was just my personal internalization), it seemed that being loved and chosen by a man of God to be his wife was tantamount to being loved and chosen by God. Therefore, *not* being loved and chosen by a man of God was tantamount to *not* being loved and chosen by God.

No part of my value as a woman could be isolated from my relationship with men. Which meant that entering my viable marital years devoid of Brandon would make me one of "those" women at church. The aforementioned blamed-for-their-singleness, undesirables.

Within purity culture, all your pubescent years are spent being bombarded with messaging that essentially tells you to stay away from the opposite sex in order to preserve your purity. Your value does not come from what boys think of you but from what God thinks of you. Which is actually directly linked to what men think of you, because the whole reason you're saving yourself is because *that's what men of God want*.

Then, as soon as you are a viable marriage age (I've recently seen as young as nineteen in my hometown), at all costs, *do not be single*. Engage with the opposite sex in the most extreme way—get married *stat*. Because being single once you *can be* married means there's something seriously wrong with you.

This results in women having zero tools to actually date and interact with the opposite sex without it needing to end in marriage. So that when/if a relationship doesn't end in marriage, you're not really sure how to navigate being a nonmarried person who is "old enough" to get married. And your value is all messily intertwined with what God thinks of you and what men think of you and ...

You buy this book.

And if you're single because you're gay, well. Good luck.

At the time I didn't realize how fucked-up it was that my value as a human being was so heavily attached to being chosen by another human being. That I'd only developed scraps of autonomous self-esteem, thanks to my parents. I also didn't realize how absolutely asinine it was that I believed the ultimate gift *the God of the universe* could come up with for me was a straight dude in his early twenties. Be better at gift giving, God.

But these were my unconscious-to-fully-conscious beliefs, and I was truly distraught.

What did I do to deserve this plague of singleness into my twenties? Was it second base? Okay, no more second base!

Was it not spreading the Gospel enough? Okay, more Bridge
Analogies! Should I be trying to lead more Bible studies in
my sorority? Just tell me what to do, Jesus!

One night, over Skype, we revisited this troubleshooting-our-rela-
tionship-post-graduation conversation.

"Brandon, I love you. We can make this work. What if we just do
... really long distance for a while? I can fly back on weekends and ...
holidays?"

"MJ, you already miss so much of your life at college to spend weekends with me. You're going to do the same in New York? I can't let you
do that. Plus, all that money on flights when rent and just living in New
York City is so expensive ... Just, no ..."

Every time I offered a solution, Brandon came back with some very
sensible reason why it could not work. Ugh. So brainy.

"Also, you have to admit, MJ. Our personalities just ... clash."

Well, this took a turn.

"What do you mean?"

"I dunno. You know ... you overwhelm me sometimes. I'm starting to
think I want someone ... quieter. Less ... Just less. You're too much."

Oh.

So that's what I'd done to not be chosen. *I was me.*

"Well. Then I think it's best if we end things here," I replied, somehow,
without so much as a hitch in my voice.

Brandon, on the other hand, totally lost his shit and sobbed, just like
the first time we broke up. "Are we really breaking up over Skype right
now?"

"Brandon, doing this back-and-forth about our future is like ripping
a Band-Aid off a nearly healed wound. It hurts more every time and I
can't do it anymore. I love you and probably always will. But I have to
go. Rehearsal."

And just like that, my first love story ended in my boyfriend telling me,
over Skype, that he didn't want me because I was "too much."

At least, that's all I heard.

We hung up. I went to rehearsal with a bag full of my LaDucas, leotards, and harmful stories I'd carry around about my self-worth for the next half a decade.

> *I am the reason I'll never be chosen. My personality too large. My aspirations too big. My laugh too loud. My "too much–ness" too much. Women like me are undesirable.*

What do you do when you were raised to believe your value lay in being chosen by a man to be his wife and to only sleep with him? But now you're single and likely moving to New York City to follow your own dreams, which you always liked the idea of but never imagined doing unattached to a spouse?

You move to New York City in your early twenties to find a husband.

12

New York Is My Boyfriend/Wild Love Affair

I HAD JUST BROKEN up with the man of my dreams, and was now bitter, single, and twenty-one in the City of my dreams for my annual New York spring break trip.

I'm not sure what I expected from that trip to New York, but I can assure you, my experience far exceeded anything I could have imagined. "I did the most," as the youths say.

First things first: alcohol.

Although I had turned twenty-one six months prior to spring break in NYC, I really didn't drink that much before that trip. Depending on what brand of Evangelical you were raised, the okay-ness of alcohol consumption varies. I was in the land of BYX[1] and Baptists, so if you were calling yourself a Believer, the message was "don't do it."

Even if you're not "drinking to get drunk" (a sin) people won't know that. They'll see you with a red Solo cup and assume you're sluttin' around like the rest of the seculars. And then, once again, you're unintentionally damaging the message of Christ with your actions. So just, *Don't do it, promise?*

I chose not to drink until I was twenty-one because of this social influence, my family's long line of addicts, and because I didn't want to spend money on a "minor in possession" ticket. I was, above all, fiscally responsible.

Also because on the weekends I would leave to visit Brandon in the town where he was teaching, instead of staying at my college to get white-girl wasted with my sorority sisters. Once he was out of the picture, however, I let my inner Ke$ha run amok.

Despite getting drunk technically being a sin, I justified my drinking by asserting that my actions while drunk were more important than the actual "sin" of getting drunk. So as long as I wasn't committing any undoable sins like sex before marriage during drunk time, the severity of my blows to the message of Christ wouldn't be *that* bad. *What if, because I'm more relaxed from the booze, I get wild and end up successfully beach evangelizing?*

Not to mention, my experiences with Evangelical culture were subconsciously compounding to make me more okay with not being anyone's "example of Christ." Between the church's homophobia, my "super stress no sex" situation with Brandon, and JBL, I was slowly *fucking over it*. I stopped formally leading any Bible studies or stepping into discipleship relationships, and didn't care about telling my sorority sisters about Jesus. I just wanted to practice my faith as my own for a while, pressure free.

Lastly, Jesus's first miracle was keepin' the party goin' (well, at least in John—the timeline of this changes in the other Gospels ...) so I think he's okay with people having a good time is all I'm sayin'!

The point is, I was in New York and I could drink alcohol! *Game changer.* I spent a lot more money, but I had a lot more fun.

At bars in the Theater District, with a fancy cocktail in hand, I met Broadway stars and talked to them like they were my best friends, because alcohol made me more outgoing than I already was. Who knew! I explored the bar scene of the Lower East Side, went to rooftop clubs, and stayed out ... very late.

Having real nightlife experiences also meant I was kind of a terrible guest. My hosts were friends I'd met on a previous trip to New York who lived in Washington Heights. They were incredibly generous to let me stay on their couch for an entire week, and I was unintentionally an ungrateful asshole in return.

A logistic I had missed on my previous trips to the Big Apple was that late-night transportation is very unreliable. Trains come about every fifty-two minutes, so you usually have to take a car to wherever you wish to sleep, and that costs a lot of money I didn't have because I'd spent so much on fancy cocktails. Washington Heights is very far away from the happenin' night life I was experiencing, so I was either going to be completely broke after that trip, wait around for the train, or sleep on a bench in Central Park. At least I had options?

Another logistic: rules around replicating keys for NYC apartments vary from building to building. You can do it regardless of the building's rules, but certain keys are harder to replicate than others, and that can be super expensive. My hosts had one of those hard-and-expensive-to-replicate key situations, so I wasn't able to let myself in whenever I wanted. Which left my hosts waiting up for me or meant I had to be done with my adventures before they went to sleep at around 11 p.m.

Since 11 p.m. is literally an hour before Cinderella's curfew and I was on vacation trying to numb my heartbreak with as much adventure as possible, I didn't keep the curfew. I also didn't want to be rude and make them wait up for me, because I'm a Midwesterner with manners. If I was still out and about by 11 p.m., I became selectively pious and implemented my "just trust Jesus" technique.

A.k.a., I had faith God would find me a place to sleep.

One night I'm out, it's past 11 p.m., and I get to talking to this really good-looking dude whom I met through mutual friends. We'll call him Model, because he was tall, had a ridiculous jawline, and was straight-outta-a-Taylor-Swift-music-video hot.

Despite this guy being very hot and my being incredibly flattered that he was flirting with me, I had not forgotten a very important detail: I didn't have a place to sleep for the night. Maybe … he had some extra bed connects?

"My room is really small. But you can have the bed and I'll make a pallet on the floor."

Internal monologue:

> *I would NEVER just go home with someone I met hours ago even if they are super hot and I'm super horny and sad.*

Check the purity ring, Model. Also, you could be a serial killer!

What I actually said:

"Oh my gosh, you're so kind really?!"

And then we had a sleepover.

This was the beginning of my Necessary Pendulum. All Recovering Evangelicals experience this to some extent. It's the time in your life when you inexplicably go from following the most extreme rules about purity and Christlike morality to a T to not even knowing if you believe in God and having a slew of one-night stands.

I wasn't quite to the "questioning the existence of God/having one night stands" phase, but I did go from making very strict rules about sleeping in my bed with my boyfriend of two years to sleeping in a total stranger's bed after knowing him for two hours. All within three days. Religious recovery is weird.

We stayed up for hours chatting and I was lowkey not really paying attention to anything he was saying but instead staring at his jawline when just *you guess* what I learned about this guy. He's a Christian! See, he's not a serial killer—he loves Jesus!

How had I managed to stumble upon such a gorgeous, generous man of God in the city of my dreams, days after breaking up with Brandon? *God, are you gifting a husband in New York before I even move there?! That is so sweet!*

But then my wedding-pictures-atop-the-Empire-State-Building fantasy was abruptly halted with another detail:

He had a girlfriend.

Um. *Wut?*

Okay, not only was I, like, pretty bummed my wedding plans were so short-lived, but also ... that's ... weird? I mean, not that I thought he was trying to sleep with me exactly, but *what are you going to tell your girlfriend about this, Model? You were just trying to be a hero? Platonically helping a damsel in distress by allowing her to sleep in your bed?*

I didn't know what an open relationship was at that time, but I assume they didn't have one since, ya know, the Christian thing.

Whatever, I won't judge him. This is the part where I just go to sleep.

Then he asked to kiss me.

Of course this is happening to me! I didn't come to New York and meet my husband. I came to New York and managed to go home with a spiritual player! Asdhfkajsdhfjkahfdjkasfhd!

Spiritual player is a term I coined in high school to describe guys who "really love Jesus" but also really love blow jobs. And since those two things cannot coexist in Evangelical culture, dudes are supposed to love Jesus enough to resist acting on their love of blow jobs. But literally no teenage boy loves God more than getting their dick sucked, so of course these spiritual players are totally getting premarital BJs.

Premarital BJs are not the part that makes these guys the worst. The problem with spiritual players is they use their Christ-centered sex appeal to lure young ladies in and, after the BJ receiving, break things off. They do this because they now see the BJ giver as "not wife material." Spiritual players pawn off all the shame of the sexual act on to the woman, taking no responsibility (or shame) themselves.

Spiritual players are Christian fuckboys, and they don't always grow out of it in high school. Some of them become grown-ass men who are still abiding by their Madonna-whore complexes. And if a woman isn't woke enough to recognize these unhealthy, Oedipal, mentally infantile behaviors in the man, she'll take on all the shame for being the whore and not the wife. I lived very fully in this dichotomy for a long time.

Back to your paid programming.

So Model here was a spiritual player, ready to use his spiritual sex appeal to lure in the vulnerable. Thing is, he probably couldn't find any girl in Manhattan to work his disciple-dick-magic on, because women in Manhattan don't give a shit about spiritual sex appeal. Unless you're, like, a hot-yoga teacher.

Lucky for Model, he had conveniently stumbled upon a brokenhearted, "please want me, Man of God!" single woman from Missouri. I was spiritual player catnip, in the perfect emotional position to make terrible choices because I needed to feel loved and affirmed by a man who had a relationship with Jesus. The best predators are the ones who understand their prey.

"You have a girlfriend," I replied. Remember, he asked to kiss me.

"I know. And I'm thinking about proposing soon."

Oh my God.

He continued.

"Actually. I have the ring and she's visiting next week."

HOW DOES THIS KEEP GETTING MORE FUCKED-UP?

"But part of me needs to know, for sure, that I don't want to be with anyone else."

Did I mention Model doesn't drink? Yeah, so this is a *totally sober* justification for cheating on his soon-to-be-Evangelical fiancée. I kind of wanted to throw up in my mouth. And then kiss him. Take that, spiritual player!

But actually, my response was throw-up-in-my-mouth–worthy.

No, I did not slap Model in the face and say, "So you want to USE me as a means of knowing for sure that you don't want to get married? Perhaps you even having these thoughts and, I dunno, being twenty-one is enough reason to not follow through with this proposal?! I feel very sorry for your future wife and the person she thinks she's marrying. You suck!" Then dramatically slam his door, run into the streets of New York in nothing but his giant T-shirt, and sleep on the ground before I went anywhere near that asshole again.

No, that only happens ... well I don't know when that would ever happen, but in real life humans are rarely ballsy heroes who will voluntarily sleep pantless on benches instead of in a warm bed next to a model.

Instead, I kissed him. And we enjoyed second base every night for the next week until his girlfriend arrived.

It didn't end there. Even after Model proposed, we stayed in touch. The next time I was in New York, the same pattern ensued. I assume he never told her. According to Instagram, they are still happily married.

Despite knowing our little love affair was never going to amount to anything real, I was hurt. After all, this whole situation had once again proven that I was not enough to be chosen. Not wife material. Chillin' out on the spiritual side-eye-lines.

I also felt horribly guilty. I had capital-S sinned with this guy! I was the "other woman," and it was 10,000 percent consensual. Enjoyable, even.

I didn't think I was "that kind of person." The kind of person who could let themselves fall for someone in a committed relationship. The kind of person who could be so dishonest. I didn't think I had it in me to be so *bad*.

After a few months of this dirty secret eating me alive, I decided to talk to my older brother Eddie about it. Eddie left Jesus culture before me and was always a little ahead of my Recovering Evangelical curve. He was the only person I knew who, at the very least, wouldn't shame me more than I was already shaming myself for this adultery.

"So, you made out with a guy who is now engaged? So what?"

"So. *What*?" I expected Eddie to be non-judgy but to completely dismiss my abhorrent behavior as not abhorrent behavior? I wasn't seeking *that* level of support.

"Mattie, that is so not a huge deal."

Eddie would say that. He was a liberal LA hippie screenwriter. He didn't understand *the depths of my sin.*

"It is totally a huge deal, Eddie!" I shot back. "I should have held myself to a higher standard in this situation. A Godly standard. I'm a follower of Christ, I can't just be out here acting worldly and saying it's okay! And the worst part is ..."

"You had fun?

"Yes. How did you know that?"

"Because you are human." He turned down the Flaming Lips CD he'd pirated, so I knew he was getting serious. "Look, Matts, this guy being a confused twenty-one-year-old is not your problem. You were both acting honestly out of exactly where you are in life: just trying to figure things the fuck out. If you're committed to truly figuring things the fuck out for yourself, and not letting someone else tell you how to figure things out, you're going to fuck up. You're going to make mistakes. That is part of indulging the spectrum of life with abandon. Your experiences will be rich, but they will also sometimes be shitty."

Your experiences will be rich, but they will also sometimes be shitty.

Eddie carried on with his Exvangelical Yoda sermon. "The cool part about doing things you've always deemed 'bad' is you start to develop empathy. The more of the human experience you allow yourself to indulge, the more honestly you'll be able to relate to yourself and other humans. Refining who you want to be and how you want to be with others could never be a bad thing."

I wanted to believe he was right. That it was totally okay and necessary to make mistakes along the path of figuring life out. The problem was, I had to dissect some deeply ingrained messages I'd heard my whole life that suggested just the opposite.

I learned that all sin makes the gulf between me and God bigger and bigger. If I want to keep my God gulf small, I must keep my sins to a minimum. The way to keep my sins to a minimum is by doing exactly what God tells me to do.

How do I know what God wants me to do? By reading the Bible daily. I have God's breathed words at my disposal, giving me a "blueprint for life."

If I follow that blueprint for life, my sins stay small and so does the God gulf. Staying close to God guarantees an amazing life on earth and, ultimately, in Heaven. If I chose to go against this Godly blueprint, I would be choosing a blessing-*less* life. I would be choosing hell.

Furthermore, I'd heard many sermons that said "mistakes" are not real. It's all sin! Non-Believers use the term "mistakes" to justify their harmful behavior in order to "figure things out." They're watering down what they're actually doing—creating a bigger separation between themselves and God.

I, Mattie Jo Believer, do not need to figure things out for myself, because I already possess all the answers in this Godly blueprint; no mistakes needed! I will live a fuller, richer life than Non-Believers because I won't be distracted by all my do-*bad*-ing. I will connect with others better because I am so closely connected with God!

So if I decided I did not want to live according to this Godly blueprint for life, I would be telling God I know what's best for me more than He knows what's best for me. This was, according to scripture, the greatest sin of all: blaspheming the Holy Spirit.[2]

Pastors in my life described blaspheming the Holy Spirit as humans basically giving the middle finger to God's guidance by choosing their own. This is the unforgivable sin: Knowing the Godly path and rejecting it for my own knowledge (Hebrews 10:26–29).

Since I am, at my core, a sinful bag-o'-shit, I could never know better for myself than God knows for me. I cannot be trusted to guide me.

I had learned through repeated but subtle and therefore seriously insidious messaging that the ultimate unforgivable sin was *trusting myself*.

It was not Satan who was my biggest threat to being close to God and doing good with my life on earth; it was me.

Between the whole flesh-versus-spirit internal war, original sin, and not being able to trust yourself, you can see why existing as a Recovering Evangelical is mental and emotional gymnastics nobody fucking asked for.

Eddie was offering an out of this Evangelical mind-fuckery. If I decided I wanted to pave my own way instead of following God's way, not only would I probably be sinning a lot, I would be committing the unforgivable sin of trusting myself.

Can you trust yourself though, Mattie Jo? Look what you did in New York left to your own fleshly devices. This is proof you need to stay on the Godly blueprint!

Was that true though? Maybe it wasn't proof that I needed to stay on the godly blueprint, but just that I, for the first time in my life, was allowing myself space to fuck up, and that was *okay*. I was *learning*.

If I made mistakes with the intention of personal refinement, maybe I would become a really fantastic version of myself? Maybe I was on the precipice of living a really exciting life that I would not be able to live if I was tied to a husband in Missouri? Maybe this exciting life was what was meant for me, and not the "godly" blueprint. Maybe living my fullest life meant making my own blueprint up as I go?

Would God be upset with me just trying to live my fullest life? He came so that I could live abundantly, right? (John 10:10. Also realizing now what a hilariously unfortunate verb to use for this specific verse... #cumjokes). To me, making my own blueprint sounded hella more abundant than nailing my feet to the ground because the Bible tells me so.

I wanted to trust myself to make my own blueprint for life, but I was still terrified that in doing so I was choosing a blessing-less life. Could a life that belonged to me be more abundant than a life that belonged to God?

Only one way to find out.

13

GOD IS SO GOOD

DURING MY SENIOR YEAR of college, amid reconciling the fact that my big adult life plan of getting married soon after graduation would no longer be realized, I threw myself into my dream of moving to New York to pursue acting professionally. The alternative was to rot as a single straight woman in Missouri with the other mid-twenties old maids. I hadn't gotten student loans in musical theater to do that, so *On My Own* it was.

Many things had to be in order before I would make this move. I am not one of those reckless, artistic types who could move to New York with $13 and pray I didn't have to move back in with my parents within the year.

No, no. I am a Virgo. I had faith, but I also had a checklist.

My list included saving at least $5,000 as my New York starter fund, having professional theater credits under my belt, and finding a place to live for under $850 a month in Manhattan. (*Dear Jesus God don't make me move to Brooklyn. I am not that cool.*)

But how the hell was I going to accomplish all that? When was I going to have time to work and save $5,000 between being a full-time student and nightly rehearsals??

The preemptive stress I was enduring over the hunt for an affordable apartment in Manhattan was crippling. I cried so many virgin tears into countless bowls of instant mashed potatoes that year. In hindsight I should have bottled those up and sold them to a weirdo on the internet. Voila! All the moving money!

Anyway, my anxiety was quickly spilling over into depression. But since Christians aren't so good at the whole treating-mental-health thing, I just did what I knew how to do:

I prayed. I prayed fucking fervently.

I knew I couldn't do all this by myself. I needed God to do me a few solids. And since I had some shit to make up for from the whole spiritual-player love affair, I got to work. I had to prove my devotion to the Lord if I wanted his blessings.

Every morning, I journaled *hard*. I read books written by nuns while I was on the elliptical at the gym. I went to Mass during the week with my Catholic friends and made it back home to nondenom cool church with my family on Sundays. I read the Bible while I tried to relax on Saturdays with HGTV in the background. And I was still not having sex. I was "pray fervently" personified.

My hope-full-ly devoted plan totally worked. I managed to get four part-time jobs senior year that all worked around my class and rehearsal schedules. I got a theater gig that covered housing and food, so I saved a ton of money. God had provided more than $5,000 and a great resumé builder! Now I just needed Him to come through with an apartment.

I had visited the City enough to have realistic standards of what my first living situation in New York would probably be like. Somewhere in Washington Heights, with twelve roommates, no elevator to the fifth-but-actually-sixth floor, and a noisy view of the George Washington Bridge.

I was okay with this reality, as long as it was within my budget and close to a train, so I could get to work and early-morning auditions fairly feasibly. I also knew I wouldn't have this sorted out until a few weeks before the move, because that is how real estate works in New York City. Brokers won't even show an apartment until two or three weeks before the move-in date.

Awaiting the most important moving detail—*where I would live*—was eating apart my insides, but I knew I just had to be patient. *Keep praying, Bible/nun-memoir reading, not-sex-having, Mattie Jo.*

All year I had been so disciplined—jumping from rehearsal to work shift to church service to devo time—I was very ready for my annual spring break trip to New York City. As soon as I finished some very important industry meetings and performances required to graduate, I proceeded to enjoy one last trip to the City as a nonresident. I took in all the sights, whiskey shots, and Broadway shows without any other responsibilities.

That week was chock-full of miracles I had earned from a year of unrelenting devotion to the Lord. Obviously.

After my stunning performances for industry people, in order to celebrate getting some laughs and not completely flubbing the high notes, I got irresponsibly intoxicated and passed out on the subway. I woke up at Coney Island to an MTA employee nudging me:

"Scuse me, miss, where was your stop?"

"Prospect Ave.," I muttered sadly as I noticed vomit on my new peacoat.

"Come with me."

Kind MTA employee/my guardian angel walked me onto a different train car, pointed to another MTA employee, and said, "This train conductor is going to make sure you get off at Prospect Ave. if you fall asleep again."

"Thank you," I replied, nearly in tears of drunken gratitude.

Spoiler: I fell asleep again.

I was awakened *again* by some other random guy/guardian angel #2:

"You should really put your bag in your lap and the strap around your shoulder so someone can't easily steal it."

He sounded like he had firsthand experience in the matter, so I took his advice.

"Thank you," I mumbled before, you guessed it, I fell asleep again.

I eventually got to Prospect Ave., where the new train conductor made sure I exited safely.

It was 4 a.m. by the time I made it to my friend's apartment where I was staying. He answered the door to a shamelessly drunk me covered in my own vomit. "I told you not to fall asleep on the train."

I pushed past him rudely, and exclaimed "Wait until I tell you about the angels I met on the train!" and promptly fell asleep on the couch for good in my puke coat.

Later in the week, while on a fun day trip to Princeton, I received news that I had been accepted to attend a musical theater industry training in the City that upcoming August. I couldn't believe it! I was planning to move in September, so God was providing the perfect window for apartment hunting WHILE networking with musical theater casting directors, choreographers, and other Broadway professionals right before I officially moved to New York City!

After receiving this news and thanking God for more blessings, I called my dad and to discuss the logistics of how the heck I was going to pay for the intensive.

"You're going," Dad said.

"But, Dad, it's so expensive and I'm already saving for my move an—" Dad cut me off.

"Mattie Jo, you've done this before. Remember French Woods? You can raise the money. Your community will support you. God will take care of ya."

Given my recent Olympic-level devotion, I knew Dad was right. God had already provided so much for me to move to New York seamlessly. I knew I could trust Him to provide this money too.

After my mild panic attack over being poor but ambitious, I called up my brother's ex-girlfriend Lisa.

Quick rewind.

When I was fourteen, Eddie met a girl at USC who had grown up *Gossip Girl* level Upper East Side royalty. Lisa and I became fast friends because she was the only person I knew who, when I told her I wanted to do musical theater, didn't say, "Well, Branson is the perfect place for that!" Instead, she said, "Then we have to get you to theater camp."

She's the one who'd helped me research the top theater camps in the country and found the place that set the stage (actor pun) for the rest of my life. While Lisa and I didn't keep in constant communication, I always had immense gratitude for how she'd truly changed my life.

Almost a decade later, I called her up and asked if I could chat about the details of my actual dream coming to fruition over Chinese takeout. I told her about the intensive and the apartment hunt and asked if I could have a place on her couch for a few weeks while I scoured Upper (Upper) Manhattan for a home.

"Oh, of course you can stay with me! When are you trying to move?" Lisa replied.

"September," I responded.

"Oh, crazy! I just ran into my friend and he's looking for a roommate in September."

"Really? What are the details?"

"Looks like it's four bedrooms, four bathrooms, two stories, a terrace, cleaning lady, doorman, laundry in-unit, on the Upper West Side . . ."

"Haha, I know you don't understand how money works for normal people, Lisa, but I can't afford that."

I didn't say that, but I was definitely thinking it. I didn't know it yet, but having thoughts like this and biting my tongue around the 1 percent would soon become my new normal.

I actually said, "That sounds amazing! But there's just really no way I can afford that. Thanks though!"

"It's only seven fifty a month."

SHUT YOUR FRONT DOOR MADE OF TRUST FUND RENT MONEY I HAVE TO SEE IT.

The next day I made plans to tour the place with the friend who was looking for a roommate, Colin.

The first thing I noticed about Colin was that he was handsome and well-dressed but looked very tired. *Is this how all rich guys look up close? Hot and exhausted, wrapped in a great suit?* I was learning so much already.

We met outside of the apartment building's foyer (which, I would learn is "properly" pronounced "foy-YAY" not "FOY-yer" after I moved in), shook hands, and he led me in.

I was definitely not in Kansas (City, Missouri) anymore.

A doorman held open the giant, gorgeously designed glass/steel door.

A doorman? What is even the point of a doorman? The closest thing I'd ever gotten to a doorman was a front desk worker at an Econo Lodge. *Will he bring me extra blankets if I'm cold at night? Is there a continental breakfast here?*

We walked into the lobby.

It was massive, but not in a corporate-office way. It reminded me more of Daddy Warbucks's mansion, with marble floors, a chandelier, gold-trimmed mirrors, a rug I'm sure cost more than Colin's private school kindergarten education. And everything was so shiny.

You know those scenes in movies where the camera spins around the actor while they're looking up, having a moment of deep awe at what is taking place around them? That was me in that foy-yay. I felt like Annie. Or Cinderella. Either way, I was clearly out of place. I was ready for someone to hand me a mop so I could get back to the working class where I belonged.

We got on the elevator, and Colin started chatting me up. Which probably should have made me nervous, as it was definitely a lowkey interview. But I didn't know that, so I just spilled all the details of my life, because I am a Midwesterner, and what is the point of small talk?

"You have four jobs and go to school full-time?" he asked.

"Yes. I'm selling my car soon too. I have a savings account I opened at a credit union three years ago, specifically for this move."

We talked about how I was going into musical theater, how I knew Lisa, and what the rest of my family was up to. I shared that my father was a Christian pastor, a detail I hoped wouldn't frighten him too much. He opened the door to the apartment.

It was ... unreal.

The living room was huge and full of natural light, a true luxury in New York City. There was original art on the walls, which didn't exactly mean anything to me at the time except that I'd never seen original-art decor unless it was framed finger paintings by a toddler. I eventually learned original art is an investment for the rich, so their pieces are a sort of posturing to other wealthy people. I even started learning the names of the artists so I could seem impressive to rich people I worked for. "Wow, you have an original Alice Neel?! I love her work. I went to her exhibit at the Met last fall."

There were sconces and a credenza, two words I definitely didn't know before that apartment tour. In Missouri we have "lamps" and "dressers." But I just nodded and said, "Yes this credenza *is* gorgeous."

Colin showed me to the room I'd be renting.

It was what is known as the maid's quarters. This, I learned, is where rich people lodge their live-in help. The room is usually off the kitchen or in another wing of the home, away from the family quarters, and is much smaller than the other bedrooms.

These maid's quarters were basically a closet with a window and could fit a twin bed. And I got my own bathroom! (that didn't have a sink but *whatever I'll brush my teeth in the shower.*)

My first thought was *Damnit! I'm graduating college to still sleep in a dorm bed?* My second thought was *How am I going to have sex on that thing?*

Uh-oh.

Oh My God. Why did I just say that in my head? I don't have s—

Colin interrupted my fleshly thought diversion. "It's not great for company," he said. "But it's why you pay the least."

Oh my god, again. Did Colin just read my mind? This is not good, MJ. Not good.

"Oh, I won't be 'having company,'" I replied. "I don't *have company.*"

Did he get what I was saying? Maybe I should just tell him about the purity ring.

Before I could embarrass the literal hell out of myself, Colin just said, "Great. I'll show you upstairs."

He led me up the spiral staircase to the master bedroom, an additional living space, the in-unit laundry area, and the terrace entrance.

"New York actually has really great sunsets," he said. "It's just that most people aren't high enough above the buildings on a regular basis to see them."

As I looked over Broadway toward the Hudson River, at the cotton candy sunset that would eventually be mine to view every evening from a sixteenth-floor terrace, I thought about all the ways God had blessed me that year in support of this huge life change that did not involve being a wife:

- The four part-time jobs that worked around my class and rehearsal schedule

- The perfect theater contract

- So much money saved

- A fantastic showcase performance

- MTA angels even though I was a total drunky

- A musical theater training intensive

- A penthouse apartment in a doorman building, living with the one percent as my first New York City apartment

God really is so good.
And very easy to manipulate.

14

V Day

"So how does this work?" I asked Colin. "Am I in the mob now? It's totally fine if I am since I get my own bathroom. Just let me know."

Colin chuckled and, to my surprise, said, "Let's just shake on it. Send me first month's rent, and the apartment will be waiting for you in September."

Shake on it? Was this the 1930s?

Wait, did I die?! Is Heaven for virgins painless, affordable luxury apartment rentals in New York City?

I did shake on it.

Then promptly called my father and had him call Colin to make sure I wasn't going to be required to enter a sex trade or something in exchange for this sick apartment. Dad had Colin draft up a written agreement, and I sent first month's rent a few weeks later.

Moving to New York was actually happening. As the reality of that set in, I recalled that fleshly thought I'd uncontrollably had while looking upon my future bed in the maid's quarters.

The truth is, in my time of stillness and devotion that year leading up to my move, I often had to bounce my thoughts[1] from this quiet internal proposal. My New York Move checklist subconsciously included a little, teeny-tiny, very-nominal, not-really-at-all-super-important task I'd written in invisible/disappearing ink and told absolutely no one I was considering:

Have Sex.

Despite being overwhelmed with gifts God was giving me for being such a devoted follower, I could not shake the fact that I just did not want to be a virgin upon moving to New York City.

This might come as a surprise, since I haven't at all alluded to what a frustrated ball of can-I-get-fucked-already I was. But my reasons for wanting to do the hibbity-dibbity were actually very logical and levelheaded, not mindlessly lustful as I'd assumed my sinful motivation would be.

Of course there was the general feeling of "Haven't I waited long enough, God? *Let's Call the Whole Thing Off!*" But after I stopped negotiating Godly commands with show tune titles, I got more specific with the boss of the universe.

I was now set on a completely different path than I had expected to pursue as a woman of God. Namely, that I wouldn't be getting married anytime soon. Which meant, I wouldn't be having sex anytime soon, if I stuck to God's commands.

I mean, I *could* have gotten married upon moving to New York City. There certainly isn't a shortage of rich old creeps who would have been willing to wife up a naive twenty-three-year-old had I been willing. But wasn't God perfectly paving the actor path, not the young-wife path, for me? Why would I ignore all that to immediately put a ring on it/penis in it?

I was moving to become an actor. What that meant was that my life was going to be rather unstable and unpredictable, especially in my early twenties. This chapter of my life was not exactly the time to be making decisions around lifelong matrimony.

How old is too old before this virginity-losing-within-a-marriage is just ... weird?

I thought about dating in New York and how I didn't want the state of my hymen to be something on my date-night resumé. I didn't want to have to stress about when I was going to bring this up every time I went on a date with a dude who didn't grow up in purity culture and then await their looking at me like a martian.

When I thought about no longer waiting until marriage to have sex, I quickly realized that so much of my life had revolved around this ONE thing. I was about to step into a whole new world of experiences and opportunities, where I could be known for so much more than abstaining from sex for God.

Is this really that big of a deal, God?

Then I'd feel bad for applying logic to a God who isn't logical. Hadn't I just been totally blown away by how perfectly He'd aligned all my plans to move to New York City, beyond what I could have ever imagined? Logically I wasn't supposed to move into a penthouse apartment for less in rent than most people pay for a really shitty apartment, but you know. "God is good all the time. And all the time, God is good."

> *I should just trust God will take care of this "I don't want to be an old weirdo" problem! Deciding to have premarital sex will be going directly against God's teachings. And if I go directly against God's teachings, He will stop blessing me. If I forfeit God's blessings now, what if I become homeless, can't get a job, and He takes my voice so I can't pursue musical theater?*

I honestly thought that if I had premarital sex, God would cease being an endlessly bountiful rich guy of the stars and immediately become Ursula of the mysterious fathoms below.

And lastly,

I continued the internal soliloquy to only me,

> *If I have premarital sex, who will I be? My entire life has been defined by being a virgin who loves Jesus. Who am I without my purity? And since having sex will cause God to abandon me, who am I without God?*

Having sex meant losing God being on my good side, therefore, my entire identity. Was I really ready to lose all that for the sake of not being embarrassed on some potential Tinder dates?

Fuck me.

But actually, don't.

15

THE BITTER END

ALL OF THIS CALLED for a celebratory drink. Or, at least, an intimate concert in the West Village.

On a previous trip to New York City, I'd met this singer/song-writer—we'll call him Pop Singer—at the New York Musical Theatre Festival. I saw him perform in an angsty teen musical, and we chatted a bit at the festival after party. We stayed in touch via Facebook when I wasn't in the City, but not like "frequent messaging and flirting" stayed in touch. More like "I remember his face, that he was a really good singer, and see him post about upcoming shows sometimes" stayed in touch.

Back in the City a year later, I saw on Facebook that Pop Singer was playing a little concert at a well known venue in the Village—the Bitter End. I decided to go to hear a familiar face sing pretty in a cool neighborhood, get a beer, and brag about my new blessings. After the show, Pop Singer introduced me to his band.

I had been eyeing the drummer all night, and I think we flirted a little. I asked if the band wanted to grab drinks after, but they had to take their instruments back home, so it was just me and Pop Singer for drinks. I was bummed I couldn't flirt with Drummer more and lowkey hoped he'd meet up with us after dropping off his cymbals or whatever.

I felt high, like, actually. I was enjoying the time of life in my beloved city. *I had a penthouse apartment waiting for me.* I was out sipping drinks, flirting with a drummer, hanging with a cool singer-songwriter, *and* I was wearing a cool fitted graphic T Eddie had given me that I'd cut into a crop top. *Missouri Mattie Jo? Are you still there?*

It had been a long day of blessings from the Lord for me, so I needed to call it a night before I got drunk and tried my luck with the MTA angels again. We got the check and headed out.

"Do you need a car?" Pop Singer asked.

"Uh, no, I'm going to Brooklyn," I replied.

"Are you?" he asked with a slight smile and unexpected swagger.

Holy heck. Is Pop Singer ... hitting on me?

We got into a cab, and he did that thing they do in movies where he says to the cab driver, "One stop," confidently. It's the lamest, most unnecessary flex straight men do to strangers. Like the guy in the turban up front cares if you're getting laid. Also, the driver is clearly on the phone. Don't interrupt him. How rude.

Anyway, the entire cab ride, I'm trying to decide if I even like this guy. I mean, up until he started hitting on me, I truly didn't even consider that he might find me attractive, or whether I found him attractive. I thought he had a sweet face and a lovely voice but seemed like too much of a douchebag for me to like in general—definitely not for my first bangy-bang.

And then, Pop Singer leaned in slowly to kiss me. Slowly enough, I suppose, for me to think, *A cab make-out to end this amazing day in NYC sounds nice and you'll do,* so I kissed him back. I had gone from getting a penthouse apartment to making out in a cab with a New York–dwelling singer-songwriter while wearing a crop top, all in one day. A rom-com based on my life was writing itself at this point.

We walked into his apartment, and I noticed immediately that this kid had it made. He lived in lower Manhattan with an entire floor (and bathroom!) to himself, complete with soundproof curtains cuz singing. My survey of his parents' income and thoughts about how funny it was that all the biggest turning points in my life were suddenly associated with really rich people was interrupted by Pop Singer starting to kiss me again.

The make-out session on his couch was nothing too different from my Missouri make-out sessions. Kiss a bunch with shirts off, probably do some hand stuff below the belt, and then I'd fall asleep before I did anything I didn't want to do.

Pop Singer's hands moved pretty quickly to unbutton my pants, and I started to panic. *He cannot take off my pants!* I screamed internally. If he was going to take off my pants, that meant he would have to take off my shoes. And I didn't want to take off my shoes, because I had been walking around a damp New York City all day, so my feet smelled worse than the boys' locker room post–eighth grade P.E. dodgeball.

That's right, I wasn't having "I am about to commit the worst sin ever" panic thoughts. I was thinking about how I was not about to go into losing my virginity with a superrich kid with my Wal-mart-shoe-stinky feet. (Again, I acknowledge, "losing your virginity" is an outdated, messed up construct. But "I was about to go into being penetrated in my vagina by a penis for the first time" just doesn't flow as well. Additionally, I definitely still abided by these concepts/terms at the time.)

"Uh, can I use your bathroom really quick?" I asked.

I rushed into the bathroom, took off my shoes, and looked around for some soap. The closest thing he had was Old Spice. *Ugh, why can't he be sensible like Brandon and just use a gender neutrally clean scented Ivory soap?!* I ran the bathtub water as quietly as possible and tried to use enough Old Spice to get rid of my stinky feet smell but not so much as to out myself as having just cleaned my feet with his over-cologned boy soap.

I walked back out with my squeaky-clean feet and we made out shirtless for a while longer before the pants came off. We eventually made it to his bed and fooled around for about seventy-two seconds before Pop Singer asked, "Should I get a condom?"

What? We haven't even spent ample time on second base! We're just going to French kiss and then do it? Is this how not-Christian, unmarried sex works? Also, I've never even seen a condom, I don't know how to put one on, and I'm not on birth control, and ...

Okay, what if I just say yes and give this a go? And then if I don't want to have sex ever again with someone who isn't my husband, I don't have to! I'll just ... try it. Losing my virginity doesn't mean I'm going to start sleeping with everyone. I can totally just ... try. I'm just trying ... try ...

"MJ?"
Oh shit, he's waiting for an answer.
"Yeah."
"Yeah?"
"Yes. You should get a condom."

In a split second, I went from saving myself until marriage to losing my virginity to basically a stranger I didn't even like that much. My Necessary Pendulum was swinging *hard*.

I expected there to be a lot of pain and blood at first. And then once we got past that, we would have beautiful, pleasureful sex till the wee hours of the morning. Because I'm a spectacular actor, I would make it through the whole experience without Pop Singer ever knowing he was my first time. Unless the blood gave it away. *But maybe I'll just tell him I'm at the end of my period.* And then I'd leave and immediately ask God for forgiveness.

That is not what happened.

What happened was, I barely felt a thing, and the entire endeavor was complete in around three minutes and twelve thrusts.

As I lay there, after having participated in what I had been told would be the pinnacle of my existence as a woman, I expected to have all kinds of existential dread and immediately start praying for forgiveness. I've heard of women in similar situations getting hives and being rushed to the ER for some unexplained penetration PTSD response. But, much to my own surprise, I was not thinking about God, getting into Heaven, or enduring PTSD at all.

Instead, I just lay there, thrusted into, thinking, *what if I had married ... this?*

I was taught—not so explicitly but definitely implied—that if I didn't have sex before marriage, any man would be totally amazing for my untouched holy hole. I was told that so long as you both love the Lord, even if you have literally nothing else in common—especially sexually, since that is not part of your premarital Godly relationship—things will just "work out." God's got it, MJ.

And then it occurred to me.

> *Wait. Is this complete bummer of bumping uglies punish-ment for not waiting? If I had waited, would I have gotten a better experience with Brandon? Ugh, I miss Brandon. Omg, MJ, stop thinking about your ex while another man is inside of you, you pervert!*

I moved on to think about all the ways cis-straight-people sex had been built up to be this overwhelming, life-altering act. The beautiful Egyptian cotton sheets would flow around us while we changed each other's lives for the better. We would sip wine afterward, kiss lightly, and laugh together at the amazing time we'd just had.

What I had just experienced felt like riding a rickety roller coaster at a theme park. I hadn't enjoyed myself at all, my hips and pelvis kind of hurt, and I couldn't wait for it to be over. Also, I didn't want to drink wine with him. I wanted to leave and eat some French fries. Alone.

While I lay there reviewing all the ways I'd been lied to about sex in my life, Pop Singer had gotten out of bed and moved on to a very important daily task as if everything in the world was just exactly as it'd been three minutes and twelve thrusts earlier.

"I'm going to humidify if that's okay? I have a voice lesson tomorrow," he said. And then proceeded to humidify and check his phone.

"That's fine," I said sweetly and agreeably, even though *what the fuck?*

Had I missed something? We'd just *had sex.* And, okay, I'll be the first to admit it was not good, considering the very little base-traveling, some wet-humping that didn't even feel as good as dry-humping, but come on, bro. You're going to immediately get up to humidify and check your texts???

Life as an Evangelical in the Midwest had not prepared me for the real world of early-twenties bachelor douchery.

It gets worse.

"Ha! Drummer just texted me," Pop Singer said with a chuckle. "Says he thinks you're super cute and can he get your number."

"What?" I was actually not following.

"My drummer, remember him from tonight? He thinks you're cute. Can I give him your number?"

Oh.

My God.

I washed my feet (just like Jesus) before I lost my virginity in New York City while wearing a purity ring. It was very bad because, I think, he's bad at sex, but I can't be sure because I've never before had sex. And now he's 1) ignoring me to look at his phone and moisten his vocal cords instead of, IDK, MOISTENING ME, and, 2) passing me off like a goddamn track baton to his bandmate? And worse, it's the one I was originally interested in, so I should have just gone home with him. *Bet he'd bang me like a cymbal, not this bullshit!*

So naturally I replied, "Sure."

"Cool. He'll text you. Drummer's a great guy."

Not sure I trust your judgment, asshole.

"Great," I said instead. "I think I'm gunna go."

"Right now? It's so late."

"Yeah. I'll take a car. It's fine."

"No, stay." He paused. "I want you to stay."

Is he flirting? The audacity.

So, I stayed, because I wouldn't develop the capability to do what I want to do over what men want me to do for ... a very long time.

Pop Singer finished humidifying and crawled back into bed with me.

"Thanks for coming over," he said with a kiss on my cheek. "I had a really great time."

Oh, good for you.

"Me too," I said.

"But just so you know, I don't really like cuddling." And then, without missing a beat, he plopped a giant body pillow between the two of us, creating a physical barrier after just having been #oneflesh.

I rolled over to look at the opposite wall, wanting nothing more than to fall immediately asleep and have one of my iconic recurring sex dreams with Chad Michael Murray so the night wouldn't have the worst ending. There was a bit of silence before Pop Singer interrupted it with the dumbest, stupidest thing he said all night.

"Hey, MJ?"

"Yeah?"

"Am I, like, the second person you've ever slept with?"

A decade later, I am still trying to wrap my mind around this question. "Second person you've ever slept with"—so specific. Like, what about that evening suggested I'd had exactly one other sexual partner? Was he just trying to get me to admit that it was my first time?

"No. Of course not," I replied.

This wasn't a lie. I couldn't lie. I couldn't afford any other sins that night.

"Cool." Then he rolled over and fell asleep.

I'd finally had sex and that was ... the end.

The bitter end, indeed.

16

Welcome to the Fallout

I LEFT QUIETLY BEFORE he woke up. I did not want to speak another word to him.

Another lie they told me about sex is that I would be forever emotionally attached and desperately clingy to any man I was sexually involved with, especially the guy with whom I lost my virginity.

I was experiencing quite the contrary. I hoped to never see or speak to Pop Singer again.

Not because I thought him to be the worst person ever. We were in our early twenties, and I'm sure he was raised to think sex is all about the man, which is actually not different from how I was raised, so I absolutely hold nothing against him. We were both clueless and operating from a deeply ingrained, male-centered-society preset; I just had better manners.

I walked myself uptown to clear my head. I found myself in Port Authority, of all places, because I knew I needed to make an important call and wanted ample places to sit that wouldn't be as intimate as a restaurant or coffee shop. I didn't want anyone eavesdropping on my tales of debauchery! Lol as if disappointing sex with a musician is the worst story New Yorkers have overheard.

I called a friend from high school small group to confess what I'd done. She'd lost her virginity to a college fuckboy while on ecstasy (the Necessary Pendulum!), so I knew I could trust her not to judge me.

"How do you feel?" she asked.

"Is 'I want French fries' a feeling?" I responded honestly, and then: "Do you think I need to get Plan B?"

I'd heard of Plan B from girls in my sorority. And a few times when I was asked to buy it for purity ring friends who were too afraid to purchase it themselves. I'd drive to a CVS well outside of city limits where no one would recognize me and get the goods. I was the Morning After Mother Teresa.

"Didn't you use a condom?" she asked.

"Well, yes. But aren't they, like, not very effective? And I'm not on birth control!"

In abstinence class I was told that condoms are only seventy-percent effective against pregnancy prevention and STD contraction. Which, I would later learn from a Planned Parenthood nurse, is such a bogus percentage/statistic, these teachers could have been measuring the increase in hair shine on a Pantene Pro-V commercial and it would have been more accurate. Anyway, I genuinely didn't think the things worked, which is probably why I would fail to use them in the future way more often than I'd like to admit.

I walked to the nearest Duane Reade and shamefully purchased my overpriced pregnancy preventer. I finally got my French fries and washed my Plan B with Diet Coke, all before 10 a.m. I kept the Plan B box in my purse for the remainder of the trip. I'm not sure exactly why. Is that how I wanted to commemorate my first time in my memory box? What a strange old-lady-hoarder thing to do, but it did prove useful.

A few days later, in the cab to JFK with my best friend, Candice, I stared quietly out the window at the New York City skyline. I thought about the events of that week and how utterly shocked I was at how everything ... turned out. I was going back to Missouri with an Upper West Side penthouse and no more virginity. Spring breaks, amiright?

I looked over to Candice and thought about how I was going to tell her about Pop Singer. Candice was raised Catholic, but not Brandon-version Catholic. Just like, "we go to church sometimes and are generally good humans" Catholic. So, luckily, unlike some of my other friends, who told me they were praying for me incessantly upon learning Brandon fingered me once, Candice was a safe space for sexy talk.

I just went for it. "Candice, I have to tell you something," I started. And then I didn't speak. I took the Plan B box out of my bag and handed it to her.

Her jaw dropped.

"Mattie. *What*?" I nodded. She started to cry. "Are you serious? Tell me everything. *Why am I crying*?"

Candice is the kindest, sweetest, most perfect human being you will ever meet in real life. She also actually looks like a Barbie. The huge boobs on a tiny frame and lusciously long blond hair and everything. It would be disgusting if she wasn't the best listener, advice giver, "let's eat our feelings in [gluten-free] pasta and ice cream together" healer as well.

I shared the tale of washing my feet in a singer's bathtub and then having sex with him and then buying Plan B at the Duane Reade on 42nd and 8th and then purifying my sinful insides with fried potatoes.

"How do you feel?" She, like my ecstasy-fuckboy-small-group friend, was concerned.

I'd had some time for the whole ordeal to sink in, so I felt a little more than a carb craving at this point.

"I feel ..." I started, "exactly the same as I did before. I'm still me. I'm honestly just pretty pissed I was told *that* was such a big deal."

She laughed through her tears and said, "Well, I'm really happy for you."

Strangely, I was happy for me too.

It would take months for the memory of having sex for the first time to elicit a real emotional response in me. But I kept going back to my friends' question: *How do you feel?*

I knew how I was supposed to feel.

I was supposed to feel like a new woman, magically transformed and made anew via straight-people penetration. But I didn't feel any different, and I was angry that so many women told me a *male penis* could have that kind of effect on me.

I was supposed to feel mentally unstable, void of any logic, leading only with my uncontrollable emotional attachment to Pop Singer forever and ever amen. When actually, I never even really thought of him in the weeks, months, years following that experience. Except that Pop Singer did become kind of famous. He won a few Grammys for songs he wrote and went on to have a song I would hear everywhere from dumpling restaurants in Taiwan to H&Ms in Manhattan. While trying on swimsuits with my girlfriends once, I recognized his voice and exclaimed, "I definitely fucked this guy!"

Juxtaposed against feeling metamorphosed, I was also supposed to feel dirty, used, worthless, and ashamed. I have of course felt those things in my sex life and non-sex life. Particularly when I knowingly ate at a Popeyes that was featured on the news for finding a rat in their fryers. But post–bye-bye virginity ceremony? No.

Here's what I did feel: enlightened, grateful, and kind of scared.

In one night, so much of what I had been taught about sex was completely disproved by just having it. I thought about my friends who were going to get married before experiencing this disappointed enlightenment. *Is it my moral obligation to tell them?* I decided no. They'd probably just tell me—as I had already suspected—it was bad because I didn't wait. It wouldn't be that way for them. *Yeah, okay...*

I was genuinely grateful I didn't have to find out about all these sex-lies after exchanging vows with a person who was also trapped in them too. I wouldn't have the added shame burden of divorce following me amid my already-very-thick shame fog. Or staying in a terrible marriage because that relationship so effectively perpetuates the lies.

As a single person, I could proceed in life discovering what else I had been lied to about without dragging another human along for my journey of bitterness and rage. I was free.

And of course, I was scared that God hated me now. I was going to have to move to New York without God's blessings, so I'd probably never be on Broadway or get a husband. (I have yet to be on Broadway or get a husband, so maybe I was onto something. Although, I have made out with a man I deeply loved atop the Empire State Building and I met Lin-Manuel Miranda backstage at *Hamilton*, so maybe God needs to alter His rewards system.) This fear of not having any goodness in my life because God hated me became the quiet but powerfully ruling undercurrent of my life.

But alas, my New York Move checklist was complete. I moved to New York the following September.

The streets, concert venues, bars, terraces on 5th Avenue, park benches, NYU practice rooms (where I would sing and have sex, sometimes at the same time) of New York became the sanctuary where my entire identity imploded, one capital-T Truth revealing itself to be capital-B Bullshit at a time.

PART TWO
Dismantling

17

BAPTISM BY *TINDER FLAME*

MY PARENTS DROVE ME across the country for two full days. Until we reached the George Washington Bridge, it didn't feel real. Once we tried to find parking for a minivan on the Upper West Side, however, it was very, very real.

We unloaded three giant pink tubs full of all my belongings onto a fancy 1920s-hotel-like cart from my building, with assistance from a doorman, then onto the shiny elevator. My parents met Colin, shook hands, and I internally prayed my father would not bring up religion with him in the next forty-eight hours. We got some sleep before a few days of New York City adventures, complete with a Sunday visit to a megachurch led by a famous Christian author—Tim Keller—that was conveniently two steps from my building. I believed God had placed me there to remind (haunt) me about where my priorities should lie in my new home. I would go on to attend many services there very hungover.

The day my parents left me in New York, I really let my shit go. I held my mom in the foyer of my prewar luxury building and cried into her shoulder in public like a kindergarten lunatic. Mom reiterated how much braver I was than she could ever be. Dad told me how proud he was of me and whispered a prayer while he held me a little longer.

They drove off, and I went back upstairs to cry some more.

I officially live in New York City.

I sat on my twin bed in a room designed for live-in paid help and thought about all the ways my present moment was very, very weird. Even then, I knew I was about to begin living a life no one from home would believe was actually happening. *Mattie Jo in a penthouse in Manhattan? In a room made for maids?*

I took a deep breath, audibly thanked God for this weird but amazing situation, and promptly downloaded Tinder.

I didn't know where to begin with dating in New York City, but lucky for me, app dating had become normalized among the youths. Online dating was no longer a thing for old divorcés who couldn't get a date IRL. Now, even the most charming and cute of individuals could handpick through a screen the person with whom they wanted to spend their Friday night.

I matched with a Hottie McHotster we'll call First Tinder Date. We planned to meet up that weekend.

First Tinder Date was from Long Island, worked in the Financial District, and lived in Murray Hill. I now know that is a winning combination for "I'm not looking for anything serious but I make way more money than any twenty-two-year-old should, so I'll buy you expensive cocktails I know you can't afford, actress." I didn't know that yet, so I first-date grilled the guy like we had serious potential. I was *intentional*.

In the Evangelical world, intentional is a buzzword in dating; mostly for dudes toward girls. "Do you feel like he's being intentional with you?" your small group leader and friends ask. Or, if a Godly man wanted to posture his religious commitment, he'd begin a conversation about #boundaries with "I want to be intentional with you..." It basically means "I'm setting this up as if we are going to get married." If a dude doesn't tell you he's being intentional, he's not Godly enough and you're probably not equally yoked.

Based on my upbringing, there were a few very important things you must know and do before and during the first date as a woman of God.

First of all, one must never go on a date with someone unless you think they're marriage material. Kind of like the Catholic teaching that you shouldn't ejaculate without intent to procreate, there had to be a Godly purpose behind your actions otherwise what a waste of time (and sperm).

This teaching is heavily rooted in purity culture as it suggests the more men with whom women give their hearts, time, and bodies, the less of the woman there is for the future husband. I watched so many of my friends experience massive anxiety over whether or not to even go on *one date* with a person if they didn't know *for sure* that person would be their spouse.

"But how can you know if someone will make a good spouse unless you...*date them?*" God will tell you who your spouse will be of course!! Isn't that great news?! No need to have any lived experience and make that decision on your own. Just listen to God's voice and you will know who you should marry!

Can't hear God's voice? Oh, that's probably because you're too much of a sinner and not close enough to Him. Commit to no dating and just work on your relationship with God so you can more clearly hear His guidance. Don't, like, actually go on dates to see if you like a guy.

Once you're Godly enough and have heard God's voice and decided this person is a viable marriage option, then you have to go on the date. The date should include a coffee shop with some Biblical reference in the name like "The Potter's House" and, of course, swapped testimonies.

Swapping testimonies is very important in determining your compatibility because it reveals the extent each of you loves The Lord. Without this information, you cannot know if you are equally yoked. And if you are not equally yoked, you will be sinning against Jesus and setting a bad example of Godly relationships to the world. Your mutual love for the Lord is the only measure of true compatibility.

After hearing their testimony, you need to exchange dating history. If he's a "real" Man of God, he will volunteer his sexual history as well because #integrity. You need to know this because it will tell you a lot about his character. How can you feel truly special if he's had so many relationships before you? Why weren't you worth waiting for?

So I went into this first Tinder date in New York City with the exact same dating dogma as my Evangelical world. Therefore, it was not at all weird for first-date conversations with my viable spouse option to include discussing faith and exes.

I quickly learned how incredibly uncomfortable it is to traverse topics such as religion and relationship baggage on a first date in the secular world.

I could say I felt bad for him, but I actually feel bad for me. How embarrassing that I actually conducted myself in such a manner on a date at Jocob's Pickles in New York City?! The good news is, I'm pretty self-aware so I stopped asking guys their testimony and relationship and sexual history pretty quickly after that night.

Here's how my equally yoked interrogation played out:

"So have you had any serious relationships?"

"Umm ... yeah."

He was uncomfortable, but I didn't get the memo. I hadn't yet learned that in other cultures, people opening up is not required, especially to strangers. This is a stark difference to the Midwest where you can be at Dollar General and the cashier will tell you, toothless and completely unsolicited, about their current custody battle and trailer park explosion. I kept drilling.

"Okay, when was that?"

"College, obviously."

"Obviously?"

"We just graduated college?"

Oh. Duh.

"Oh, right but like, it could have been high school."

"Why would I tell you about a relationship from high school? High school relationships are never serious."

Clearly, he'd never landed in a Flyover State.

"My parents met in high school."

"Yeah, but that was like, the 70s. No one does that now."

"No one on Long Island gets married young?"

"Young like teenagers or young like, early thirties?"

Early thirties? Was this guy looking for a geriatric wife???

His coastal cultural differences were blaring.

"Wow, back home getting married in your thirties is like, way old."

And then, because clearly he wasn't going to share anymore about his ex, I volunteered my relationship resume. "I've only had one serious relationship—my college boyfriend—and I was going to marry him."

"Whoa, you were like, engaged??"

"Well, no. Not exactly."

"So, what do you mean you were going to get married?"

The fact that I had to explain this to a person was one of many explanations that helped me realize my little slice of Evangelical reality was not everyone's.

"It was just kind of the expectation. Where I'm from, everyone is a really devout Christian so I guess it comes with the territory of saving yourself until marriage."

"Saving yourself?"

Ugh don't make me say it.

"Yeah. Like, waiting until marriage to have sex."

He laughed and looked at me, all incredulous like.

"What? Be a virgin until marriage? That's a real thing people do?"

Every bit of the disappointing experience with Pop Singer was worth my affirmed suspicions that continuing to wait until marriage would make me a total alien person to New Yorkers. Which is, you know, completely unfair and shouldn't be an indicator of a person's worth on either end—to wait or not wait—but, anyway ...

"Yeah, mostly everyone I know is waiting or did wait."

"Not like, actually though? They're lying."

"I don't think they are."

"They are."

To be fair, I knew a decent number of friends who had "slipped up" (penetration pun!) a few times and had sex before marriage. But they all, at least to their small groups, seemed very remorseful and would "not do it again." I'm not sure why it took a rando finance guy calling it out over whiskey cocktails for me to flag the fact that most of my friends were actually not super successful in waiting but, I guess he was not entirely wrong.

"I know they aren't lying because I was one of 'them.' I was very successful at the effort."

"Wait." He turned away from the bar and positioned himself directly at me. "Are you a virgin?"

FUCK.

"No!"

I could not have been happier to respond so quickly with this response that, lucky me, was not a lie!

"Right, because you lied and actually did fuck your college bf."

This is where I should have lied. I should have just been like, *yeah, I will never see this guy again so who cares if I tell him the truth*? But I am, after all, a shameless over-sharer and not great at improv so without thinking, I replied

"Well, no. We didn't have sex."

I expected his next question to be "Then who did you have sex with?" But because he was a secular, well-adjusted person who understands sensible first-time-meeting-someone boundaries, he didn't implore about my sexual history. He just said, "Bummer. So, you're super Christian?"

I didn't know how to answer that, and I wouldn't for a very long time thereafter when anyone asked about my specific faith identity. So, I just delivered the autopilot answer from my Evangelical days.

"I wouldn't say I'm 'super Christian.' I would say my faith is really important to me but doesn't look traditional. It's not about the religion aspect so much as the actual relationship I have with Jesus." I used this as the perfect segue into seeing if he was a Christian. I should have known there was very little chance of that being the case considering him being so flabbergasted at the idea of saving oneself until marriage but, "What about you?"

"I was raised Jewish but I don't really practice anything outside of the big holidays. It's a chance to see family but that's really it."

Not only was that a very succinct and casual answer given my incredibly thoughtful and thorough one, I was also completely caught off guard.

Jewish? Like, a Jew? Why aren't you wearing that tiny hat thing? Where are your curly Q's? Do Jews simply walk among us like totally normal people??

I was obviously very new to the Upper West Side.

He's not a Christian? How will he intentionally date me? What will I tell my parents?! How will we raise our children!

I was hit with the reality that most men in New York would not share my specific brand of religious beliefs. I'm not sure why this was surprising to me, but it was, and I was sincerely distressed over the matter. This guy seemed great and was a total babe but like, *we are not equally yoked, so how can I go on another date with him if we will never be married*?

The next morning—because I was still working on breaking my whole "tell everyone everything" Midwestern tendency—I shared my religious compatibility stress with Colin who, turns out, was also a Jewish day-walker.

"So, you met on Tinder, went on one date, and you're planning on approaching him about your religious differences because you think that means you aren't compatible for marriage?" Colin needed clarification. Why, I wasn't sure. It seemed pretty black-and-white (cookie. I'm sorry) and reasonable to me.

"Yes. Exactly." I replied.

"And you don't think that's weird?"

No, I don't think it's weird. Is it weird?

"I just ... how can I date him if he doesn't have the same religious views as me?" I answered. "Isn't that a waste of time? Like, I would never date a *Mormon*."

"Oh yes, because Mormons have very strange beliefs."

He was trying to insult me, I could tell. So, I shot back, "Do you know what Mormons believe, Colin? Golden tablets that have never been found, the Garden of Eden is in Missouri, they each get their own planet when they die. I just can't see myself ever truly being compatible with someone whose religious beliefs are founded on essentially unsupported, made-up information."

"Right because your religious fantasy is superior to others' religious fantasy."

Fantasy? Who did this guy think he was?! Clearly Colin had never read The Case for Christ.[1]

"I mean ... archeology, history? I wouldn't call Christianity and/or the Bible 'fantasy.'"

"Of course not. Virgins have children all the time. Guys die on crosses and then rise from the dead. Dudes have walked on water *a lot*. Oh, and water into wine thing. Woo! See that all the time at bars around here. Very real."

Oh.

"No, no I get it!" Colin continued. "Christians get miracles, everyone else gets 'stuff they made up.'

Fuck.

"Look, you can date this guy or not, and I agree Mormons are a little out to lunch. But I think there's a bigger issue here, MJ. Here's a book I suggest you start reading. Enjoy the rabbit hole! Happy enlightenment."

Or something like that.

This conversation proved Colin to not be the scary, tired business guy (still not sure what Colin does exactly) I thought him to be. Over the next few years, he became my rich-big-brother Jewish Jedi master. He helped me traverse my new world from questions about the Bible to "why do all the rich kids I babysit have their initials sewn on everything? That seems like a weird thing to pay a seamstress for, like, if you're gonna pay a seamstress."

"Summer camp." he said succinctly, as if I should have known that. I stared at him a little longer and waited for a more thorough explanation.

"When you go to summer camp, your laundry gets sent out to get done, right? So you have to have your initials on everything so you know what's yours."

"They don't know what their own clothes look like?"

"Well there are clothes that look really similar such as tennis whites and..."

"Tennis whites?"

"Most beach clubs and country clubs require white clothes only for tennis."

Of course, only people who have paid laundry help have an entire wardrobe of white. For kids!

"Oh. Got it."

My new life was so strange, but Colin was very helpful.

Anyway, the book Colin suggested to me was *Zealot* by Reza Aslan and it became the catalyst for my ongoing study of scripture from a non-white-American-Evangelical perspective.

I devoured the information in *Zealot*. The more I read, the more I questioned and needed answers, so I read more books. On subway rides and in audition holding rooms, I read and highlighted and scribbled notes of fury at my findings.

I had officially entered the *stress ball of scriptural skepticism* spiral of my deconstruction.

18

GOD-BARFED

THIS CHAPTER OF MY deconstruction was grueling and painful. I felt a grief and devastation I didn't know how to describe. And, in New York, where no one could conceptualize a deeply personal faith determined by Biblical "inerrancy," I felt isolated (and insane) in my grief. But it was the most essential part of my de-shackling.

Much like after I lost my V-card, once I started to study the history of scripture outside of a Christian context, I repeatedly uncovered a few absolute truths that are actually not absolutely true. In fact, one could argue these "truths" were actually "lies" and I had founded my entire life on these lies being true.

But before we dive in too deep here, I want to make clear that this is by no means a thorough investigation of the Bible's inconsistencies, full history, and therefore overall validity. For that, you will need to consult my "further suggested reading" section and check out the experts. This is just skimming the surface of some information that really busted open how I viewed the Bible and its role in my life.

The greatest two "truths" I found in my research to *not* be so true were:

1. The Bible is God-breathed, absolute truth, without error.

2. Jesus was without a doubt God incarnate, the son of God, the Messiah.

For starters, history taught me how we got the canonical collection of holy books known as the New Testament. Turns out, God didn't write the Bible; *people* wrote the Bible! *People* arranged the Bible. *People* translated the Bible. *People* preach(ed) the Bible within their societal and cultural understandings.

The Bible is an incredibly human book with lots of wild stories, funny one-liners, and great wisdom. But it is not—in any way—literally directly from the Lord's tongue and without error and absolutely true.

When this topical challenge came up in my church days, leaders would say that despite humans being authors of the texts, God would never allow anything to be put in His sacred text that wasn't absolutely true. This, (shocker), was also not true.

There are other contemporary texts of the New Testament about Jesus that didn't make it into the final Bible draft. Why were these versions of Jesus any less legitimate than the twenty-seven books we now call the "The Word of God?"

When Christianity needed to become organized for political reasons, the guys at the Council of Nicaea were like "Okay dudes, what do we want the Christians as an organization to believe? It appears, based on texts and what we know through oral tradition, there are some varied perspectives. Some people think Jesus was fully a man, living a pretty profound life worthy of admiration. Others think he was a full-on spirit walking among us (let's hear it for the Gnostics!). And some think he was a combo of both God and human. So what's the consensus on who/what Jesus is, y'all?"

Then some dude in the back was like "Let's just throw 'em all in, call it the Trinity, and break for lunch."

Thus, we got the Father, Son, and Holy Spirit aka The Trinity.

Then there's the whole Messiah thing.

Early Christians, much like current Christians, were not a monolith. Their perspectives on Jesus were incredibly diverse. I guess the only difference is that now, thanks to the Council of Nicaea, though Christians may vary in how often they take communion or their liturgy practice, all current Christians believe Jesus is the Messiah, sent to earth to die for the sins of humanity.

Back in the day, however, this was not the case. Many people did not believe Jesus to be the Messiah, but the church as a force decided that would be their stance. This belief would be the biggest detail that set Christians apart from Jews (which was the goal. So, in many ways, the very foundation of Christianity was antisemitic.) So, we got Jesus the Messiah out of the council of Nicaea too.

Therefore, the books of the Christian canon were selected based on the belief of the Trinity and Jesus as the Messiah, savior of all souls. Only texts which supported this belief were included in the official canon. Which is why we don't have the Gospel of Thomas or Phillip in the Bible, but we do have Revelation. Great for Kirk Cameron's production company, not so great for my ongoing effort to not be afraid of hell.

Furthermore, a "son of God" who performed miracles and was martyred, was not so uncommon in those days. There were others before Jesus who lived similar lives—performed miracles, had large followings, spoke about the "Kingdom of God," and were ultimately crucified. (What a strange fad everyone was just okay with. Imagine if instead of TikTok dances, the cool thing to do was claim you're God and then be publicly murdered.)

What set Jesus apart from other Messianic figures was his disciples proceeded to be martyred for their claims of his resurrection. His closest followers were, at least based on oral tradition and texts written about 65–300 years after Jesus's death, willing to die for the truth that they saw Jesus alive post-cross hanging.

Martyrdom is a little dramatic, yes. But it got people's attention and definitely helped the Christian movement spread rapidly, which was the goal.

Then there's the inconsistency of Jesus's qualities in each Gospel, what he did, and his family history. This was totally brushed over in my understanding and teaching of the Bible! There was little honoring for what each Gospel author intended to portray about Jesus—especially if the details directly conflicted with another Gospel. Instead, all of these details were combined to create a sort of super Jesus who did it all.

Learning this new way of reading the Bible "horizontally"—putting the stories side by side and comparing them—was very enlightening and very frustrating. When studied closely and individually, Jesus is a different figure in each Gospel, and doesn't knowing that tell us a fuller story about who He was? Rather than disrespecting the individual stories and just throwing them all together like a Jesus story stir fry?

An example of the problem with this different Jesus different Gospels issue is stated in an interview with Bart Ehrman author of *Jesus Interrupted: Revealing the Hidden Contradictions in the Bible* on NPR:

> In Mark's Gospel, Jesus is not interested in teaching about himself. But when you read John's Gospel, that's virtually the only thing Jesus talks about is who he is, what his identity is, where he came from. This is completely unlike anything that you find in Mark or in Matthew and Luke. And historically it creates all sorts of problems, because if the historical Jesus actually went around saying that he was God, it's very hard to believe that Matthew, Mark and Luke left out that part—you know, as if that part wasn't important to mention. But in fact, they don't mention it. And so this view of the divinity of Jesus on his own lips is found only in our latest Gospel, the Gospel of John.

That last part really fucked me up. *Jesus only claims to be God in the book of John?*

Jesus calls himself the "Son of man" a lot, but that doesn't necessarily mean "God." It also doesn't mean "God's son who is going to rule over huMANkind" in the literal God-impregnated-Mary family structure kind of way. "Son of man" was used to describe Adam and prophets—the humans on earth who were liaisons between humans and God—but we don't think of them as the Big G God.

In the rest of the Gospels, the authors either decided to leave out this "small" detail or Jesus was just selectively braggadocious. Either way, an interesting observation about the guy who was ostensibly God incarnate.

What about the fact that Jesus never talked about establishing a whole new religion? According to Jesus's actions, he really enjoyed being Jewish and was just trying to renew justice in what had become a pretty corrupt system. He was trying to right the wrongs within a faith he loved. *Can relate, JC.*

Also, the Christian God was a practicing Jew, so why the heck don't Evangelicals know shit about the Old Testament? It is the canon of the religion their God practiced! That's like only ever watching *Grease 2* when we know *Grease* is available. Unacceptable!

You still with me?

Just like Colin predicted, dissecting scripture is a massive rabbit hole, which is why I believe many people will never do the research. It's time-consuming and emotionally draining. While you're absorbing the information, you're also having to process the "What the fuck do I do with all of *that*?!" mental and emotional exhaustion.

It wasn't that I found all of this to completely invalidate Christianity. It was just ... so *incomplete*. I had been taught to base my entire life and worldview on a story without being given the full story. And the full story really changed some shit!

It was like being told the best beaches, views, and experiences in the world exist in Panama City Beach, Florida. And then one day you get to go to the Philippines or Spain and you're like *there's a whole earth that isn't Florida out here; why didn't anyone tell me?*

After months of burying my face in books, listening to lectures, and annoying Colin with questions about the Torah, I was depleted, but also sure of one thing: the Bible was not God-breathed; if anything, it was God-barfed.

One morning, with coffee and a swollen cry face, I looked out my Upper West Side window and let my heart fully sink. I let a reality I never ever expected to confront, let alone in a penthouse overlooking the Hudson River, set in: *Jesus is not who they told me He was.*

Accepting this was going to change my entire life, whether I wanted it to or not.

Yes, many of my ideas about God had slowly changed over the years. Maybe gay people aren't going to hell and I don't have to be a missionary in the 10/40 window and all that. But I never expected to be asking myself if I actually believed Jesus was the Messiah; to be asking myself if I was, by definition, even a Christian.

If my belief in Jesus as God was to be blown up—and it was—then what? *I'm no longer a virgin and, now, no longer a follower of Christ? Who am I?*

First Tinder Date and I, miraculously, did go on seeing each other for awhile. Why he didn't run away the minute a Shiksa from the Bible Belt uttered the words "relationship with Jesus" on a first date, I'm not sure. But I decided, at least for the time being, I could give dating a guy of a different faith background a try. So, accompanying our very fun weekends of shooting picklebacks and eating at restaurants I certainly couldn't afford, I privately wrestled with essential questions in dismantling my identity:

I don't even know what I believe, so how can I require someone else to abide by a certain set of beliefs?

Should I be thinking about marriage with a finance guy in his early twenties? Do I even want to get married to the guys I'm dating right now? How do I date if not to marry?

How I learned the Bible was incredibly limiting and, frankly, wrong.

And finally,

Jesus is no longer my God.

And that is how going on a Tinder date with a Jewish finance guy catalyzed the final death of

@MattieJoCowsert
Lover of Jesus
Committed Christ-follower
Proverbs 3:6

I saw First Tinder Date on the subway recently. I should have said thank you.

19

FUCKING RICH PEOPLE

THIS CHAPTER OF MY life was so weird, sometimes I think it could not have actually happened.

Up until this point in my life, I think the richest people I'd ever met were my uncles who owned their own dental practice. Then I met Colin. Then I met ... the Hollanders.

Once again, my brother's superrich ex-girlfriend came through with some sweet generosity by helping get me a job. She connected me with a woman who needed occasional, part-time, cheap personal assistant help, and I was the perfect candidate. So thanks to my living, and now work, situation, basically any time I wasn't at an audition or sinfully indulging dates with non-Christians, I was hanging out with millionaires and getting to see all this excessive income culture very up close and ugly-like.

Upon going in to be interviewed for the position, I was sent up the elevator by, of course, a doorman. Who I now knew how to conduct myself around, because, you know, I had one too.

Every time I entered a new building, I learned all kinds of things that denote a person's income bracket in New York. Back home it was whether you wore clothes from Rue21 or Abercrombie. In New York, it was things like what kind of doorman you had. Was he a uniform doorman in a conductor hat and a shirt of many buttons? Were they there overnight or just during the day? Was it a doorman or an "elevator guy," because there is a difference! Elevator guys stand on the elevator with you and ask you which floor, then take you there on a manual lift. (Like the ones on *Titanic*!)

Sometimes buildings have both an elevator guy *and* a doorman. This constant company sort of stressed me out. *Do I say hello and strike conversation with every single building employee I encounter on my way to the destination?* I soon learned; no. Very few New Yorkers will ever take offense to you leaving them alone.

Past the Hollanders' doorman was the elevator that opened directly into their apartment, another thing I learned is an indicator of income. The amount of money you have can be gauged quickly by how many other residences you share your floor with. My penthouse floor, for example, was shared with three other residents. So although we were on the top floor, we were on the top floor split by four apartments, separated at each terrace. We weren't rich enough to own the *entire* floor with a wraparound terrace.

The Hollanders, on the other hand, were *that* rich. They had the entire penthouse floor to themselves, complete with an unseparated wraparound terrace. So, yes. Wealth can be communicated by not subtly saying with your giant apartment, "Look! I have so much money, I don't have a *shared* foyer or any neighbors!"

I stepped into a personal foyer and was greeted by the family's full-time maid—another indicator of their level of wealth. Most upper-middle-classers of New York have weekly to biweekly *cleaning ladies*. Cleaning ladies are different from maids, in that they are paid hourly and only come every so often.

Colin had a cleaning lady who came once every two weeks. I remember asking Colin why we needed a cleaning lady, and was it an extra charge? In Missouri, to not do your own cleaning is lazy. To pay someone else to do it is considered stuck-up and rude.

"I have very little free time in my life, and in general, limited time on earth," Colin started, quite morbidly. "I don't want to spend any of the time I'm not at work doing things like cleaning a toilet. I want to spend it with my friends, reading the *New York Times* (He did this. Like, the paper version), or ..." He paused as I gave him a *you know not everyone is this privileged* look. "I think of my time as cost per hour. So I'd rather spend time making way more money per hour than it costs me to pay someone to do the thing I don't want to do." I'd never thought of it that way: Time is the real thing being spent. How much was my time worth?

"The point of making money, MJ," Colin continued his economics Ted Talk for one "is to give you freedom to live the life you want, right?" This was another thing I'd never considered. Where I was from, the point of money seemed to be to complain about how you never had enough, and then give what you did have to God in the form of tithing. It wasn't to provide freedom; it was to cause stress.

"Well, the life I want includes spending my weekends relaxing and not arguing with my roommate over whose turn it is to clean the kitchen." I liked Colin's money ideology. It seemed more fun than how I was raised.

So anyway, most quasi-rich people in New York have cleaning ladies. But a full-time, *salaried* maid like the Hollanders had? You rich as hell! I wondered what the heck this maid could possibly do for eight hours a day, five days a week. Cleaning this apartment couldn't take *that* long. Oh, I would find out ...

Her name was Alena, and she led me to a sofa I was scared to sit on for fear that my sale-rack dress would pollute its upholstery. "Mrs. Hollander will be right with you," she said. I nodded, sat up as straight as I possibly could, and tried not to nervous-fart on the fancy couch.

Mrs. Hollander came into the fancy-couch room and seemed mostly pleasant. "Lisa speaks very highly of you! That you're a hard worker and very smart," she shared, sounding almost *surprised*. I wondered if Lisa had also mentioned anything about my brother and how my family lived. See: humbly.

She offered to give me a tour as we discussed my "duties." I guess I'd already gotten the job? That was easy. But didn't she, like, want to make sure I wasn't a psychopath first? Or at the very least, qualified for the position? She seemed unconcerned, so I just went with it.

I stood up to begin to see this museum of a home, and as we left, I caught Alena doing something strange to the sofa. "Uh." I stopped Mrs. Hollander. "I'm sorry, did I mess up the couch?"

"Oh no, dear," she replied. "Alena is just smoothing out the seat marks."

Okay ...?

In weeks to come I asked Alena why she did this, because I still didn't understand. "The velvet all goes the same way, so it looks nicer." *Huh.* For as long as I could remember, my mom bought our furniture at garage sales, and we covered those suckers with chocolate milk, Monopoly cash, and Cheeto puffs. I'd never once considered that seat marks would be an issue on a thing ... designed for seating.

As we toured I thought, *this place looks very different from my penthouse.* (A thought I never imagined would actually occupy my headspace.) Every room seemed like it was an isolated interior design showroom. There were rooms like "the den" and "the cigar room." "Oh, and we converted part of the office into my shoe closet." There was even a *library.* Was I in a real-life game of Clue? *Am I going to get murdered with their Cartier candlesticks??*

We discussed my role and duties, which Mrs. Hollander assured me would be "very relaxed" and "no pressure." "I just need some help with things like retail returns, a filing system, and keeping up with my calendar ..." I didn't understand why a woman who didn't have a job, whose kids were fully grown, AND who had a full-time maid didn't have time to do these menial tasks, but I didn't argue. I assumed it also had something to do with the "paying for how you want to spend your time" rich-people freedom Colin described. If she wanted to pay me to do these things, live ya life, lady.

She also made this job sound as though it included enjoying the life of luxury by proxy. "You and my son, Jackson, are about the same age, and his best friend's girlfriend, Michelle, will be staying with us for a bit. I imagine you all will be friends so, if you're hanging out and you need to stay over, the guest bedroom is yours! You can have friends over as well, and you're welcome to anything in the fridge..."

I'd hit the absolute jackpot of a first job in NYC. I now had *two* fancy penthouses to sleep and hang out in! And rich (like, Rockefeller rich) friends! All because of my brother's very kind ex-girlfriend who liked me more than she liked him. Praise the Lord!

I started the job and quickly discovered that "personal assistant for a multimillionaire's housewife" is code for "babysitting a multimillionaire's wife and being asked to do impossible tasks while hanging out with the full-time maid."

There were perks, like getting to show up whenever I wanted after auditions, getting paid in cash, and adding additional income on top of my restaurant job. But this role was incredibly stressful and not at all "no pressure." Each shift consisted of Mrs. Hollander giving me impossible tasks to complete such as trying to get an $80K Bed Bath & Beyond store credit from a decade ago honored.

So many questions.

First of all, how does a person even spend that much money at Bed Bath & Beyond? Did she *buy* a *Bed Bath & Beyond*, and this is actually an outstanding mortgage balance she forgot about?

"We were outfitting the house in Quogue," she told me.

WTF is Quogue?

Any time I had questions I was too scared to ask Mrs. Hollander for fear of seeming like the country bumpkin I absolutely was, I'd just save them all up and bother Colin later.

"Quogue is a part of the Hamptons," he told me. *Of course it's The Hamptons.*

Her trying to return things way past their return policy didn't stop at Bed, Bath & Beyond. It was basically a way of life.

I traversed the Upper East Side every day, going to stores with names I could barely pronounce, let alone have any business stepping foot into wearing a dress from T.J. Maxx. Then, once I felt perfectly uncomfortable and completely out of place, I'd have to request full refunds on items purchased well outside of the return window, and most of the time, without a receipt.

The first time she had me visit the flagship Ralph Lauren store to return a pair of Jackson's pants, I almost passed out from feeling so poor. I mean, I'd only ever been to a Polo outlet! WTF is a flagship anyway? *Googles "flagship."*

Upon entering, I was asked by a large man in a suit if he could take my coat. "Um, why?" I asked. Why did he need my coat? Was it that ugly and cheap-looking that he didn't want me to embarrass myself by being seen in it??? "Coat check, miss," he replied. *These stores have coat check?!?!* I ended up saying no, because I didn't know if I had to pay for coat check, or how much that would cost at the Ralph Lauren flagship.

I then walked up to the desk with two women who looked like—combined—they might weigh as much as my right calf, and told them I had a return. "Oh, this is the women's store," they said matter-of-factly, as if I should have figured that out by all the androgynously shaped mannequins in collars. "The men's store is right across the street, on the third floor." *Oh, thank God. At least I wasn't supposed to go to, like, Quogue.*

I walked across the street, up three flights of velvety carpeted stairs with a bunch of pictures of white dudes on horses, and eventually got to the men's counter for my return. "I don't have the receipt," I told them. "But I do have a proof of purchase on this credit card statement." I tried to pull up an email while carrying multiple bags of returns and my coat, since I hadn't, you know, checked it.

"What's their name and address?" the associate asked. I gave it. "Oh, we see. Okay, it's past the return policy window for a full refund but we'll give them a $365.78 credit on their house account." *They have a house account? At Ralph Lauren flagship?! Those pants cost $365?*

I obviously didn't say any of that. I just said, "Sounds good! Can I get a receipt confirmation of this transaction?" and then got yelled at by Mrs. Hollander later for not getting an actual refund.

"You didn't have a receipt, and it was past the return policy window. I explained wondering how, with a college degree, I'd landed a job explaining retail return protocol to a 50-year-old.

This explanation did not suffice. Mrs. Hollander sharply retorted, "Return policies are not real. Money spent is money spent. Money doesn't expire and I spend good money at those places. They should always honor a return."

It didn't stop at Jackson's pants.

Other ridiculous return requests included

- Jonathan Adler, to return a vase that had been gifted to her, and she didn't have a gift receipt. She wanted the money back for something she hadn't even bought.

- Zitomer (a fancy pharmacy), to return a pair of pajamas from, according to the associate, "three seasons ago." The Hollanders had a house account there, and I got a store credit. Any time there was a house account and store credit given, I counted it as a win.

- Benefit Cosmetics, to return lip-gloss and powder without a receipt. After fighting with Mrs. Hollander on the phone, the associates agreed to a gift card.

And then, the most mortifying.

- Duane Reade, to return an *opened bottle* of mascara, you guessed it, without a receipt.

I was relieved to be going to a recognizable store for plebes like me but was absolutely speechless when Mrs. Hollander yelled these directions after I told her Duane Reade will not accept this return:

"MJ! Just walk in and ask for the Indian woman in the back. She'll accept the return!"

I did not try to take that mascara back. I distracted her with suggesting I organize all the souvenirs she'd collected from flying Delta First Class over the years.

I was never going to get out of this impossible returns thing. Alena showed me an entire closet filled to the brim that Mrs. Hollander had her organize in preparation of returns. *Ah. So, this is what Alena does after she finishes dusting their grand piano for the 185th time. Hides Mrs. Hollander's compulsive shopping habit from Mr. Hollander!*

I asked Colin about it. He was rich. He'd know why this other rich family was so weird.

He explained the tendencies of old money and new money. The Hollanders were new money, so there was likely a lot of "keeping up with the Joneses" going on. Perhaps they didn't have as much money as they presented. This is common in the very wealthy world.

The other option he proposed is that many wealthy people are where they are because they actually know exactly how and where their money is spent. Apparently, it is a misconception that all rich people just spend frivolously and mindlessly. In fact, the ones who stay wealthy from generation to generation do so because they are intentional and responsible with their money (/weirdly stingy and unnecessarily parsimonious).

"So Mrs. Hollander is just being a conscious budgeter?" This felt like a stretch, and far too forgiving of her irrational tendencies, but I went with it.

"Well, that's part of it, yes." Colin didn't let her entirely off the hook. "She's also bored and unhappy, looking for ways to exert power and purpose, so she hires people like you to boss around."

Ding, ding, *ding*.

And that is how a woman averse to receipts taught me about old money, new money, power dynamics in people who otherwise feel completely out of control of their lives, and how some folks would rather develop psychological conditions in the form of compulsion and obsession than admit they're poorer than their neighbors (with whom they don't even share a terrace!).

And then there was the time she told me to call the super to fix their AC. When he arrived and I chatted him up about being from Armenia, she scolded me. "Mattie Jo, you cannot talk to the help."

"Bitch, I am the help!"

That's not what I said. I said, "Yes, ma'am," and later asked Colin why I was not allowed to talk to other home staff. I learned it's likely because she's suspicious of them meddling in her personal life, and she's (probably) being racist. She doesn't view *them* the same as she views me, because they're immigrants.

This would be confirmed when it happened again and she explicitly told me she didn't want other people in the building wondering why the super was spending so much time in their apartment. And the other time, when she tried to schedule a doctor's appointment during Yom Kippur and complained that all the good doctors in New York "are the Jews. Ugh!"

She once told me I couldn't play my own music while doing other ridiculous tasks like organizing her seventeen make-up drawers or her husband's scotch collection. Apparently, her cat could handle "only classical music or NPR."

She also not-so-lowkey insulted me, like, constantly. I had a big blond stripe on the left side of my head that did indeed scream strip-mall-salon flare, but did she really have to tell me my hair was tacky and insist I dye it because her "husband didn't approve?" Also, I wasn't making $15/hr for her to dictate my hair color(s).

She told me my career choice was impractical and I should go into interior design instead. "That's artistic *and* financially practical," she unsolicitedly suggested. I wanted to ask about how her choice in career was going.

One time, when she was accusing me of drinking some Limoncello from the freezer she was "saving for Thanksgiving" she went, "MJ, do you even know *how to drink* Limoncello?"

"Of course I do, Mrs. Hollander. It is a refreshing Italian liquor poured over ice at the end of a meal and/or mixed into delicious cocktails!" How dare she assume I didn't know that!

I did not know that. I didn't even know how to pronounce *limon-chell-oh*.

Jump to Thanksgiving, where, while she had me peeling parsnips for the dinner they hosted, she made fun of me for not knowing what a parsnip was. *Um, sorry that in Missouri we just stick to regular root vegetables like the magnificently versatile potato.* And then she berated me for wearing leggings as pants for a catering event.

First of all, they were my nice, expensive, leather-looking leggings, so, rude. Second of all, was this youth group? First the hair, now "no leggings as pants!" dress code? Third of all ... she did not tell me I would be catering! She made it sound like I would be part of the dinner and evening entertainment. That Jackson would play piano while I sang "because Taylor Swift's producer will be in attendance!" I have no idea if the Taylor-Swift's-producer part was true. I was in the kitchen peeling parsnips all night.

Between her firing insults at me, I would let her cry in my arms. In total meltdown mode, she would tell me how trapped she felt. How she "never asked for this life." I'd hold her, not having the slightest idea how to react. She'd collect herself and get back to insulting me/asking me to organize her medical files from 1977.

Included in this absurd reality I was sucked into during work hours was another home staff member: their son Jackson's live-in, undercover life coach.

You read that right. *Under * cover * life * coach *

The son of these multimillionaires—according to them at least—had a lot of issues. He'd attended a prestigious boarding high school and flunked out of a fancy private college where rich kids who don't get into Ivy League schools pay to go. He ended up at the Manhattan version of community college, which, according to Colin, was very embarrassing for his parents. But instead of doing what parents who don't care about status would do—cut the kid off financially and make him "figure it out"—they moved him back into their home and monitored every single detail of his life.

Part of making sure he could do basic life things like go to class was hiring his best friend's girlfriend, Michelle, to live in their home and coach him at life without him knowing that was the purpose of her being there. They told Jackson they were generously giving her a free place to live while she applied for internships in the City. Meanwhile, Michelle would have to inconspicuously suggest Jackson do his homework and, at the very least, smoke weed on the wraparound terrace, not in his bedroom.

I didn't want to hate these rich people, but I kind of hated these rich people. And I didn't think I could go on working for them, so I didn't.

I refused to stay for Christmas even though, "that's when my life is the most hectic, MJ! I will need your help." I'd already been conned out of Thanksgiving with my family, I wasn't going to lose Christmas too. Not for fucking parsnips.

I told Colin I was going to quit and vented, like this:

"It's not like she needs me. Mrs. Hollander doesn't even have a job! Personal assistant, my ass! I'm her babysitter, as is Alena! I mean, a full-time maid?! And a live-in undercover life coach for her son? I understand not wanting to deep clean your apartment in your free time. But literally, all Mrs. Hollander has is free time! She doesn't even parent!"

"You gonna be okay?" Colin seemed more amused at my anger than genuinely concerned. And then we had another conversation that was far more consequential than I could have ever imagined. About, of all things, rich people.

"It's just ... unnerving that they get away with being assholes because they're rich. That's all."

"Do you know poor people who are assholes and bad parents?"

"Yes, of course."

My family is equal parts *7th Heaven* and *Winter's Bone*, so I knew shitty poor people who were terrible parents in my own lot. Parents who, despite having support to get help and improve their lives, wouldn't take on that responsibility so their kids ended up in foster care and then, prison.

"Okay, well then that's the first thing. People aren't assholes because they do or don't have a lot of money. They're just ... assholes. Money typically amplifies what a person already is at their core. If they're kind, they're money is used for generosity. If they're dicks, they'll become even bigger dicks."

How simple. *Assholes be assholes.*

Then Colin went on to give me emotional insight as to what was probably occurring within each member of the Hollander household.

"Your parents gave you something Jackson doesn't have, MJ: emotional support and freedom. He probably just wants to be in a band and make art. And instead of getting to figure out how his passions can translate into a lifestyle; he is being pressured by parents who raised him to go Ivy League to be something he absolutely is not. He knows how ashamed his parents are of him. Can you imagine how that weighs on a person?"

I did not know. I knew my parents may not have been pleased to hear about my recent religious view shifts and sex action, but I never once felt my parents were *ashamed of* me.

Colin then shared his own struggles with addiction, mental health, and rehab at a very young age. How he was the exception in this arena, as he actually took the help that was given to him.

"I learned my addictions were the result of me not liking myself. And no one else could fix that or give that to me except me. Jackson is going to have to do the same."

That one hit too. As I moved through the messiest part of my identity deconstruction, all my actions stemmed mostly from a deep-seated hatred of myself for not being enough, sexual shame, and fear that I would never be successful in my career choice. I mean, I'd been in New York for six months, and all I had to show for it was an identity crisis and zero callbacks.

"Then there's Mrs. Hollander." he continued "Yes, she's miserable, but it's a familiar misery. While she could probably divorce and make bank, she'll stay because familiarity feels safer."

"Safer than alimony?" I thought but didn't say. Colin had a point, though. As I was slowly starting to climb out of my own prison of familiarity, I knew firsthand just how not fun or easy it was. It was painful and I had absolutely no idea what I was doing. I understood why people just "stayed put." Struggling through the unknown is fucking hard.

I know our situations were not at all the same, *but* these conversations helped me see that some problems are not poor- or rich-people problems. If you dig deep enough, most of us are just experiencing people problems.

That being said, I did quit that job. Mrs. Hollander and I sort of mutually ghosted each other after I told her I wasn't working Christmas.

I flew Southwest Wanna Get Away rates to Missouri, and she took the family yacht to Greece. *Samesies.*

My time with Mrs. Hollander taught me pragmatic working-for-rich-people things like don't waste your time wondering why unemployed individuals need so much help managing their lives, how to tell the difference between old and new money, and how to prepare parsnip mash. I learned how to stand within and witness a wacko world of which I will never be part and pretend like it's all totally normal. I learned that "survival" jobs can be a great stage for practicing acting. Most importantly, I learned not to resent rich people because at their core, they're just people.

I didn't expect rich people to be my first in-your-face teachers of compassion, empathy, and loving people who are hard to love. You know, that real-deal *Just Like Jesus*[1] shit. Just because a person has a wraparound terrace to display their wealth on the outside doesn't make them less of a human Jesus could care for on the inside.

Though I stopped working for the Hollander brand of uber wealth, I did go on to make a survival-job career out of very generous, kind rich people/celebrities who needed an emotional-support Midwesterner.

Hurt is hurt.

People are people.

Why eat the rich when you can eat their personal chef prepared Wagyu steak, take their private jets to stay in your own suite at a Ritz-Carlton, and get paid cash to drop their kids at the Harvard club for squash lessons?

20

CHRISTMAS JEWS

To THIS DAY, THERE is nothing that makes me question my decision to make New York City my home—until winter, when I oscillate between wondering if I have Stockholm syndrome or if I'm just a masochist.

The one redeeming quality of winter in New York is Christmas into New Year's. There are lights and decorations everywhere. The tree at Rockefeller Center. Every restaurant and bar is decked out in greenery, shiny gold ornaments, and sparkling lights. I just *love it*. If it's going to be miserably cold and I'm going to have to dress like I'm ready to hunt the Abominable Snowman on the way to the A train, at least there are twinkle lights.

My first winter in New York was abhorrently cold, and it never stopped snowing. But it was December, so at least I could be in the Christmas spirit, because no one does a love for the birth of Jesus Christ and the peak of consumerism like the Ozarks. It is still the thing I love most about growing up in those meth-filled hills.

I came home to Colin eating one of those delicious-looking meals he always prepared for himself (and then told me down to the cent how much he spent on it; he was always impressed with his frugality), and I headed for my peanut butter.

"Oh, Colin!" I exclaimed. "I have never been to New York at Christmastime and I am *loving it*. It's so magical! They even decorated the medians on Broadway with Christmas trees!"

"I hate Christmas," Colin replied.

I laughed, assured he was joking. How does anyone actually hate Christmas? It's such a hyperbolic concept, Dr. Suess invented an actual monster to personify the idea.

"Okay, Mr. Grinch," I said. "Wait. Are you serious?"

"Yes. One thousand percent."

"How can you hate Christmas? The decorations, the songs, the joy!"

"Christmas is oppressive."

Okay what the actual fuck is this guy talking about?

"Not everyone grew up celebrating Christmas, MJ. And yet, your holiday celebration—not even a day, like a full two months of this bull-shit—is forced upon the rest of us. I went to Starbucks today and they gave me a red cup with fucking bows on it. I handed it back and said, 'Uh, can I get a big-boy cup, please?'"

A big-boy cup. LAWL.

Colin continued his Christmas-sucks diatribe: "It's just annoying. No other holiday is internationally smothering like this one. And companies don't even consider that it's not for all of us."

Oh, damn. Again, Colin was blowing my mind with some deep religious inequity I'd never considered as an Evangelical.

"Um, okay," I replied. "That is a very good point."—*bleak quiet stare*—"Does this mean I won't be able to put a Christmas tree in the living room?"

"Yeah, absolutely not"

Damnit.

This wasn't the last time I would accidentally get excited about Christmas in front of someone who didn't celebrate it. I asked the kids I babysat, "So where are you going for Christmas break?" "We don't celebrate Christmas," they smugly replied. "But for *winter* break, we're going to the Galapagos."

Another thing I learned about rich people—any time there isn't school, they're in a foreign country, or, like, Palm Beach. Then I'd feel stupid I just asked a Jewish kid where they'd celebrate Christmas and then feel even stupider I didn't know what the fuck the Galapagos was. "Oh, nice!" I replied. "So then will you be celebrating Hanukkah while in the Ga ... ?" *mumbles something that hopefully sounds close to 'lapagos'*

"Hanukkah has already passed," they said.

Turns out, the Jewish calendar varies year to year, so Hanukkah may sometimes land on Christmas, but other years it lands closer to Thanksgiving. Who knew? Other than, idk, the world's Jewish population, all of Manhattan and Brooklyn, and probably most of the Bronx, Queens, and Staten Island.

"And no. We don't really celebrate."

"Why would someone *not* celebrate Hanukkah?? It's like Christmas for eight days!" I asked Colin later, not wanting to look anymore ignorant in front of a third grader.

"No, it isn't," Colin replied, clearly (and understandably) annoyed. "Hanukkah is not a big holiday on the Jewish calendar. We are way more invested in Rosh Hashanah and Yom Kippur. But those don't fall close to Christian holidays so you don't pay attention to them."

I wanted to ask what those holidays were but, again, ignorance threshold.

"In parts of the country where there isn't a large Jewish population, schools teach Hanukkah and even Kwanza in an attempt to be inclusive and diverse or whatever. You probably learned that Hanukkah is synonymous with Christmas, but without the whole Messiah birth, right? Well, it isn't. And all of this furthers the Christian-centered approach to the November-December ordeal."

I *had* learned that Hanukkah was basically Christmas without Jesus.

I'd go on to still make this Christmas-tidings-to-Jews mistake a few more times before I finally learned my lesson.

I once purchased some candy as a sweet little gift for a guy I was dating. It was a Reese's Christmas tree, and he was Jewish. Oops.

I wished my friend Arye a Merry Christmas one year. His name is *Arye Zucker*. How could I be so Christian-ly dense? Anyway, he sent me back a bitmoji saying the same thing, so I don't think he was offended. (I have met plenty of Jewish folks who embrace and love the jovial nature of Christmas. I once babysat for a little Jewish girl who loved Christmas.

Instead of an Elf on the Shelf she had a Mensch on a Bench. I'd never heard of this tradition, but I thought it was both hilarious and brilliant. "It's the one 'jolly' thing my parents let me do for Hanukkah that's like Christmas," she explained. "Christmas is so jolly and fun! Hanukkah is just ... blah. When I go to college, I am *getting a Christmas tree!*" And then I went back to reading her *Anne of Green Gables* while she bathed in a clawfoot tub.)

Experiences and conversations like these were little ways I slowly learned to exist in a world that didn't assume every single person believed the same things. Back home, if you told someone you'd just enjoyed some "worship" they'd assume you meant an acoustic set of Hillsong United songs on a Sunday evening. In New York, people might ask if you'd just gone to an ayahuasca retreat.

In Missouri, I was rarely confronted with how my specific practices or beliefs might be anywhere from insensitive to abhorrently offensive to others. Back home the word "tolerance" was an abstract concept. What exactly did we have to be "tolerant" of on a daily basis? Everyone was exactly the same!

In a homogenous community, you can make a racist comment and call it a "harmless joke." When there are no people of color around, who is there to offend or outright threaten? You can constantly insist your religious views and practices are superior to others' when no one around you practices or believes a different religion. You can more easily insist that gay, transgender, and gender nonconforming people are all mentally ill and don't deserve basic rights when you do not interact with any of the aforementioned identities.

Anyway, it may seem like a small something but Colin was helping me realize I had a default way of seeing the world. My default wasn't "bad" necessarily. It's just that my default isn't everyone's default.

I can't assume everyone wants a cup with fucking bows on it.

21

CASUAL CHRISTIAN

IT WAS MY FIRST Christmas back home. One of my best friends had just gotten married, the other was getting married the following June, and I'd recently gone on a first date where I hooked up post–drunk eating three bodega chicken breasts with yet another finance guy.

When people asked, "How's New York going?" I wanted to say, "Oh, it's great! I'm trying to get my footing as an actor all the while having zero footing as a person. No one can tell though! I cover up my fear of aimless unknowing with an impressive daily to-do list. If I seem productive no one will know I am internally spiraling!"

But instead I'd say, "I love it!" and then share stories about crazy rich people and try to avoid stories of my dating debauchery.

Being back in "God's Country" smacked me in the face with the paradox my first half year in New York was proving to be. I was successfully executing all that New York required of me financially, personally, mentally, and spiritually, which was way more than my married-right-out-of-college friends could do. But I also had no clue who I was or where I was going, which they seemed to have figured out.

I was a strange combination of exceptionally responsible and completely unhinged. On the outside I was making all my work shifts, paying rent, and going to countless auditions. But on the inside I was screaming silently in shame, anxiety, and serious fear.

I wanted to answer all my faith questions so I could go on knowing who I was and how I wanted to show up in the world. To my understanding, there was no way to know anything about life if I did not know where I stood with *the Lord*.

Every day I spent being unsure of my Christian identity was one more day I could get hit by an MTA bus or fall on the subway tracks then go straight to Hell. I had enough stressors on my plate, I couldn't add "Definite resident of Hell" to that list, or I was going to need a psychiatrist I couldn't afford, which would also stress me out.

Therefore, I just had to sit myself very uncomfortably in the proverbial (and literal, if I died, I guess) faith limbo.

This was a mindfuck for a few reasons.

First of all, as a soldier in the Army of the Lord, I was supposed to have an "unwavering faith" and devotion to Jesus. I had vowed that to Him multiple times throughout my life. "No matter what the world throws my way, Lord," I'd pray, "I will always believe in you and follow you ..."

Until I move into a penthouse with a rich Jew, have sex, and read some history books, I guess.

Did I lie to Jesus?! Was my faith really that fragile? Did I even ever love Jesus? Was I ever a "real" Christian?

So much change was happening around me. Therefore, so much change was happening within me. It makes total sense that the very foundation of who I was was being shaken!

But I didn't see it that way. I just saw myself as a piece-of-shit devotee.

Second of all, not knowing if I was a Christian meant I was something worse—I was a "Casual Christian."

A Casual Christian is someone who goes to church but doesn't actually "live out their faith." Maybe they call themselves a Christian, but they have sex, drink, have non-Christian friends but don't actively try to convert those friends. There is even a worship song called Casual Christian! A sung commitment to Jesus that we will *never* be "lukewarm" like those detestable half-assed Christians.

Unlike what many secularly raised folks might think, the opposite of following Jesus was not Satan-worshiping, it was being casually committed to the Jesus cause. If you claim to be a Christian, but are not actively exemplifying it in your life, you're leading others astray from the Gospel. Therefore, being a Casual Christian made me the biggest enemy of the Kingdom of God.

Not only was I afraid to *not* call myself a Christian and lead myself straight to hell; I was also afraid of calling myself a Christian and being to blame for leading potential believers to hell!

I discussed all of this with Eddie, my Christian ... *ish?* confidant.

I shared all my aforementioned stressors, and included "God gave me this amazing penthouse because of how faithful I once was, and now I'm doubting Him as a thank you!"

"First of all, you didn't get that penthouse because God loves you for being a devout Christian."

"Yes I did."

"No. You got that penthouse because I did cocaine in college."

"Oh my God." I burst into laughter. I truly had never considered that it was my brother's partying with a lot of rich kids that got me this real estate miracle, not my untouched hymen and daily devotionals.

"Here's the thing, Matts" Eddie continued to, more elaborately, help alter my perspective, "You have to distinguish between *knowing* something is true and *believing* something is true. Knowing something is fact. We know very little in life beyond scientific findings, but even those are changing all the time. Believing something, however, is a *choice*. Sometimes when we have lived experiences that prove something to be true in our own lives, we conflate the two concepts, and then try to project what we 'know' onto others because we 'know' it's true, but we actually just 'believe' it's true. Evangelicals don't *know* Jesus is the son of God, came to die for our sins, and is our way to Heaven; they *believe* it, and treat it as fact. It is entirely okay to believe whatever you want in your own life, but when you insist others take on your personal beliefs as facts—or else they will rot in hell and/or suffer shamefully on earth—that's when shit gets dicey. And wars get started."

"Okay so ..."

"So my point is let yourself off the hook. You don't 'know' if Jesus is God and neither do the Evangelicals; they just 'believe' it. Besides, no one in New York is going to ask about your religious beliefs on a regular basis. So you've got at least until your next wedding in Missouri to surmise an answer to this hypothetical faith question you're stressing over."

"Okay, but ..."

"You're not going to hell. You're doing everything right, kiddo. I promise."

My brother hadn't witnessed me step in my own vomit upon getting out of bed for church after a regretful Saturday night, but sure sure. I was "doing everything right" and definitely "not going to hell."

This perspective of "knowing" vs. "believing" reminded me of a conversation I'd had with a professor years prior. The year I was so annoyed with JBL, met Arma, and decided the church was wrong about the whole gays-being-evil thing, I asked to have a discussion during office hours with my religious studies professor.

I happened to know this guy was a Christian, because he went to my church. I was curious why, given his expansive religious knowledge, he'd chosen Christianity.

"After knowing so much about so many other religions, why have you settled on Christianity?" I asked him.

"Well," he replied "I haven't exactly 'settled' on anything necessarily. This is just the religion I've decided to implement in my life as I go. I guess it could change at some point."

It could change at some point! Hadn't he gotten the "unwavering faith" memo?

"I've just always been more invested in the adventure of seeking answers than the finiteness of the answers I seek," he continued. "And I think you're the same, Mattie Jo. We are the forever seekers. It's okay to not know."

This professor was presenting a faith driven by journey, instead of absolutes. At the time I continued to be an unwavering faith-haver, but the conversation never fully left me.

It's okay to not know? To be a forever seeker?

Deeper than fear of hell and fear of sending others to hell, was my fear that I no longer had access to a God I once loved. I'd spent my life in a profound, constant connection with a specific God. And now, that specific God was disappearing. *Who I was when I loved and connected with that God was disappearing.* Was I even allowed to pray if I didn't know in my bones, without a single doubt(ing Thomas), unwaveringly that Jesus was God? Didn't you have to have faith in *that* God in order to have access to *that* God?

The thing that scared me the most about "choosing" to no longer believe in Jesus as my personal savior was that I would be completely alone in this big, terrifying, brand-new world I had decided to plant myself in as a grown-up. Not only would I be alone because I didn't have Jesus with me; my friends and family wouldn't "get me" anymore.

There's this belief among Evangelicals that people who leave the faith are doing it because, basically, they can't hack it morally. They'd rather have sex and drink and go to drag shows than live the way the Lord calls us to live. Because that way—the worldly way—of life is *easier*.

This lie makes me so angry, if I could put clap emojis between every word in the next sentence, I would. Read it like I did.

There is nothing *easy* about losing how you have always defined yourself, having to redefine it with no direction, and losing your loved ones along with it.

This is another way the manipulation of staying in religiously oppressive systems is so effective—the threat of losing social support, love, and approval is too scary for many to brave.

This is why I believe that, in order to truly, fully have the space and freedom to leave the influence of Evangelical culture, you have to geographically leave it, at least for a time.

In the darkest parts of my deconstruction, I was in a new city with opportunities to build a new community. Though the threat of losing the approval of my family and friends back home was scary, and I didn't at all want that—especially from my family— subconsciously I knew I could and would build a new community for myself. A chosen family.

Of course, theoretically, there was a way I could opt out of this aloneness at any time.

If only you'd just believe, Mattie Jo. Just proclaim you know Jesus is Lord!

As if, after all these new experiences and learning, having faith in Jesus was as easy as believing New York would recycle my cardboard because that was what the signs near the recycling bins in my apartment building said.

It's not that easy ...

I wanted so badly to "just believe." I didn't want to be a Casual Christian, a lukewarm-believing turd. I wanted to be the zealous, Jesus-loving, so-sure-of-everything girl I used to be! Instead, I spent hours studying, dissecting, and trying to make sense of the faith that once brought me connection with the divine, joy, and a strong moral compass but also shame, self-hate, and sexual confusion.

Over time, I began to realize how fucking insane it was that I was taught faith should be immovable, never-changing, forever solid.

Without consent, we humans change all the time. I mean, between ages ten and sixteen, women literally *grow* boobs. Young men's voices drop. We get taller, our hips widen. Some of us privileged folk get those fucked-up teeth that grew into our heads fixed with the modern ortho-medical miracle of braces.

We don't just change physically; we are expanding our brains constantly! You know why toddlers need naps? Because their baby brains are overwhelmed with all this new information they're absorbing about being a human on earth every single moment and *they are tired.*

As a Recovering Evangelical, I *was* uncontrollably growing and changing all the time. Like a toddler, I was getting new shit thrown at me constantly. And since I was not prepared for real adult life outside of a very specific culture, my brain, emotions—everything!—was overwhelmed.

The difference in being an adult rather than a toddler is, not only was I absorbing so much new information all the time; I was trying to unlearn so much old information at the same time. And damn was I tired.

This message of immovable, unwavering anything—especially faith—only works on people who never leave what they've always known. If at any point you are brave enough to leave where you grew up and/or the comments section of Facebook to go actually live, you will be uncontrollably growing and changing all the time.

I am a forever seeker. It's okay to not know.

I didn't know much of anything, but I did know this: As long as I was truly living, wavering would occur. Change would happen. And since I was really into this truly living thing, I decided the adventure of the journey was more important to me than the finiteness of having unwavering faith.

Through a murky, confusing culture of idolization of the Bible, purity, and social reward I'd always known, I kept seeking a God of love I hoped was still there for me. Even if that meant I no longer called myself a Christian, not even a casual one.

Except now that means I am FOR SURE going to hell.
Ugh.

22

HELL YES? OH, FUCK.

A STRANGE THING HAPPENED when I became one of the people I had spent my entire life hearing I needed to save. As a doubter, questioner, and not-quite-Christian-er, I got a VR experience of just how the flawed faith I was offered—and taught I needed to offer everyone in my path as my life's purpose—was not at all "faith." It was simply all fear.

I was sold an unconditionally loving God, unlike all the other Christian denominations that were "fundamentalists" and "dogmatic."

The God I was sold says, "All are welcome. I love you, not because you earned it, but simply because I created you." This God who sacrificed His "one and only son" as the ultimate testament of His love for me. His love is not transactional. There is absolutely nothing I can do to earn His love or take it away. What a relief! Divine, unconditional, non-capitalistic love!

Love, love, love, love, love, love. *God is love; do you hear me?!*

The closer I looked, the more I realized that was not at all true. Just because hell and dogma were not delivered violently and frighteningly at my church, didn't mean I wasn't receiving messages involving them. The faith I was offered as a nondenom was no different from those other denominations; it was just packaged differently. Same song, different choir robes.

Upon joining the Christian club, I promptly began being told all the ways I must now conduct my life in order to say thank you to God for all His love. *If you don't live your life in these very specific ways, you can't really call yourself a Christian. If you can't really call yourself a Christian, you're going to hell.*

In other words, God's love is, in fact, conditional.

Once I stopped abiding by the ways I could receive that love—namely, once I no longer knew if I identified as a Christian—I realized how much of my "faith" was just me behaving and believing in ways that would assure I got to Heaven and didn't burn in hell.

During my "Am I going to hell?" psychological crisis, I remembered a conversation I'd had while on my mission trip to Indonesia with Laurel, Karen, and Larry. (Remember those fuckers?) They were discussing Rob Bell's—a prominent Evangelical leader and author—newest book: *Love Wins*.

I'd heard of *Love Wins* in college but didn't dare read it then. I knew what the overall message of it was: Hell cannot exist under the umbrella of an all-loving God. hell and "all-loving" are directly in conflict. When Rob released this book, it sent the Evangelical community into a faith frenzy (but got him in cahoots with Oprah, so I'm sure he took the loss well).

"It's just terrible what he's doing," Laurel said. "The way he's leading people so clearly away from the truth of scripture."

With a mouth full of noodles, I piped up, "I mean, it doesn't sound wrong. God is supposed to be all-loving, right? Hell sounds ..."

"But it's scripture, Mattie Jo!" Laurel retorted. "God is a JUST God. He gives us so many opportunities to receive His love. If we don't accept His gift, that is on us, not Him. That's why we are here in Indonesia. To help God give this Muslim country an opportunity to receive His love!"

So then I said, "Okay then, *Laurel*. If God is a *just* God, He cannot also be an unconditionally loving God. Justice and unconditional are conflicting ideas. So, either this God we worship is a mess of conflict, or He's just *just*. Oh look, I don't even need to read Rob Bell's book. *I get it.*"

I didn't actually say that because the frustration of an un-kissed engaged woman in her late twenties is not something to agitate.

I shut up and kept eating my noodles.

Years later, I realized how this conversation fully exposed the fragility of Evangelicalism. The second a prominent Christian leader offered that maybe hell wasn't real, Evangelicals freaked out because they knew they were losing their biggest marketing tool. If hell isn't real, why would anyone buy into the rigid, impossible, anxiety-inducing, limiting, traumatizing life of Evangelical culture?

As I was discovering, people probably wouldn't.

One evening, exhausted from an existential journaling session, I walked out of my bedroom in my pajamas and ran into Colin.

I looked down at my feet in deep thought, and without considering whether he even wanted to engage in this conversation with me, I word-vomited: "I think I've been conned. I just realized I've been living my whole life on the moral ethic of trying not to go to hell."

Annoyed, but not going to completely ignore me, he responded, "That checks out."

Embarrassed at what a simpleton I probably sounded like, but desperate to share this revolutionary discovery with anyone who would listen, I continued to word-vomit.

"But I never thought it was that! I thought my faith was based on the all-consuming, unconditional love of God. But actually, it's based on the all-consuming, completely conditional fear of hell!"

Then Colin articulated so well, like only someone who went to a $25K-per-year kindergarten could: "Ah. So you've discovered the highly effective tool of successful religious and political movements alike—fearmongering manipulation for the purpose of social control."

Was I, a personal relationship with Jesus Christ–haver, a victim of *fearmongering manipulation for the purpose of social control?*

Yes. Yes, I was.

If I feared a bad enough punishment, my behavior was controlled. And if they can control my behavior, they have the power. I wanted to shout from my terrace in my underwear, "So I don't have to follow this shit anymore because it is not and has never been about love!!! And I shan't be controlled any longer!!! Look at my sexy underwear!!!"

I didn't do that. Mostly because I didn't own any sexy underwear, but also because I was already an outsider on the Upper West Side and I wasn't going to make it worse.

Instead, any time I got the chance, I'd have angry conversations with friends and family back home like this:

"How can we say God is unconditionally loving blah-blah-blah if He'd send me to hell for maybe not seeing eye to eye with Him on certain things? Especially when, hello, *He made me with this brain to think.* Is God really such a weak-ass bitch He can't stand to participate in a simple debate?"

Then they'd give me some version of this bullshit response:

"God's ways are not our ways, MJ. Yes, it's hard for us to understand how God could send someone to hell because they don't believe in Jesus, but we are not God. He is beyond us. And He did not make us with *these minds.* He made us with pure minds but then our minds became sinful when we chose sin."

Then I'd reply with some snarky response breaking down all their bullshit:

"Um, not true. Humans fully comprehend a system of 'do this equals reward, do that equals consequence.' I have been existing in that space since I started fighting nap time! From the time I was in preschool, I've learned that certain behavior gets me a prize from the treasure chest, and certain behavior gets me time-out. I was raised in capitalist, working-class America! I understand earning my keep. What I actually don't understand is total grace, a gift freely given. Simply because I exist."

"Your description of this 'totally-beyond-us God' sounds actually *exactly like us.* He doesn't sound beautifully divine; he sounds human as fuck.

"Furthermore, you are basically suggesting that the God of the Universe, who created asteroids and fuzzy caterpillars, set up a booby trap for humans within their first week of involuntarily being created on earth. And then made humanity for all future generations suffer for eternity because of a decision we had nothing to do with? Also, He couldn't like, see the sin thing coming? Did he miss that in the whole 'all-knowing' part of himself?

"So, I'm supposed to worship an all-knowing God who got blindsided pretty quickly by humans? Who created sin but also created the system

GOD, SEX, AND RICH PEOPLE

to get out of sin? So we have to rely on Him to escape the suffering *He created*? God sounds like an abusive-narcissist, shit boyfriend. Not a 'beyond-me, all-knowing, worthy-of-praise, loving Creator.'"

There was also sometimes this response, which I totally loved:

"Justice and love are not exclusive. Serving justice can be loving. Like fighting the Taliban in Afghanistan. Serving justice to evil in order to lovingly help innocent civilians live a better, freer life."

And then I'd point out:

> Believing Jesus is the Messiah is not the same as fighting Taliban terrorism! Also, Evangelicals rarely reference the Old Testament unless it serves them. The warlord God of the Old Testament serves you in this case. He seeks Justice against His enemies, leading his Jewish VIPs to victory in battle. Or, if someone commits a heinous sin, He makes them offer a sacrifice. Tit for tat, this Old Testament God.

> Until the New Testament, when Jesus says love your enemy. To turn the other cheek. When they mocked him at the cross, He didn't fight back. I thought God was always supposed to be the same? Constant. Never changing. And yet the violent, angry God of the OT became a pacifist in his physical manifestation?

Anyway, you can see the holes in all this are a total spiral. Also, I am thoroughly impressed with how much I still know about the Bible.

So, there I was, twentysomething years old, probably drunk, on my twin size bed in a Manhattan apartment, coming to terms with yet another layer of Evangelical trauma malarkey: I didn't know how to make decisions in my current life that didn't boil down to my fear of experiencing damnation in my afterlife.

So, then I sort of, subconsciously anyway, came up with a sifting question for my own moral/ethical guidance: If the threat of hell isn't real, how do I actually want to live my life?

If God is truly all-loving and hell isn't real ...

Do I feel free to stop attending a church that makes me feel shame, and instead build community where I feel celebrated? *Yes.*

Do I need to tithe to a Christian church? Or can I just donate to organizations I know are philanthropic and aligned with my personal passions? *No, and yes.*

Can I stop believing my sexuality makes me bad unless it's within the context of a heterosexual marriage? *Yes!*

Do I care about identifying as a Christian? *No.*

Do I want to still be a compassionate, kind, honest, generous person? *Yes.*

Do I want to apply the Golden Rule, especially in my sex life? *Yes!*

Can I perhaps actually start having really amazing, worshipful sex on the regular by choosing the parameters within which sex is fulfilling and healthy and orgasmic for me? (Find the clit, live abundantly. *That's in the Bible, right?*)

These questions helped me sift through which parts of my Evangelical faith were useful and which needed to go to the morality-compass dumpster forever and ever amen.

What's frustrating about the Recovering Evangelical process is that even once I intellectually shifted certain beliefs, the emotional resonance of those beliefs didn't cease. Although I no longer believed I would be eternally tormented in hell by God for not necessarily claiming Jesus as my Lord and Savior, I still believed releasing my Christian morals was the reason for everything bad that happened to me on earth. It was as if the second I started to have thoughts that could lead me to some kind of freedom, I'd remember some other trope to keep me imprisoned in Evangelical Mindfuckville.

And then I'd console myself with the thought: *Maybe I am going to hell. But perhaps that's okay if hell is full of fabulous gays and Rob Bell, and Heaven is full of ... Evangelicals.*

23

A QUICK NOTE ABOUT
FRIENDS AND FAMILY

SOMETHING I WISH SOMEONE would have told me during what I refer to as my Rubble Years—the years of constantly knocking shit down but not yet having the understanding to rebuild, so I was just kind of sitting on top of the spiritual, mental, and emotional rubble—was that being a zealot is being a zealot, regardless of your belief system, and I needed to not impose my new beliefs so aggressively on others. Basically, I needed to live and let live.

Many of my closest friends were preparing to marry people they were, if they got really honest with themselves, marrying because of these ideas I was in the process of busting open as lies. Many of my family members were living comfortably in jobs and communities which were founded on these "absolute truths" I was in the process of contending. I wanted to share my findings with Christian family and friends. This was my new mission!

> Did you know a lot of people have very good reasons to not believe Jesus is the Messiah? Did you know some people who are not Christians are actually legitimately happy? They don't have a Jesus-shaped void in their hearts? I think I'm slowly becoming one of those people ...

> Did you know there are a bunch of books that didn't make it into the Bible because they were written by women or because the writers thought Jesus was a ghost, but somehow Revelation's legitimacy still held up?! What

about all the feminist theology that contains loads of stories that support God as an androgynous force, not a man figure furthering the patriarchy?

Did you know Jesus repeatedly claimed He was going to come back "within this generation" and then just ... didn't?

Do you realize most of our faith is just leveraging the fear of hell for the purposes of social control? And that you're being controlled by entering into a marriage just to have sex so God doesn't hate you? *You don't have to get married! You can be free!*

I wanted to make the blind see! What can I say? Old habits die hard. My need to proselytize and change people's minds was another thing I needed to unlearn. This was definitely not the last time I would see my Evangelical tendencies seeping their way into my new worldview and way of life.

But the people I grew up with were not my audience. Anytime I tried to bring any of this up, they didn't take me seriously. They thought I was being turned by the liberals of New York into an angry woman. Which was absolutely true. I was turned and I was angry.

But under that anger was really a lot of hurt.

I wanted so badly for others in my Evangelical community to understand the betrayal, pain, and justified anger I felt about the things I'd been taught about my faith, sexuality, and general existence in the world.

I felt like I was the only one going through this shit, and honestly, I just wanted some company. It was sad and lonely atop my rubble.

Don't they want to know all this information too?! I thought. The answer was no, they didn't want to know. And I should have let that be okay.

I remember after one of my "Isn't this insane? Why didn't anyone tell us this before?!" tirades, my mother responded, "Well, I don't need to know all the facts for it to make sense in my life, Mattie. That's why it's called faith. It's a mystery."

"Mom," I retorted. "A mystery is 'Why does this blue Dum Dum taste like a strawberry?' Not 'Here are all of these archeological, historical, textual, and sociological studies that show Evangelical Christianity is utter bullshit.'"

"You're overthinking this," she said.

"I am not overthinking! I'm giving all of this the thought it deserves! It's everyone else who is being mentally lazy here, not me! God gave us brains for a reason!"

And then she'd get upset and say I was yelling at her, and we'd stop the conversation only to have a similar one a few weeks later. To be fair, my mom did agree with a lot of what I said about Evangelical culture. It was always the "Jesus may not be God" stuff that didn't sit with her.

In a much more honest, less dismissive conversation, a close friend responded to my talking points, "Honestly, I'm afraid to know everything you know. I'm afraid of what it would do to me. I kind of don't want to know."

I kind of don't want to know.

I fully understood that.

In my rubble years, I found myself wishing I didn't know. If only I'd never become privy to all these different studies and cultural perspectives, I could have stayed blissfully ignorant in my piety. *Comfortable.* Very suppressed and horny, but also very certain I was going to Heaven. So, ya know. Balance.

But that was never going to be me. I didn't leave a town of 3,000 people with a trailer park called "The Yacht Club" to move to New York City and become an actress (and work for people who belong to actual yacht clubs) because I like being comfortable.

What I had to accept in those years, as infuriating as it was, was that some people are okay with *comfortable.* They do not want to seek more or know more because they do not want to do the hard work of reconstructing and redefining their identity and that is *okay.* I would hate to live that way, but it's not my life! It's theirs!

Eddie once told me, "Mattie, if you live your life insisting everyone do things the exact way you would do them, you will be constantly disappointed. You will be tired for all the wrong reasons."

Remember in Evangelical culture when they told us that if we just "live like Christ" people will get curious, ask why we are so joyful, and then we can tell them Jesus, whip out the bridge analogy, and turn people's hearts toward the Lord? Well, in a very bare-bones way, I think the same applies to living out deconstruction.

You don't have to convince anyone of anything, you just have to live your life. And if people have questions, they can come to you. Then conversation will begin. Unlike our Gospel-spreading training, however, maybe disconnect from the need to have a particular outcome from that conversation.

Boundaries, personal responsibility, and releasing the need to change anyone? These were not skills we were taught as Evangelicals, but they are imperative in maintaining respectful relationships as we all develop and grow.

I know it's frustrating, but I promise trying to convince those nearest and dearest to you to be on your same journey is fruitless. Instead, meet them with grace and allow them to stay on their own path. And if you have the capacity, go to church with them when you're home for the holidays and chuckle to yourself when the Pinterest-y crafted wall decor in the lobby reads "Come all those who are thirsty. Isaiah 55:1″ IT'S ME: the thirstiest bitch.

PART THREE

Sex, Singlehood, and
Searching for Purpose

24

ALMOST FAMOUS BY ASSOCIATION

IN ADDITION TO GOING to auditions and scrubbing toilets from 9 p.m. to 12 a.m. for discount dance classes at Steps on Broadway, I also bounced between multiple gig jobs, including being a hostess at a restaurant in the Theater District. Just reading this paragraph makes me very tired.

My hostess job was super exciting because we got a ton of traffic from famous Broadway performers. Actors I'd admired on YouTube in college would walk in, and I'd have to not lose my shit. I couldn't believe I got to add *this* novelty to my New York reality!

Being the total schmoozer I am, I *thrived* in this setting.

I once had a full-on conversation with Andrew Rannels about the trajectory of my career. He said, "You are doing all the right things, MJ. It will happen for you, I'm certain." I didn't believe him, but him saying so did mean a lot to me. (Ten years later I got to tell him at the opening night of *Gutenberg! The Musical!* that those words meant a lot and stuck with me all these years. And that I quoted him in my book! Living in New York is hard but rewarding in these little ways.)

The cast of the show next door was always in the restaurant, so I became quite close with them. (Which once included being invited to drink wine backstage during the show. My life!) One of the actors—the lead actor—was kind of a big deal in Hollywood, and now Broadway.

He was also ridiculously hot and very tall. We'll call him Hot Lead Actor, or HLA.

At the time, I didn't know he was a big deal. I just knew he was the physical manifestation of every dream husband I'd ever prayed for. He was also effortlessly charming, which was both annoying and alluring, as charm on men over 6 feet tall goes. I didn't talk with him much, mostly because I didn't trust myself not to say something absolutely embarrassing to his perfect face, but also because I assumed the star didn't want to be bothered.

One night, my new friend Michelle (remember Jackson's live-in undercover life coach?) asked if she could meet this famous actor I had access to. She was a big fan of his TV show and heard he was just the nicest guy, so she was sure he wouldn't mind a quick picture. Against my better judgment—because celebrities are people who want to enjoy their burger and whiskey alone sometimes—I agreed to introduce them when I was off the clock.

I walked up to Hot Lead Actor, my heart *pounding* but also thinking *isn't it so cool I'm here and not Evangelical married to Brandon right now?*

"Hey, HLA, I'm so sorry to bother you but my friend is a really big fan of your show and she just wants to say hi. Is that okay?"

"Oh my gosh, you're not bothering me at all, Mattie Jo! Of course!"

Ugh, wow he is so nice and so dreamy and 6'6" and he knows both of my names and ... *Oh right, let me get my friend.*

Michelle and HLA proceeded to sit at the bar for the better part of an hour discussing politics and religion. I didn't know much about politics at the time, so I dared not chime in and make myself look dumb, but I did learn that HLA was a Christian, *Not a Jew*. His last name sounded very Jewish—which I had learned to pick up on by that point—so I was shocked. Michelle was shocked too, and very disappointed, as she was Jewish and hopeful to have Abrahamic banter of the Jewish variety with him. But she already had a quasi-famous boyfriend. *Move over Michelle!*

I could barely keep my clitoral throb from being visible through my pants with that detail. This perfect human is *also a man of God*?

How was he real and how did I encounter him in New York City? *God, are we friends again?*

I didn't say that, I just piped up for the first time in the conversation and said, "You're a Christian? My dad's a pastor. I'm ... er ... uh." Then

I remembered I didn't think I was a Christian anymore and didn't want that to ruin my chances at marrying this Man of God so I just shut up.

The conversation died down and HLA needed to head backstage. On our way out, HLA placed his hand on my lower back.

What the fuck.

Then, I shit you not, he said, "Hey, Mattie Jo, can I get your number?"

What the fuck times two.

"Uh, sure it's ..."

"Great. Maybe we can get coffee sometime and talk about Jesus?"

(!!!!!!!!!)

"Yeah! I'll bring my journal, Bible, and highlighters."

I could still hold my own with Christian banter.

"Perfect. We'll talk soon."

And then he leaned all the way down from his 6'6" atmosphere and kissed me on the cheek.

He walked out, and I think I just stood there in shock.

"MJ! He is into you," Michelle said.

I wanted to brush it off like she was wrong, but, like, I don't think she was. He touched my lower back, asked me to coffee, and then kissed my freaking cheek!

Does this mean God doesn't hate me for having sex before marriage and maybe no longer believing Jesus is the Messiah? Am I being rewarded with an amazing Godly guy, despite my not-so-Godly recent approach to life?

And then: *Shit, what if HLA finds out I'm questioning my faith? That I'm not a virgin/Godly woman. Is he gonna want me anymore?*

A few nights later, while up watching YouTube videos of *Damn Yankees* parodies until way too late, I received his text.

HLA: Hey! I was just at 54 Below. What are you up to?

Me: Just chillin. Having trouble sleeping for some reason.

The reason is I was wondering when/if you were going to text me.

> **HLA:** Well, you're welcome to
> come down to the West Village.
> But that would probably just end
> in trouble ;)

What the fuck times three!

It's past 11 p.m. on a school night. Was HLA ... booty-calling me? I think I was supposed to be mad—according to my previous Evangelical dating blueprint—that he was doing this *after* he suggested coffee and Jesus-talk.

But, I'm me, so I was mostly really excited to brag to all my Evangelical married friends that this Hollywood Christian hottie just offered to maybe "trouble" together.

But also, *What the heck? Do Christian men in New York City "trouble" unmarried? Not only that, do they "casually" trouble, like the secularists? First no testimony-sharing on accidental dates with Jews and now this?*

I could not keep up with expectations for New York City dating.

Then I thought, *If this is not God divinely orchestrating my eventual matrimony with HLA, I am going to have to prove myself and earn this marriage.*

How I responded to this booty call would determine two things:

1. HLA's continued pursuit of me, and

2. God's blessing in the form of a successful marriage

WWWMD: What Would Wife Material Do?

Wife material would say no. Even though I wanted to "trouble" with this famous hottie in the West Village, I had to think about my ultimate goal here—marriage. To my understanding at the time, men do not respect booty calls, and they certainly do not *marry* booty calls. They respect and marry women with whom they talk about Jesus over coffee.

But also *also* ...

WWMJLTD: What Would MJ *Like* To Do?

MJ would like to fuck him. I wanted to go to the West Village and fuck his charming, famous brains out. Despite the fact that I wasn't really sure how to "fuck someone's brains out," he wanted it! He wanted *me*.

I had reached a decision.

I texted HLA back.

> **Me:** Ha! Well that is tempting. But it's late. We better stick to that chat about Jesus over coffee ;)

> **HLA:** There ya go! ;)

There ya go? There ya GO?

Did that mean he approved of my choice? That he was so blown away that I said no to sex with him, I would *definitely* stand out as a marriage candidate in his brain??

Flustered yet proud of myself, I went back to my room and fell asleep (probably also masturbated in order to put out that fire).

HLA and I did eventually get together. Unfortunately, it was not the romantic pursuit I had hoped my not having sex with him would elicit. We got salads at Just Salad, and it truly was ... just salad.

Our meetup was not a date, let alone a marriage proposal. We didn't even get coffee and talk about Jesus/swap testimonies/me maybe admit I wasn't sure what I believed anymore. He talked to me like I was a child who needed guidance. Which I suppose wouldn't have been insulting or slightly weird if our previous interactions hadn't been flirtatious.

HLA never took me out properly, but he did ask to have sex with me again. He was visibly intoxicated those nights so, although I was flattered, I said no. He would also randomly ask if I wanted a latte during my shift and before his show. I assumed he was doing this, not because he was interested, but because he felt bad for the booty calls and not paying for my salad.

Also worth mentioning, this guy was older than me and used his status to try to sleep with someone much younger, hoping her naivete would help him get his way. What a sleazeball, creep thing to do. Almost a decade later, HLA was back in the city to promote a new movie, and he sort of pulled the same shit.

Long story short, instead of meeting at a bar like we'd discussed, he last-minute suggested I come back to his hotel room for that drink.

Classic.

I declined, not because I thought in doing so he would miraculously want to marry me, but because I genuinely did not want to be in his hotel room alone together! I wanted to reconnect as a more mature, established actor/writer and generally more insightful woman! Anyway, he showed up to the bar very pouty and perturbed. He insulted my choice to get the Covid vaccine and went on some political tirade about how the government doesn't care about ending Covid, just making money. And then, once he calmed down and we started to chat about my current projects, he said, "A blog huh? Are blogs even like a thing anymore?"

He did pay for my drink this time. True growth.

Anyway, I mulled over the details of my interactions with HLA for weeks following our Just Salad non-date. I was truly puzzled. I had done all the right things to get a specific outcome, and not only did God not gift me a husband at the end of my great behavior; I didn't even get a free salad! (To be clear, while I personally love a chivalrous man who plans and pays, I understand it's not within every man's means. But this guy was at the top of his acting career in Hollywood and New York. I was a hostess for $15 an hour. Be a kind human and pay for my salad, sir.)

I'd done everything "right" by Evangelical standards, and it didn't matter. Apparently, I couldn't sexually manipulate HLA into being genuinely interested in me, let alone into marrying me. And I couldn't trick God into gifting me a husband, simply by not sleeping with a guy the first time the dude asks.

Between my chastity not luring in even the Godly guys of NYC, and God apparently not spending His valuable time waiting to reward my chastity with a hot, famous husband, I thought *maybe I'm just free to have sex whenever I want!*

But ... how do I know when to have sex?

I had not learned how to gauge when *I* was ready to have sex, only to determine the timeliness of the act based on the man's opinion of me! If these regular guys in the regular world (including those who called themselves Christians but didn't adhere to the whole purity thing) were not judging my wife status based on the timeliness of our sex-doing, I had no (banging) barometer.

Though this whole sexual-withholding manipulation epiphany with HLA didn't "fix" me overnight, it did catalyze me owning the best gift New York offered me: anonymity.

If no one in New York gave a fuck who I was fucking, when I was fucking, or if I was saying the word "fucking," then what did I want to do? How did I want to define my value? How did I want to express my sexuality and what did that mean about who I wanted to be?

Take my knickers and my dignity, NYC. This purity ring is about to get really rusty.

25

FUCK THE SHAME AWAY

BECAUSE HEAVY RELIGION OFTEN brings heavy rebellion, I Necessary Pendulumed my way through sex in the city. My sexual and spiritual self-questions just sort of marinated in my brain while my soul—tired and exhausted from my implosion goings-on—said, "Fuck it all."

And I, quite literally, fucked it all.

My early-days NYC sexcapades were probably, by definition, not the most reckless they could have been, but I also wasn't ... picky. "Quantity over quality" was my subconscious sex motto.

I had the kind of sex I think most people experience in college: You don't really remember it; you don't even necessarily *want* to do it? You just kinda think you have to because "everyone else is."

Okay, that's not entirely true. I did want to have sex. But the more sex I had, the more I realized I wanted to have sex in, like, the abstract. I wanted to be sexually active, sure. But then I would meet dudes, start making out, and think, *oh, we should have sex now probably*, when I really wanted to stop at second base.

But I'd still "do it," because I felt like I needed to make up for lost time. I needed practice! The only thing I feared more than being not married by thirty was still having bad sex by thirty. *If I am going to be a fornicating jezebel*, I thought, *I might as well be good at it.*

I also genuinely thought that if I had enough sex, I wouldn't feel bad about it anymore.

I hoped that with experience, I wouldn't want to wash my entire body and insides with peroxide after every single time. I thought I could fuck the shame away, and maybe improve my performance quality while I was at it. Two birds with way too many dicks.

Most of my sexual experiences were one time per dude, and then we were done. Not only were my experiences mostly one-and-dones; the sex was also bad. But I didn't really know the sex was *that* bad at the time because I had nothing except my own masturbation sessions to compare it to.

My experiences over the next two to three years included but were definitely not limited to ...

I once slept with a guy and he later told me it was the best sex he'd ever had. I was convinced he was lying to me, or was having terrible sex before me, because I didn't remember anything about our encounter. Except that I was really excited to get bagels the next morning. There were many nights in my future where I'd be—mid-fuck—dreaming about postcoital carbs.

After a Broadway show opening-night party I attended on Easter one year, I had a little rendezvous with one of the actors. Nothing says Necessary Pendulum swing like hooking up with a Broadway actor after an opening-night party on *Easter*. (There's an erection/resurrection joke in here somewhere, but I'm not quite finding it so I will just say: "He is come.")

Okay, in truth we did not have sex on Easter. We waited until a few weeks later because I subconsciously could not bring myself to have intercourse on the day of Jesus's resurrection.

Blow jobs, however? Totally. If I was going to do dirty things on the holiest day of the Christian calendar, I wanted it to be reflective of my servant's heart.

I slept with a friend of the groom at my best friend's wedding, because getting laid at a wedding where I was the maid of honor like in the movies sounded like a fun story. Because I was Necessary Penduluming, I was very drunk for this encounter and implemented zero decorum. I didn't take into consideration that I was staying at her deceased grandmother's home with her parents, which was probably not the best or most respectful place for coitus. I carried on with my living-out-a-movie drunken dream.

I woke up feeling actually pretty proud of myself that I'd marked *maid of ho-ing* off my bucket list, until I realized I had started my period and turned the bride's deceased grandmother's guest bedroom into a crime scene. As I tried to discreetly carry period-sex sheets to the washer, I ran into my best friend's dad, Gary, in the kitchen. He offered me and Wedding Hookup Guy some donuts. And then, as if I couldn't get any more divinely punished for my impure behavior, the rest of the bridesmaids (who were all married or Evangelical purity princesses) walked through the door to deliver some wedding gifts.

I just stood there frozen in my bridesmaid's dress, eating a donut, with literal blood on my hands.

I felt—as after most sexual experiences in my life at that point—a combination of very proud of myself for getting laid as a literal and metaphorical fuck-you to the Evangelical system, and very ashamed at my shambly behavior. Perhaps, maybe at some point potentially, I could think about having sex *not* entirely drunk? Then maybe I could have sex and it *not* end in eating donuts with period-blood hands? Shoot for the stars, ya know.

Furthermore, I was bothered knowing I had become "that" girl in my previous life's peer group. The one everyone was spiritually side-eyeing and internally slut-shaming. Or at least, from what I've learned in therapy, that's what I assumed and was projecting onto them. This projection, however, was experientially confirmed when my best friend—the bride at that wedding—threatened to end our friendship over the ordeal.

I left that wedding, and my flight back to New York got canceled. Another divine move, I was certain, happening as punishment for my debauchery. I awkwardly saw Wedding Period Donut Sex Guy at another wedding a few years later where I, shocker, made out with a different friend of the groom's. Bless my horny, repressed soul.

I met a dude on a dating app who had attended this super religious private school right by my house in Missouri and ended up stationed at the coast guard base on Staten Island postgraduation. After we met up, my love story projections a-fluttered. *Omg, what if I move to NYC and still end up marrying a guy who graduated from College of the Ozarks? This will make such a great love story!*

C of O Coast Guard Guy and I didn't get married. Instead, we went on a few great dates, and I listened to Carly Rae Jepson's "I Really Like You" on repeat until I saw him again. Even though we never explicitly spoke about our current stances on premarital sex (because I didn't even really know, let alone adultlike articulate exactly what my views were to another person ... just that I'd like to get it in plz and thank you), I appreciated my roots being understood. There was a safety in knowing someone in New York City spoke the native tongue of Evangelical fuckery and, therefore, maybe understood the complications of post-Evangelical fucking. Oh also he was very ripped.

I took the subway, ferry, *and a bus* to see him again. I then watched his impeccable set of military abs above his actually quite nice penis jackhammer me all the way back to Manhattan. Never to return to Staten Island. Ever. Again. No set of military abs or quite nice penis could justify repeating that commute.

I eventually became a bartender in Hell's Kitchen, so I was basically on a playground for really poor decision-making. I often went home with strangers, completely intoxicated, and did not use protection.

My boss at this bar was a total asshole, but he did have one redeeming quality—his very hot nephew. Hot nephew was from Ireland, so not only was he hot, he was extra hot 'cause #accents.

Long story short, one night after one too many picklebacks, I brought Irish Nephew back to my place, and we somehow figured out how to have intercourse on my twin size bed. I've always been a determined individual.

I showed him out the next morning with my badass female roommates witnessing the exit.

In addition to having Colin as a roommate, landlord, and culture-shock mitigator, I eventually had two lovely female roommates who came into the picture a few months after I moved in. Thank God too, because I could not have navigated New York dating with Colin's perspective alone. He was great but also ... a man.

Aneesha was a beautiful Indian American who worked as a public defender. Katrin was from Sweden and had come to the States after getting her PhD. There was more diversity in my four-bedroom apartment in New York than all of Missouri.

Together, they were a hybrid of what I hoped to be one day: well-established in their careers, on top of their mental, physical, sexual, and financial health. I sought their advice on secular dating often.

I kissed Hot Irish Nephew, said, "see ya later," and absolutely never saw him later. I turned around and immediately started defending myself to Aneesha and Katrin, mentally thanking God Colin was not there to witness such a shameful event.

"I did not expect him to come over, it just kind of happened. I ... I think we are going out later this week ...?"

"MJ, did you have fun? Were you safe?" Aneesha asked.

Because I was now a New Yorker and very worldly, I knew "Were you safe?" did not mean "Do you carry an EpiPen?" It meant had we used condoms. And the answer, because abstinence-only education is the best way to (ironically) fuck yourself in sexually active adulthood, was no. I was not safe.

"I think I had fun? But no ... I wasn't ... safe."

"You *think* you had fun?" Katrin asked.

I started to cry.

I was never going to see that guy again. And, as discussed previously, because my having sex with a man was supposed to tie me emotionally to him forever, I should have been very sad that I would never see him again. But I wasn't sad I'd never see him again. I was sad that I never *wanted* to see him again.

How did I get here?

I was having a moment of sincere incredulousness at my own actions. I thought about how, just a couple of years earlier, I had been a virgin saving myself for my husband. I was the girl in college who everyone knew by her faith in Jesus Christ and commitment to not being "of the flesh."

And here I was, in New York City, saying, "see ya later!" to a dude I hoped I never had to see later, hungover, post-barebacking sesh. It doesn't get much more flesh-ly than that.

My very sweet roommate hugged me and offered some encouragement.

"Okay then. You learned something valuable here. You learned you don't want to do one-night stands. And you definitely don't want to do unprotected one-night stands. This is great! Now you know and you won't do this in the future because you know it's not something that makes you feel your best. Doesn't seem so bad?"

"But what I did, Aneesha. It's awful."

"Which part?"

"All of it."

"Why?"

"Um ... because it's wrong?"

"What does that mean?"

Aneesha was good at asking questions. *Lawyers, amiright.*

She continued. "If it truly feels wrong for you, MJ, that's all that matters. Move on with a new personal boundary, let it go, enjoy your Saturday. Also go get Plan B. And look into getting tested in a few weeks."

First of all, clearly Aneesha had never been exposed to the imperative self-flagellation of being a woman in Christ. I couldn't just walk away from a night of unprotected sex with a stranger and think, *Hmm, never wanna do that again. Glad I know now!*

I needed to punish myself for my sins. I needed to feel the depths of how flawed I was as a human being without God's guidance. I needed to find a church that could smell the stale stranger sperm in my nether regions and let me repent STAT.

Secondly, *only slutty girls need to get tested, right?* I didn't know that regular STI testing could be viewed as medically healthy, not morally loaded. I lived in a perpetual state of subconscious self-slut-shaming and getting regular STI tests made it seem ... official.

Lastly, Plan B? For ... *me? Again? Maybe I need to finally get on birth control ...*

I didn't have time to go to church for confession; I had to get to a bartending shift (but I did get the Plan B). Instead of repentance, I mulled over my roommate's advice and tried not to look my boss in the eye.

Could I really just "let myself off the hook?" Could I just look at this situation as something I hadn't known before and now I knew? And now that I knew, I wouldn't do it anymore? Could I seriously be learning a positive lesson from an *unprotected* one-night stand?

Could I be that *easy* on myself?

The Church taught me that if I make light of something that is actually a very bad sin, then I'm minimizing the worst thing in life: my contribution to widening the gap between humanity and God. And just like wildfire, one-night stands are super okay in every human's eyes. No one needs Christ to fix us. No one gets saved. Every human soul is going to hell forever and ever amen all because I drunkenly fucked my boss's hot Irish nephew.

After this situation with Hot Irish Nephew, it appeared I had two options: my autopilot self-flagellation for the Kingdom of God or an in-depth experience inventory for the sake of creating better experiences for myself.

The Evangelical-shaming way of making decisions is, at its core, based in fear of punishment and self-hate instead of critical reasoning and self-empowerment.

If I never stopped to understand the deeper reasoning behind not wanting to make certain choices again, how would I alter my decisions based on their motivations? Just labeling it "bad" or "sin" wasn't proving to be very productive.

I decided that in-depth experience inventory was the way to go. Instead of beating myself up, I would simply pay better attention.

Which parts was I not okay with? Was it the sex part? The unprotected-sex part? The fact that I didn't want to see him again? Why do I not want to see him again? Do I want to be able to have an enjoyable morning with a partner instead of embarrassingly kicking them out? Will I feel more comfortable to enjoy myself if we use protection?

If I answered these questions, perhaps I could set myself up to have better sexual encounters in the future by acting on these new lessons I'd learned, instead of doing the same thing and continually feeling like a "bad" person.

In other words, I couldn't fuck the shame away; I had to Aneesha-lawyer-level-question-and-answer the shame away.

Stopping to ask these questions and, consequently, quit behaving from a place of shame, was the beginning of me slowly swinging out of my Necessary Pendulum. I'd done the purity ring thing, and now I'd done the a-lot-of-one-night-stands thing. Now I just wanted to do the *Mattie Jo* thing.

26

DATING TO MARRY

DOING THE MATTIE Jo thing included going on a lot of dates. That I hoped led to marriage.

I genuinely wanted a boyfriend, mostly to get some productive sex practice, which I thought would be better achieved within a committed relationship. I also wanted to prove I truly could have it all. *A glamorous life in New York City AND a New York City level hottie huzbo?* My friends back home would be so jealous.

I went on many first dates and very few second dates.

Much to my disappointment, finding a boyfriend in his early twenties in New York City was kind of like teaching your grandparents about preferred pronouns. You can put in a lot of effort, but at some point you just give up because you're not really going to win this one and also, how exhausting.

When dates consistently didn't end in me getting a boyfriend/husband, I internalized that to mean I was unlovable.

"It's not you, Mattie Jo," Aneesha assured.

"I think it is though. Like, clearly, I am doing something wrong for none of these guys to even be remotely interested in being my boyfriend. Maybe I'm being punished."

"Punished for what?" Katrin replied.

For not following the Christlike path of early marriage and weekly small group meetings and instead moving to New York City and turning away from my faith, moral code, and Jesus.

I was learning to better bite my tongue about the weird churchy shit no one in New York understood. Especially the liberal intellectuals, so I said "Never mind."

"What exactly are you looking for?" Katrin asked.

I paused, knowing it was going to sound crazy, but if I wanted honest help, I needed to give honest answers.

"I want to get married."

"Right *now*?" Aneesha shot back incredulously.

"All my friends back home are getting married! It's not *that* crazy. And it's what I want. I mean, what is even the point of going on dates if it's not going to end in marriage?"

Katrin and Aneesha were quiet and just kind of stared at me, thinking of their next tag-team mentor move I guess.

"MJ, you're like twenty-three years old," Aneesha started. "Most people in New York City in their early twenties are having a lot of big adult life 'firsts.' Their first real jobs, managing an income, paying insane rent, navigating what life here specifically is. Not to mention, they're probably not even sure of who they are. Many are coming off lives that were created for them and now they're trying to create their own. Perhaps many of those people just aren't prioritizing marriage; they're prioritizing themselves."

Wait.

What Aneesha described is exactly what *I* was doing. Or, what I was attempting to do. *Should I also not be prioritizing marriage, and instead actively prioritizing myself. How do I even do that?*

"Hmmm ... good point," I replied calmly, still trying to figure out how I would actually execute this non-pursuit-of-marriage concept. I continued, "But like, how do I do that?"

"Do what?" Katrin asked.

"Date without the intention of it ending in getting married?"

"I think you just let yourself have fun and learn," Aneesha offered. "Take it as an opportunity to meet new people, and if something clicks, yay! If not, so long as you are having a good time, what's the problem?"

What's the problem? The problem is, the more men I date, the more undesirable I will be to my future husband, duh! I will have less of my heart and body to give to him, so I need to find the man I want to be with forever very soon so as not to risk leaving debris of my goodies all over Manhattan and Brooklyn, but never Queens. (Just kidding. The best lover I've ever had lived in Astoria. But that's why I say I only go to Astoria to get laid. And now every guy I've ever fucked in Astoria is reading this and wondering if they're the best lover I've ever had. Haha! You will never know!)

I truly thought that casually dating would make me a less desirable wife option to future husbands. I continued attempting to inquire about this new concept without sounding like I'd been raised by cows and inbreds.

"But won't that make what I have with a future relationship like, less special?"

"Why would it make it less special?"

"Because, I don't know, I'm not like ... saving my feelings of love for just the man that I end up with forever?"

"So, you think," Katrin said slowly, needing clarification, "if you date for fun, it will make a future marriage less special?"

I'd learned the fewer the better when it came to relationships. My two best friends married their very first boyfriends. Purity culture didn't just stop at our hymens; it extended to our hearts. Therefore, the more men I was involved with emotionally in my life, the less of my heart I'd have for my husband. And since I would probably be emotionally involved with every single man I went on a date with, that was a whole lot of nothing I'd have left for my special guy.

"Yeah. Like, won't that make the guy I end up with feel like he wasn't important?"

"He isn't important," Aneesha shot back. "You don't even know him yet."

Oh my god.

She continued. "Mattie Jo, why would you need to consider a person who isn't even in your life yet? Are you just going to base all your behavior on a make-believe, potential person?"

Holy hell. I had learned to base my dating, emotional, and sexual behavior on a made-up person! That *was* insane!

"Besides, you have no idea what you will experience with many different people on life's journey. Your experiences with dating until you find the person you stick with long-term will probably make you appreciate your future partner even more."

My past relationships could enrich my future marriage? Is that true?

Katrin contributed as I internally threw all my Evangelical dating books on a bonfire.

"Your past relationships do not take away from your present life unless you allow them to. Then you're choosing to live in the past instead of fully embracing and being grateful for what's actually part of your life in the now."

As with most things in my new world, all this new information I'd been hit with was making my head explode. Most of this information, in fact, was entirely the opposite of how I'd learned to navigate my value and behavior in romantic and sexual relationships.

First of all, maybe me not "getting a boyfriend [husband]" had nothing to do with my lovability or God punishing me, and everything to do with the circumstances of many people my age—including me!—in New York City. I would try again and again to revisit this truth every time a relationship did not pan out. It was simply not the time for me or most of the guys I was going out with to be entering a relationship leading to matrimony.

Secondly, dating could be a tool for learning about myself and didn't have to be a linear path to a wedding day. I could use this as a chance to redefine what I even liked in a person. I was changing as a person, so it was only natural that my preferences in a boyfriend would change, right?

Like, maybe I wanted to marry a genderfluid Harry Styles–type hottie who could rock a dress and enjoy my watermelon sugar. Or a spoken-word soothsayer like British actor and filmmaker Riz Ahmed! Not just a straight American Christian bro who considers "game day" sacred and a sweatshirt without a hood a "nice" shirt.

Thirdly, dating a lot before finding my husband was potentially going to enrich my future marriage, not detract from it. The kinds of connections I could have with people were as vast and expansive as different translations of scripture. Perhaps if I allowed myself to experience all those different connections, I would also learn to better navigate my emotions and behavior within them. Which would ultimately make me a better wife! I mean, human ...

Fourthly—probably the greatest lie of my Evangelical dating theology—my past relationship and sexual escapades didn't have to negatively affect my future marriage; that was a choice in perspective. Everyone has experiences that shape them. It is entirely up to me to allow those experiences to shape me in a positive or negative way.

If I ended up in a marriage where my husband was thinking about me and my college boyfriend, that probably meant he was an insecure psycho. And vice versa! When you're with someone, you're choosing to be with them *in the now*. Not whatever previous iteration of them they were before you met.

And lastly, why did they keep saying "partner" instead of "husband"? Could I have a ... *partner?* Until I moved to New York, I'd only heard "partner" used by gay couples. I assumed this was because they couldn't get married and/or saying "boyfriend and boyfriend" or "girlfriend and girlfriend" sounded funny. But in New York, straight women said "partner." *What the heck?*

"Why do you say 'partner'?" I asked Katrin and Aneesha, afraid I sounded like an uncultured hillbilly but I had to know.

"Because that's what we will be," Katrin said, in her very matter-of-factly Scandinavian way. "Wife and husband and boyfriend or girlfriend, they come with this idea of certain roles within the relationship. I don't want to uphold a role simply because I've got a certain title. I want us to have a truly egalitarian, respectful partnership. I believe you should name the kind of relationship you want, and I want a partner. So that is what I say."

I thought about what the terms "husband" and "wife" really meant to me. If I was honest, they mostly meant "proving to everyone on Facebook I am worthy of love."

So if "husband" and "wife" just meant "worthy of love" to me, perhaps I needed to reconsider my semantics, redefine these for myself, not just inherit the church's definition and roles cuz "wives submit to your husbands" and all that.

I left that conversation and felt a little less pressure every time I opened Tinder. I still didn't have a game plan for how to execute this new way of normie dating super well, but just like with everything new and necessary in my life, I was determined to figure it out.

27

(Fuck)Boy Monsters

An essential, understated skill in every woman's "demolition to redefinition journey" is learning how to traverse the inevitable encounters she'll have with fuckboys.

According to Urban Dictionary, "fuckboi" or "fuckboy" has a lot of definitions but can be narrowed down to my favorites:

1. Men who act like boys and will manipulate you in any and every heartless way possible in order to get fucked.

2. Men who still rely on their mothers but disrespect women.

In my experience, fuckboys are suave pussy-seekers who sort of bamboozle us with their charm. We are upset briefly after we've hooked up when they don't call us because their cat choked on some hookah ashes and it's caused them deep psychological distress, but we get over it and move on.

"Boy monster," however, is a term some friends and I coined in our early twenties to describe the mysterious men who are a total burden on us but for whatever reason(s) we keep them around.

They are a bit more insidious than fuckboys. Masterful, manipulative fake boyfriends, Boy Monsters prey on horny women with low self-worth. They go the extra emotional mile to make the women they're fucking feel like there's "something more," something "special," but have zero intention of ever actually being in a relationship.

They know this manipulative bullshit will not work on women who actually respect themselves, so they stick to those of us who are insecure and desperately seeking love outside ourselves to affirm our lovability.

I was dealing with a fuckboy–Boy Monster hybrid. And deconstructing, very-confused-about-how-to-find-her-identity-and-value-outside-of-the-orbit-of-a-man Mattie Jo was Fuckboy Monster catnip.

Ironically, I met Fuckboy Monster the same night I met "V card receiver" Pop Singer. Fuckboy Monster was the music director for the show in which Pop Singer was performing at the time, and they both were attending NYU for various music things. When we first met, I thought Fuckboy Monster was not into girls "like that," which is probably why I was so comfortable around him, and we became fast friends.

We got together when I visited the City, ate Donna Bell's Bake Shop in Hell's Kitchen, then went to see Broadway shows together. Through our communication, I eventually learned he was not gay, just a musical theater writer. Learning this, combined with his well educated deep critiques of the shows we'd seen, turned him from fast friend to fastly fuckable. Cuz nothing says sex appeal like a strong critique of a musical.

He once invited me to see his a cappella group perform at NYU, and then to the after-party. We left the party pretty quickly after a drunk girl knocked over the entire table of alcohol. Then we ran into Alec Baldwin walking his dog in the Village. New York was so exciting!

After hooking up with Pop Singer, I met up with FBM to tell the tale.

"I'm sorry. You lost your virginity to Pop Singer?" His response was almost insulting.

"Yes. I know. It's horrible," I replied, instead of saying, "Hey, fuck you, it's not like he's ugly!"

"How was it?"

"Terrible."

"I'm really sorry. Well just know, it's not going to be bad every time."

Is FBM hitting on me? Slash insinuating that sex with him wouldn't be terrible? Do I think Fuckboy Monster is hot? Am I being turned on by this musical theater boy whose daily uniform is properly fitted jeans with a Uniqlo T-shirt??

The answer was yes. And before I left New York that trip, in the kitchen of his mother's apartment, we had a steamy make-out sesh. Fuckboy Monster pressed himself against me, and I was dangerously aroused. I could *feel it*. I unbuttoned his jeans, grabbed his dick, and audibly said, "See you at the pole!"[1]

Just kidding.

I did say, "Thank God," though. Talk about blaspheming the Holy Spirit.

Unfortunately, along with having a big dick, Fuckboy Monster was a big dick.

We stayed in contact when I went back to Missouri. He'd send me funny texts about mock-conducting *Book of Mormon* while working out, or songs he'd recently written, and ask my opinion. He'd FaceTime me before auditions to talk me down from my nerves. He expressed jealousy when I briefly started dating someone else. We communicated daily. I just knew he'd be my boyfriend as soon as I officially moved to New York!

In the weeks leading up to my move, he offered to help and said he was looking forward to meeting my parents. But when I arrived on the Upper West Side, excitedly expecting him to help me unload my things and fall in love with my family, I heard nothing from him. Crickets. Not even a quickly disappearing typing box.

He eventually followed up days later, asking if my parents were still in town and did I want to meet up. And because I had no boundaries or standards—or perhaps ANGER?—I said yes. I would love to see him.

Fuckboy Monster came over to the penthouse, and we promptly began making out. I was very ready to experience that perfect penis I'd had the pleasure of groping months earlier. Much to my surprise, however, FBM did not initiate sex. We fooled around for a little bit, and then he abruptly left. No cuddling, no talking. Just a little second base and bye-bye.

Two weeks later, he was in a relationship with another girl on Facebook. (Lol, remember when Facebook told us factual information, like a person's relationship status?)

I felt like such an idiot. Had I missed something? Why would he have spent so much time talking to me while I was in Missouri only to fully ditch me as soon as I moved to the City, *where he lived?* Not only that, he full-on just, like, had a girlfriend now?!

I had moral-conflict flashbacks of my time with Hot Model. *Not this again. Do I tell her I grabbed her boyfriend's dick very recently or ... ?*

I did not tell her. Instead, I would see Fuckboy Monster's flawlessly beautiful, big-eyed musical theater princess girlfriend at auditions and think to myself how ridiculous it was that her boyfriend and I had fooled around while they were dating and she had no idea who I was. Being reminded of my descent to the realms of forever-husbandless-slutville right before an audition for *Thoroughly Modern Millie* was my personal hell.

It stung that I wasn't his choice, but what could I do? I continued to see other people and tried to forget our seamlessly fun and sexually fueled connection.

And then a year later, I got a call. It was FBM. He'd recently cut things off with his girlfriend and would like to see me.

He came over to the penthouse and cried in my arms about another woman. We started to make out. I had physical recall of our-almost-sexy-time encounter a year prior.

This is it. This is going to be the sex I've been wanting to have for the last year. I shan't be disappointed. Get inside of me, already, Fuckboy Monster!

Post-consoling, heartbreak sex with Fuckboy Monster was not exactly what I had envisioned for "the sex I'd been to wanting to have for the last year." But he initiated it, and I was dying to get that perfect penis to penetrate me ASAP. Not my proudest moment.

ASAP penetration we did. So, ASAP we didn't use a condom. So, there I was, having unprotected sex on my twin size bed again.

He impeccably timed his inquiry into my birth control method to coincide with ASAP penetration.

"I'm not on birth control," I answered honestly.

He pulled out immediately.

"What? Why didn't you tell me that before I was inside of you??"

"Umm, because you asked after."

"MJ, what the hell?!"

Oh no. He's actually angry with me. But why? He's the one who put his bare penis inside of me without having a discussion beforehand! And he didn't even inquire about testing, only his potential for having a baby with me. Was he actually concerned with sexual health or just procreation?

It occurred to me that I was probably the first woman FBM had ever slept with who wasn't on birth control. He definitely did not expect the answer I gave him, nor did he expect me to let him inside without protection.

Had FBM completely forgotten the little tiny detail where I was raised in the sexual-education deprived Midwest and was new to this sex stuff? I was not among the coastal liberals who were handed condoms at puberty. I was handed a purity ring and Abstinence Only Education (in my public school!) Or, more likely, had he not even considered that I would not be on the pill?

The point is, he was panicking, and I think I should have been, but instead I was just mad because I thought I was getting divinely cockblocked again. Was I ever going to have good sex??

"You should get Plan B," he said matter-of-factly.

Not this again.

I just stared at him, not knowing what to say but certainly not wanting to spend $50 when it takes two to tango, FBM!

"*I* should get Plan B?" I think he caught my drift, because his response was "We can split the cost." How generous.

So I, once again, found myself purchasing Plan B on a Tuesday afternoon in a Duane Reade after suboptimal sex. Having positive sexual experiences was apparently not part of God's plan for my life.

After we left Duane Reade, we got some coffee, and I tried not to look visibly hurt.

Now that I'm a grown-ass woman who has had many years of therapy and reflection, I can look back and be furious at FBM for assuming something about my body, then putting all the responsibility for birth control and/or safe sex on me, the woman. Acting like a total titty baby when I didn't do the whole preventing-pregnancy thing for him.

I'm also angry and sad for the sexually uneducated me. Instead of using condoms and protecting myself, I thought I didn't need to because I was scared into believing they were ineffective. Furthermore—which is very common among the purity ring wearers—buying condoms meant I was planning to have sex. And even though, ya know, I *was* planning to have sex, confirming it in the form of dick rubber suits made it—much like regular STI tests—official.

Instead of learning anything about birth control, I just assumed it was all bad. I could barely convince Brandon that getting on the pill wasn't going to make God give me stillbirths forever. My mom once told me that if I was going to have sex in high school, she wasn't going to allow birth control, because if I felt mature enough to have sex, I should be mature enough to deal with the "potential consequences." Not sure I'm gonna unpack that one at this very moment, but the point is, I hadn't exactly done ample research on this stuff.

But at the time, in that moment, I was just hurt. I was not cared for in a very vulnerable situation by someone who—a year earlier—I had called a friend. By someone who *I genuinely liked*. I internalized FBM's reaction to mean I was not enough for him. I felt he only saw me as a means to an end, which I then felt maybe I deserved for being so "easy."

I just wanted to have good sex with someone I trusted. I thought, based on our "friendship," FBM could maybe be that person. But clearly, I was wrong and would continue my path of suboptimal one-and-done sex forever.

We sat in silence for a while until he finally said, " Look, MJ, if we are going to have sex regularly, you should get on birth control."

Regular sex? He wants to try sex again? That sounds nice. Wait, no. I'm mad at you, FBM.

"I don't like birth control. I've tried it," I replied.

"Which have you tried?"

None of your business.

"I've tried three different pills."

I actually had tried birth control before. A few times in college to deal with acne. Every time was a terrible experience. I was bloated, constantly angry, and couldn't get wet. Like, of course I wasn't going to get pregnant. How could anyone even have sex under those physical conditions??

"Okay, so get the nonhormonal IUD," he suggested.

"The what?" I had no idea what he was talking about.

"It's a piece of copper that goes in your cervix and makes your uterine environment completely unlivable for sperm. So the sperm, like, die upon arrival."

This Fuckboy Monster would know more about birth control than me.

"Like an infantry ... for sperm?" I clarified.

"Uh-huh."

"In my cervix."

"Right."

My interest was piqued, but I didn't want him to think I'd conceded based on his advice and also the potential of us having repeat sex sessions so I half committed with "I'll maybe look into it."

I wish I could tell you that a day of just-the-tip sex leading to Plan B over coffee and a man telling me what kind of birth control I needed to be on so he could fuck me bareback at some point in the future was enough of an experience to make me hate FBM and never speak to him again. But it wasn't.

We went on to be involved for the next two years.

Fuckboy Monster had presented a tantalizing offer: consistent sex with someone I actually knew. Someone who, at one point, I'd liked. Maybe he could just be like, my sex-practice partner and I wouldn't have to do this spaghetti-slinging sex trial stuff with Tinder dates anymore. That was possible, right?

It proved to be quasi-possible.

FBM and I did eventually start having good, consistent-*ish* sex. I say "good" because at the time, it was the best sex I'd ever had. In hindsight, however, sex with FBM is what I call "big-dick sex." Less than ideal amount of clit-focused play, because porn convinces these guys their big dicks are more than enough to please a woman. My sexy time with him would now get a 2-star review on Yelp versus the 5 I was mentally giving it at the time. We don't know what we don't know.

I say consistent-*ish* because, although I certainly desired it much more often, we'd hook up about twice a month. And it was always on his time, never when I wanted. I'd try to be a brave little sexually empowered lady by initiating sex, but he was always conveniently "busy" at those times. When FBM was available to actually fuck, however, I would drop everything to get it in.

Our meetings were sporadic, never respectfully scheduled. I wouldn't hear from him for weeks at a time and then he'd reach out randomly, saying he had some romantic evening planned for us. I'd cancel outings with friends or actual dates with actual boyfriend prospects to go spend time with him.

I believed his erratic responses to my initiating sex were continued Godly punishment for being sexually forward. I also believed they were further proof that sexually forward women are not attractive to men. That maybe purity culture was right, and I needed to remain both chaste and *chased* in order to be attractive to men. I applied this "men don't respect sexually forward women" and "this is my punishment for being sexually forward—rejection" as gospel truth in my dating goings-on.

Trying to get fucked is such a mindfuck.

He eventually started casting me in all his musicals at NYU. I loved this so much, because I was getting to work at a very well-known institution, sharpening my skills as a singer and actor while constantly learning new material, all while getting to have regular sex in the NYU practice rooms. Skill-sharpening indeed.

During a late-night recording session, FBM and I talked about how dating was going for me. I hated when he brought this up. The fact that it didn't seem to bother him that I was seeing other people made me furious. It made my blood boil and heart sink anytime I thought of him with another woman! Why didn't he feel the same level of jealousy about me?

So we were talking about how dating was going, and I said something about how I thought none of the dudes I was seeing were working out because I was sleeping with them before they were my boyfriend.

"Do you really think that?" FBM asked.

"Think what?"

"That none of these guys like you because you're sleeping with them?"

"Isn't that how it goes? I show I'm 'too easy' so they lose interest."

"Oh dear God," he said, exasperated as he threw down his conducting stick (or something). "That is absurd, MJ. Sex is not your currency. There is so much more to you than whether or not you have sex with a person. And if a dude—or anyone—doesn't see that, that's on them, not you."

Wow you think I'm so much more than sex? That's a compliment, right?

He continued. "Besides, don't these guys have sex with you too? Why aren't they slut-shaming themselves?"

OMG, *what a great point, Fuckboy Monster.*

I hate that ultimately Fuckboy Monster was the first man in my life to affirm the idea that sex was not my currency. And not in the Purity Culture way, where they tell women constantly that they are "so much more than your body and sexuality" and then make everything —from how you dress to whether you decide to have sex— about your body and sexuality. I was definitely still operating under the belief that sex was my currency, but in a different now-I'm-having-it context.

Fuckboy Monster was saying that being sexual is not a reason to judge someone poorly or positively. It's just part of being a person.

The irony, of course, is that it felt like he was saying all this to emotionally manipulate me into continuing to sleep with him. He knew what was happening between us had to be "more than sex" for me to feel okay about having sex with him. Consider the source, is all I'm saying.

He continued, "You're not an either/or, MJ. You're a yes, *and.*"

Oh Jesus, not an actor trope turned emotional manipulation tool.

"You can be a fully respected person and also want to fuck wild. I respect you and love you. And we also have sex. You aren't valuable to me only because we have sex and you aren't not valuable to me because we are having sex. It's simply just a thing we are doing in addition to"—he pointed at all the recording equipment—"all of this."

I hate to admit this, but what FBM said to me that night was quite revelatory in my sexual ethics beliefs.

This conversation with FBM offered me another new perspective about sex. Sex is really just part of being human. It is not a bargaining tool or measurement of value. It is not either your body or your being; it is both and it is all. *Look at me slowly developing my blueprint for boning!*

And, yeah, *guys*. Are you slut-shaming yourselves after the hibbidy-dibbity? You were there too, man!

That being said, I would revisit this very deeply ingrained belief that sleeping with a dude made him immediately view me as an object and not a full person again and again in my continued effort toward designing my blueprint for boning.

Though I am truly grateful for that evening of sexual-equity-ethics epiphany a fuckboy helped me discover, it didn't change the fact that our relationship was still mostly not great.

Spending time with FBM artistically and emotionally gave me a sense that things were really great between us. I was trying to keep him compartmentalized as my occasional practice dick ride, but I was emotionally involved—who was I kidding? I would start to get my hopes up again that we were actually becoming "something," and then something like him spelling my last name wrong in a program would happen, and I'd be reminded of my place in his heart/mind.

"We have been sleeping together for years, and you don't know how to spell my last name?!" I asked, truly appalled.

"Okay it's not like your name is super common," he responded.

"If you spell my name like *that*"—I pointed to the program—"the pronunciation fully changes. That means you don't even know how to *pronounce* my name."

"Okay, I'm sorry. I owe you."

What an apology.

I didn't talk about FBM to many of my friends for a long time. I knew he wasn't good to me, and I knew I was better than how he was treating me. But eventually I couldn't help it, and the stories of this Fuckboy Monster started pouring out.

As good friends do when you're falling for an asshat, they did not approve. One friend even told me, "Look, I support you, but I do not support this. If you're going to continue to entertain such a clearly toxic and unhealthy relationship, that is your choice, but I don't want to hear about it."

Slow clap for that bitch. I wasn't even mad. She was right.

At first, I told myself it didn't have to make sense to anyone else. It made sense to us. FBM just "got" me. We had an intimacy no one could "get," because they weren't around in those moments of him crying in my arms, confiding in me about his deepest pains. They weren't there when he told me I was the most important thing in the world to him, when he told me he loved me. He made sense to me, and wasn't that all that mattered?

When I actually thought about it, however, FBM didn't make any sense to me. I thought only women with unrelenting daddy issues fell for assholes. *I don't have daddy issues!*

I had a dad who celebrated my achievements, who held me when I cried during the hardest years of high school. Who encouraged me to chase my dreams, who wrote me very personalized birthday cards every year and took my mom on dates regularly and had more integrity than any other person I'd met. Okay so I do have daddy issues ... but not like, the Demi Lovato kind.

So, what was my deal? Why was I putting up with FBM?

I put up with him because, although I knew the circumstances were less than ideal, I was having "consistent, good" sex for the first time in my life. I put up with a horrific amount of shitty behavior for same-person dick, because ultimately, I wanted to keep my number low.

There it was. The purity culture monster rearing its ugly bullshit once again! Fewer men, less sex = greater value.

On a deeper level, I put up with him because, at a time when I was still learning how to give myself love and affirmation, he gave me shards of love and affirmation. At a time when so much of my value was still wrapped up in how a man viewed me, picking up love shards from a Fuckboy Monster felt better than no love at all.

28

MATTIE JO MEETS A MORMON

EVEN THOUGH FBM LINGERED in my life for way longer than I should have allowed, I did still have dating experiences within this chapter of my life that were sweet and wholesome. Positive, even. Or, at the very least, weren't IRL personifications of my projected purity culture trauma and lived out self-worth narratives.

After my best friend's wedding—the one where I bled all over her dead grandmother's guest bedroom during accidental period sex with a one-night stand—I was sitting alone, internally slut-shaming myself in the Dallas airport, when the airline announced my flight had been canceled. "Of course!" I audibly exclaimed, convinced the airline gods had heard about my questionable behavior the night before and fucked up my whole day as punishment.

As I was beelining to the airline kiosk to reschedule my flight, feeling deeply guilty for ruining everyone's travel plans with my sex drive and Necessary Pendulum sense of adventure, this dude appeared next to me:

"Hey, were you on that flight to New York?"

"Yeah, I was supposed to be. Were you?"

"Yeah ... I need to be there by tomorrow morning. What are we supposed to do?"

"We should go to the kiosk farthest away from the gate. It'll have a shorter line."

And off we went. It took me a solid five minutes of conversation to calm down about the canceled flight enough to realize this dude was actually really cute. He asked about my life in New York and shared that he was getting his doctorate in seismology on the West Coast but was on his way to a conference at Columbia about mapping the ocean floor or whatever seismologists do. The conference started the next day, and he'd be in the City for two weeks.

"Wow can't say I've ever met a seismologist. In fact, I don't even think I've heard that word since seventh grade Physical Science. But surprisingly, I know what it is."

"Ha! It's that Midwest public education! I'm from Iowa."

So this dude was hella cute—dark hair, beard, great smile, and style that says "I'm a little bit Sk8r boi/I'm a little bit very busy studying the core of the earth"—a great conversationalist, was *Midwestern*, and would be in the city for two whole weeks!

Omg, is he my husband? Did God forget about the period maid of ho(nor) debacle from less than twelve hours ago and suddenly gift me my spouse right here in this airport?

Spouse? Spouse?! We don't say "spouse" anymore, Mattie Jo.

Right, right, sorry. "Partner."

Yes. Also, we don't believe God rewards and punishes in the form of husbands anymore, remember?

Oh yes, that's true. Thanks for the reminder. Oh shit, I'm still in a conversation with this seismologist sk8r boi.

I offered to be his New York tour guide, because I am an excellent New York tour guide and also, I wanted to hang out with this guy a bunch. I'm not sure why I was so confident this total stranger in an airport was worthy of such generosity, but ya know, big risk, big reward.

When we got up to the front of the line, they offered to get us hotel rooms overnight or put us on a *super* late flight into *Newark*.

"Oh, Newark is a terrible idea," I said all "New York know it all-y." "Especially at that time. It will take forever to get into the city on NJ Transit or like a thousand dollars to take a cab." *Let's have a sleepover in a La Quinta Airport instead!*

"Well, my plate-tectonics degree is paying for this trip so I think I can swing the cab. I think we just take the super late flight into Newark?"

This dude doesn't want to spend the night with me?! Rude.

So instead of turning an airport meet cute into a(nother) night of probable regret, we spent the rest of the evening waiting for our flight, conversing over airline-meal-voucher sandwiches.

"So you're in grad school now. Where did you do your undergrad?" I asked.

"Brigham Young. BYU ... Do you know it?" he replied.

Oh. That's why he didn't want to stay the night with me. He's Mormon. Welp, there go my marriage hopes.

Despite Colin's previously calling out my hypocrisy at thinking Mormons' beliefs were so much weirder than my Evangelical beliefs, I still didn't consider getting involved with a Mormon an option. For starters, I knew Mormons could not date not-Mormons. Also, I was way too focused on getting laid at that point in my life to even consider dating someone who wouldn't have sex with me. Or would have sex with me, and then have all the guilt and shame that Brandon and I had. So anyway. My heart sank as this "meet cute" turned quickly into "meet a Mormon."

Honestly though, what did I expect? The guy was super nice, smart, good-looking, and totally respectful. Like he was going to be all those things on his own and not because a religious cult scared him into it? *Yeah, right.*

"Oh, you're Mormon? I thought you said you grew up in Iowa?" I asked, trying to seem genuinely curious and not at all disappointed.

He laughed "I did grow up in Iowa. There *are* Mormons outside of Utah. But ... I'm actually currently in the process of leaving the church. You caught me at a really weird time."

Oh, thank Joseph Smith. Meet cute back!

"Oh wow," I said with hopefully muffled elation. "Well, I'm an Evangelical nondenom preacher's kid and I'm also in the process of ... reconfiguring my identity, so I can empathize."

"Really?! Well, these sandwiches that taste like soggy cardboard just got a lot more exciting."

"Yeah, glad your plate-tectonics degree isn't paying for *these*." We shared a laugh and a moment of relief. What was that relief? An unspoken safety perhaps neither of us had experienced in our solitude of confusion and self-reconstruction?

"I know this is a loaded question," I began "so feel free to tell me to mind my own beeswax but, why are you leaving the church?"

He took a deep breath, nervously chuckled, and then started "That is a loaded question, but since you get it, maybe it will take less exposition ..." Another deep breath/long pause, like he was about to unload the most integral and deep-rooted self-exploration findings to a total stranger or something. "It's hard. I was so involved. My family is very, *very* Mormon. I went to BYU, did the mission, the whole thing. It wasn't until I left the Midwest for California, started studying science and meeting new people that I realized it's just not true. I'm not like other people who leave because they resent the church or think it's evil. I'm leaving because I just ... I can't commit my entire life to fiction."

Nothing says deep soul connection like discussing your religious hang-ups on a first date. At an airport.

For the first time since moving to New York City, I got to share this part of myself I felt no one in my world could really conceptualize: loving the faith I once knew but also knowing so much of it was not true. Physically and geographically removing myself from the culture and pressures of that belief system had revealed its lies.

In that very brief exchange, I felt seen by this stranger sk8r seismologist. I knew he understood a part of me—the deepest part of me, the *condition-of-my-soul* part of me—that I had no idea how to articulate at the time.

Up until that point of dating in New York, I'd avoided this part of myself within dating dynamics. If I did try to explain how I grew up, dudes didn't really understand it. They'd either equate me with the unhinged preacher's daughter trope of Ariel in *Footloose* or act like I'd escaped some Charles Manson–like cult. *It's not that!* I wanted to scream, but instead didn't try to explain further. I just wanted to blend in and be cool and pretend I wasn't going through an ongoing grief I didn't know how to define.

After our religious-baggage heart-to-heart, we boarded the plane and headed to NYC. Our seats weren't next to each other, so he asked the woman next to him if I could trade seats with her. Bold.

Before I knew it, I was resting my head on his shoulder, watching *Blood Diamond*. (Romantic, right?) He looked down at me and smiled. I looked up, wondering if he was going to make a move. *Do Mormons know how to make a move?* And then ... we kissed.

And that is how, three hours after washing period-blood sheets in front of my best friend's dad in my maid of honor dress, I met a soon-to-be-ex-Mormon at an airport, and we exchanged our deconstruction testimonies in the food court, then made out watching *Blood Diamond* on the plane.

For the remainder of his two weeks in New York, we spent many nights together. We went to dinner, hung out with my artsy friends and his science-y friends. I took him for oysters and his first ever cocktail. I made sure to order him the sugariest drink on the menu; he took one sip and asked, "What's your drink of choice?"

"Whiskey," I responded, without missing a beat.

He shook his head. "Okay so like, if you want a tasty liquid to consume, you can honestly tell me you enjoy whiskey over, idk, chocolate milk?"

And then I almost spat out my whiskey, because how true. Alcohol tastes like nail polish remover, and chocolate milk tastes like ice cream that makes your bones stronger. If you're talking palatability, there was zero competition between the two tasty liquids to consume.

By a few nights in, he discovered hard cider, which "tastes like bubbly apple juice!" and stuck to that. Over whiskey and bubbly apple juice, I brought up the elephant wearing a purity ring in the room. "So, where are you at with the whole no-sex-till-marriage thing? Are you gonna keep adhering to that? Do you still wear your holy underwear?"

To be clear, I didn't have any plans to sleep with Ex-Mormon. I was still working through the whole "if I sleep with a guy, he will never love me!" fear, so my question was more about me knowing to what extent

I would/could possibly make this guy hate himself if we ever went past making out on my twin bed.

With his adorable nervous chuckle, a smile on his face, and a genuinely impressed expression, he said, "You just say what you're thinking don't you?"

"I'm sorry I just ..."

"No, no! I love it. I've never met anyone like you, Mattie Jo."

Had I met a quality brainy, attractive dude who didn't think I was "too much?" Did those exist?

"I just don't want you to be upset, ya know? If we end up ..."

"Touching under my holy underwear?"

"Precisely."

We then proceeded to swap stories about how our sexual expression had gone terribly awry with each of our first loves. He had basically gone through the exact same thing I had with Brandon with his ex-girlfriend. Except his story was arguably worse, because she ended up leaving him—geographically *and* relationally—after they'd had sex. This woman literally moved away to flee her "sin."

"So, I understand how shitty it feels when you make someone feel ... shitty," he said.

"Especially when that thing that made them feel shitty ..."

"Shouldn't at all."

"Yeah." He really did get it.

"To be clear," I began again, "I wouldn't feel shitty. But I also ... we don't have to ..."

"Mattie Jo, you are amazing and unlike anyone I've ever met, but I still don't *really* know you. We don't have to have sex. I think given what we've shared, that might be weird for us both at this point."

This moment does not end in us finishing our not-so-tasty liquids and enjoying each other's not-so-tasty liquids. Ex-Mormon and I didn't have sex, and I never saw the holy underwear. However, he was an amazing kisser, and it was nice to have no-pressure PG-13 make-outs while I got to know this gem of a human.

Toward the end of his stay, he asked for my help drafting the letter he was planning to send to his parents about leaving the church. I realized how vulnerable and scary that must have been, and did not at all take for granted that he was willing to share that with me, a random girl he'd met due to a canceled flight.

The two weeks passed, and after our weird, temporary relationship, I saw him off to the airport.

Ex-Mormon started to tear up as he asked me, "What now?"

"I don't know," I replied. I truly didn't. I stood at the corner of 83rd and Broadway very confused as to what had walked in and out of my life so beautifully, so simply, and so ... quickly.

I need some chocolate milk.

"But," I continued, "I do know that I'm really grateful neither of us got married like we were supposed to, so we could do something wild like have a two-week relationship with a fellow religiously wounded stranger we met in an airport."

He laughed, kissed me, and headed back west.

Mormon is pretty off the grid, as you would expect most earth scientists to be, so I didn't hear from him much after our little love affair. However, a month or two later, I came home to a package and a thoughtful note written on a postcard. The package was full of University gear: sweats, a tank, a coffee mug, and a magnet.

I saw Mormon again a few years later, when he was back in New York for another ocean-floor-mapping conference. He had been completely Mormon-free for close to three years, and I'd been in therapy for that time, so we had much to discuss over Mexican brunch.

"People don't need religion, you know?" he said, sipping his margarita. He'd come a long way since insulting the fruity-licious cocktail I suggested. "Like we were always taught humans need religion to help us be good because we aren't on our own. We don't need religion to make us good."

"I think that's still my biggest hang-up as I still wrestle with this," I followed up. "I don't believe humans are inherently bad. I actually think religion makes all of this *worse*. Like, even after all the work I've done on myself—identifying old beliefs, creating new ones, and then implementing those into my life—I still find myself constantly up against Evangelical/purity culture narratives. At every turn, I'm working against a system I don't even buy into anymore, because these 'Truths' are rooted in me. They've made it incredibly exhausting to make any decision! Luckily, now I have better tools to navigate all this. When you met me, I was still such a confused, shambly mess."

"You seemed to be doing very well for such a confused, shambly mess," he said with that adorable chuckle-smile I remembered so well.

"Yeah, well," I affirmed, "I am a fantastic actor."

I think of Ex-Mormon every time I, God forbid, have to fly out of Newark. How life gifted us each other at such a mutually confusing time in our lives, so we could know we weren't alone in our spiritual, sexual, and identity overhaul struggle. We could know there were others engaged in the hard and brave work of a massive undoing.

But mostly so we could see that, in our chosen personal path-forging, we were getting to indulge the full spectrum of life experience.

For so much of my early journey in New York City, I was afraid I'd "gotten it all wrong." Sure, I had moments when I was really proud of myself. For my bravery and resilience. But everything from auditions to dating to not looking like an inept public-school-educated person in front of rich people was so hard. I often wondered if it being so hard was proof that I should have just stayed in Missouri. Stayed the "straight and narrow."

Meeting Ex Mormon was the first time I thought, *Maybe I haven't gotten this all wrong. Maybe I'm doing this entirely right.*

My chosen path was proving to be anything but straight and narrow. My path was sprawling, terrifying, exciting, completely uncharted, and, most importantly, mine.

29

TOO SOON?

I HAD JUST FINISHED working with some billionaire kids in Tribeca, when I got a text from another dude I had assumed was no longer interested. Instead of continuing my walk unbothered because I am a strong, confident woman whose emotions are not dictated by a simple text message, I had a total meltdown. I parked myself at the nearest establishment that would serve me white wine, started to sob, and called my big brother Eddie for help.

I'd met Roger on a dating app a few months prior. He was actually not that handsome, but I went through a phase where I was really into the bald, thick-rimmed-glasses thing, so I thought he was a babe. He was from the South and had a successful career in journalism. We matched and chitchatted for a bit, but he never initiated plans to actually see me, so I let it go.

Weeks later, I was meeting a writing mentor for coffee at her office. I looked around that bustling workspace full of real writers, hoping no one would find out all I do is write a blog, when the imposter-syndrome party in my head abruptly halted.

I spotted him. *Roger.*

Was this God bringing us together?! My heart's need for a big love story to brag about to friends back home started to envision us telling this story. "We connected on a dating app, but Roger wasn't actually interested until I ended up at his office by divine intervention. Now we are married and are both rich writers." Modern Love column, here we come!

So, I reached out again.

"Hey. This is super random but, do you work at [super official journalism office]? I know that's weird, but I was there and I think I saw you eating what appeared to be a Chipotle Burrito."

It *was* him.

"What are the odds?" he responded. "I'm sorry I never followed up about our date. I got busy with moving into this apartment I just bought, and my mom was in town for my birthday. Let's finally get that drink."

Flex to tell me he bought an apartment and spends his birthdays with his mom? We got drinks the next day.

The date went so well. There was never a lull in conversation; he was smart and laughed at my jokes. At the end of the night, he kissed me and asked when he could see me again. I told him I was pretty booked for the next two weeks, but I was free Thursday.

"Then I'll see you Thursday?"

Yay! He's into me! He couldn't wait two weeks to see me so he'd like to see me twice in one week! I was elated.

I texted my brother on the way home. "I just went on the best date ever."

He shot back: "That's great! But proceed with caution. It's only the first date and most men are trash."

Ugh. You suck, big bro! Roger is not trash! He is smart and successful and classy and wears thick-rimmed glasses. Also, he is very into me—don't rain on my parade!

Two days later I ended up at Roger's apartment where we had consenting-adult sexy time.

After that, I stopped hearing from Roger as much. His communication was sporadic and never with a "When can I see you?" When he did make plans, he would cancel at the last minute. One night I was so upset about his canceling *again*, I stayed in and got sad-drunk with the mom I was nannying for that evening. Hard times.

I was a ball of anxiety and frustration. Why had Roger, who was just *so* into me initially, lost interest?

I'll tell ya why: I slept with him "too soon."

As we've discussed, Evangelical-land combined with abstinence-only education drilled into my head that a man would not respect me if I slept with him "too soon." And that it was his right—as a person with a penis—to place judgment and shame on a person with a vagina for engaging in the exact same activity as him.

And I, vagina-having-person, would just have to accept this lack of respect from penis-having-person, because if I'd wanted him to respect and desire me as a wife, I should have waited to have sex with him. I put myself in the whore box. My bad.

After being stood up by Roger (twice), I was super bummed. But as mentioned above, I knew it was all my fault, so I couldn't be mad. *Just eat some Oreos and proceed to your next disappointing dating scenario, MJ.*

So, when he did text me randomly, post–billionaire babysitting time, I was shocked by my reaction. I went into full-blown panic/crisis mode over a dude I'd seen exactly three times IRL. What was wrong with me?

Through tears and sauvignon blanc, I expressed my sadness, anger, and helplessness at the whole situation to Eddie.

"I just ... I don't want to feel like this! I want to have sex with a guy I like and not live in fear that doing so is going to make him no longer like me because in his mind, I'm now a total ho. I am not a ho! [beat] Or maybe I am a ho! But that doesn't mean I'm not also talented, ambitious, financially responsible, kind, funny, considerate, hot, a great friend, daughter, sister, and caretaker of other people's children. *Ugh.*"

Instead of Eddie saying "I told you so," like he fully should have, he said, "Mattie, this has nothing to do with you having sex with Roger."

Um, yes it does. I wouldn't expect you to understand, MAN. You don't get harshly judged about your sex-having and then thrown into an unlovable box to rot forever.

I didn't say that. Instead, I said:

"Are you sure?"

"Yes. Roger didn't lose interest. He was never interested."

First of all, fuck you. Second of all, go on.

"But he seemed so interested on our first date! I mean, he asked to see me twice in one week!"

"Matts," Eddie continued, "anyone can put on a show for a few dates. Based on what you've told me, for whatever reason, Roger hasn't been invested from the beginning. He didn't plan to see you until you were literally in his workplace. He doesn't really text you or keep his commitments to your dates. Does that behavior make clear that he's into you or into dating ... at all?"

At that moment, I was very embarrassed that someone other than me had to point out something that should have been blatantly obvious to me.

"You're right," I said.

"Look, it's okay kiddo. This shit happens." Brother went on, "At the very least, if this IS how Roger shows interest, it totally sucks and you don't want any part of it. You don't want to be a 'yes' for this kind of treatment. You want someone who plans, who communicates, who shows he's invested with his attention and time, right?"

"Right."

"Yeah, so Roger's not that guy. Do you want to sleep with guys who don't respect your time and/or show genuine interest in *you*?"

That hit me hard. I'd had a lot of sex, but not a lot of *good* sex. This question was another step in defining, for myself, what a positive sexual experience could be.

"No. I don't," I responded.

"So maybe the only 'too soon' that exists here is if you sleep with a dude before you know his level of genuine interest," my brother summarized. "Guys who are into you are going to stick around well after sex. Guys who were never interested to begin with aren't going to stick around *just* to have sex. You can spare yourself the anxiety that seems to come up from sleeping with the latter."

sips sav blanc "I like this plan."

I didn't pay my brother for that therapy session, but I think I should have.

I know I'm not the only woman who has abided by this story. The "I feel empowered in my sexuality and chose to have sex, so that's why he lost interest. This is just further proof that women can't safely express themselves sexually with anyone other than their husband!" story.

Within it, I felt helpless and unchosen. My wanting sex, then having sex, was the reason no man would "stick around." Even though, let's circle back to the fact that there was also a man involved. Where is his socially projected shame spiral?[1] I digress ...

But none of that is true. *None. Of. It.*

Here's what is true.

If we, as women, buy into the lie that our value is solely based on our sex-having, we allow the theft of our brains, bodies, and personal standards. Furthermore, that narrative absolves the other person of having any part in why a relationship—early dating to long-term partnership—doesn't work out.

For example, when I believed that Roger ghosted me because I had sex with him, I couldn't see all the red flags the guy was basically wearing as a suit. I didn't even give thought to all the ways maybe *he* did not meet *my* standards for a potential partner. I slapped all the blame on myself.

When I took off my "too soon" goggles, I came out of a helpless fog. I paid better attention to what was happening right in front of me with the dudes I was dating. With clarity and confidence, I could assess whether or not they were what *I wanted*.

Lastly, in the cases when I would inevitably come across a dude who, even after I waited to see if he met my standards, stopped talking to me "because we had sex," I could now choose to be unbothered. That dude did not respect me (or any woman) in the first place. He was an asshat, and it had nothing to do with me or my value. No more tears in my sauvignon blanc for misogynist daywalkers.

30

YOU CAN'T FUCK THE DOORMAN

I'D BEEN IN NEW York for two and a half years when Colin broke the news.

"MJ, I've met someone."

"I have to move out?! I mean, *I'm so happy for you ...*"

My time living like a rich person was coming to an end.

"So, I am going to start my big-boy life with her and make this our home."

Colin gave me five months to find a place and offered to help if I needed it. "I'm actually quite good at real estate," he said, half-joking half-serious.

"You are? (Beat. Realizing.) Oh, is *that* what you do for work?"

"Seriously?"

I still don't exactly know what Colin does for work. Give loans to developers to build shopping malls? Something like that.

"Thank you, Colin. I appreciate you." *Even if I do have to move into a more expensive, shittier apartment like normal actors now.* "So tell me about her! Where is she from? Where did she go to school? Nightingale? Chapin? Brearley?" My time babysitting taught me all things New York elite private school hierarchy. "Did your families 'summer' together?"

"Very funny. No, she's a social worker from Detroit actually. And ... Catholic."

My work here is done.

"Are you telling me you're going to marry a Midwesterner AND celebrate Christmas upon my move?" *Pull out the bow-covered coffee cups, y'all!*

"If I can convince her, I can't wait to marry this Midwesterner. We will discuss Christmas."

I like to believe Colin marrying a wholesome, hard-working, *twinkly-light-all-winter-long!* loving Midwesterner came from my influence. But maybe I'm giving myself too much credit and she was just super hot.

"Welp, you know what this means for me?"

"You get at least a full-size bed?"

"I can finally fuck the doorman!"

The first time I ever noticed our very fuckable doorman was about a month after my official move to New York, as I was leaving for a night of Halloween debauchery.

As I walked out of my fancy, mostly-old-person building dressed as a "slutty Cub Scout" (complete with combat boots and shorty shorts, because it was uncharacteristically 75 degrees in October), I clocked the young and exceptionally hot man ready to open my door. *Omg, no way do I have a gold-doored elevator, laundry in-unit, terrace-having penthouse apartment, and live-in eye candy! My cup simply overfloweth.* I smiled with a polite "Bye" as I exited. "Have a fun night!" he responded, and then I contemplated how I was going to ask Colin about this guy later without seeming too thirsty.

I woke up the next morning after very drunk, very bad sex in not-my-own bed, to a 40-degree temperature drop and pouring rain. *Not this.*

I proceeded to do the most righteous walk of shame in the freezing rain from Washington Heights back to the Upper West Side, only to find Hot Doorman *still there*. I ran upstairs, showered away my impurities and embarrassment, and put on proper layers to go babysit for billionaires and hope I hadn't ruined my chances with Hot Doorman with that remarkable display of class.

By the time I left for billionaire babysitting, his shift was over. *Thank God.*

I saw Hot Doorman off and on for weeks but never said anything. I wanted to give enough time between our first hello and our first conversation for him to forget what a *sloot* I was. But my crush, based on nothing except him being exceptionally hot, was growing, and I needed some information.

The next time Colin and I were both home for dinner, I just launched right in. "Colin, why is one of the doormen like, my age?" So much for not seeming too thirsty.

"He's the super's nephew."

Colin gave me the lowdown. Apparently, Colin's dad hired the super when he was a refugee seeking asylum from Montenegro during the Balkan Wars of the '90s. Eventually our super brought over a ton of his family for asylum as well, and gave them all jobs in our building.

This is where I learned how Colin got this sick apartment setup. His father *owned the whole building* at one point. *How does a person just own a building worth millions and not have a reality-TV-show crew following them around? And also, still seem a little normal?* I would learn this was not uncommon at all among the 1 percent. Most kids living on the Upper West Side in doorman buildings will inherit at least one piece of property in the greater New York area.

Colin continued, "Now pretty much the whole staff is connected to Walter in some way. And Walter is actually a millionaire himself. He saved up over the years and bought properties throughout Queens and Brooklyn he now rents out. Maybe he has an apartment for you."

"Your dad really paid it forward. Literally."

"Yes. See, I told you not all rich people are assholes."

Touché.

"So [Hot Doorman] is basically just working the family business while he finishes college. I think anyway. He's always reading a textbook."

I'm not the only one who noticed his textbutts! I mean books ...

"Why do you ask?" Colin asked, playfully and quasi-rhetorically.

"He is just really young compared to the other doormen! So I was just curious ..."

"Mmhmm ..." Clearly, I am incapable of a poker face. Colin could tell I thought Hot Doorman was a total babe.

"I'm gonna go."

Then I left to Google "Balkan" and "Montenegro" and tried to contain my excitement over this Hallmark movie *writing itself*.

A few weeks later, upon returning from one of my crotch-sweat-inducing gym sessions, Hot Doorman finally struck up a conversation with me. I was so excited he was talking to me, I almost forgot about my crotch sweat.

He asked some questions about what workouts I did at the gym. And then, I told him I'd sold my car in Missouri so I would have enough money for a gym membership when I moved. "I wanted to hold myself accountable to having my proper priorities upon moving here." *I hope that impressed him and his perfect biceps I definitely don't want to touch right now.*

And then never answered his question about what workouts I did at the gym.

"That's impressive," he replied.

Yes! It worked!

"So what brought you to New York?"

And away we went.

My relationship with Hot Doorman was symbiotic in that, regardless of how disappointing dating in New York was, I was thrilled to have a live-in crush and he was thrilled to talk to someone unjaded by the city and under the age of sixty-two. We'd stand in the foyer for hours talking about everything from my acting career to his studies, my family, his family, where I grew up, where he grew up. How moving to New York was for him versus how it was for me.

He hadn't spoken English when he'd moved but was now studying medicine. I told him about my dad being a Christian pastor and what a whirlwind of constant culture shock New York was proving to be. He told me he could definitely relate to the culture shock part. A Balkan War refugee and a Bible Belt refugee: two peas in a very fancy apartment lobby.

One evening during this period when a palpable attraction was brewing between me and Hot Doorman, Colin saw us chatting and beckoned me to the elevator.

"MJ. Coming?" More of a demand than an inquiry.

"I'll be up in a few!" I replied, despite the inkling that this wasn't exactly a question.

"Dinner's waiting."

"You ordered me dinner?"

"Let's go."

Was I in trouble for something?

I said good night to Hot Doorman and made my way to the elevator. After a long, awkward few floors of silence, Colin finally came out with it.

"MJ, you can't fuck the doorman."

How dare he assume—

"I'm serious, if it goes poorly, you'll have to see him every day and that will be uncomfortable for you."

Okay good poi—

"Also, I have lived in this building my entire life and will probably live here for the rest of my life ..."

"Colin. I'm no—"

"If you fuck the doorman, I'll have the roommate who's fucking the doorman ..."

"I won't fu—"

"You. Can't. Fuck. The. Doorman."

"Okay! I won't fuck the doorman!"

I would like to say I didn't need to hear that, but I definitely needed to hear that. I sulked back to the maid's quarters feeling equal parts embarrassed and bummed.

Aside from Colin being totally classist, he did have a point. The closest thing I'd ever had to a doorman before was a Walmart greeter. How was I supposed to know "home staff" etiquette? And I *was* pretty reckless with my sex-having during this chapter of personal exploration.

That being said, I was sad to know I had to cool down my obvious crush on Hot Doorman. Those short-lived months of ignorant flirting had been so much fun.

For the remainder of my time in the penthouse, I tried to keep a professional distance, with brief foyer conversations only, because I did want to listen to Colin's good advice, but mostly because I didn't want to get kicked out of the apartment if Colin caught us late-night gabbing again.

The result was two full years of Hot Doorman and me engaging platonically with more-than-platonic tension. But, given the fact that doormen are basically just live-in-lobby spies, we didn't actually have to talk much for him to get to know me sort of well. Or at least, he knew all the embarrassing things about me like how often I'm running late or all the times I accidentally bulk-ordered household items from Amazon because I was new to Amazon shopping and often did not read the item description. I missed Walmart.

One September afternoon, about a month before my penthouse departure, I placed the bait. My heart pounding, wondering if I'd made up all this chemistry in my head or if Hot Doorman was really as into me as I was him, I told him I was apartment hunting like normal people.

"Colin is kicking me out so he can start a grown-up life with his new girlfriend."

"You're moving out?" he asked "When?"

"October."

"Can I take you out in October?"

He took the bait. Hot Doorman wanted to ask me out after years of getting to know me, my Amazon purchase habits, and my walk of shame frequency?! *Hallelu!*

On our first date, he wore a fitted cream-colored sweater, his beautiful biceps a-poppin'. I didn't know how it was possible, but Hot Doorman was even hotter when not wearing a derpy coat with eighty buttons that made him look like a Tower of Terror ride operator!

He took me to drinks at a rooftop beer garden in Astoria, then to dinner at a Southern-style restaurant. I learned he preferred fruity cocktails, which I found hilarious juxtaposed against his large muscles. He learned I still hadn't figured out my alcohol intake limit, so I was definitely drunk by the time we got to dinner. I was embarrassed, but he seemed unbothered.

He'd drive me around the city and nerd out on the history of urban planning, the architecture of bridges, and how all this contributed to New York's exceptional economy. I would get turned on by his interests outside of school and appreciation for subjects I knew nothing about. Also his car was so clean. *heart eye emoji*

Although he "wasn't a texter," he texted me every day to check in and see how I was doing. When he was working, he'd ask if I was around the neighborhood babysitting and would I like to meet up? We'd meet a few blocks down so as not to reveal anything to the residents of my previous home and his workplace. I thoroughly enjoyed living out my own New York soap opera scandal in those moments.

He showed up to one of our dates with ibuprofen because I'd told him earlier in the day my cramps were out of control. Another week, I couldn't hang, because I had a friend in town, so he offered to take us both out. He picked a fancy restaurant in Williamsburg and covered the bill.

After taking me to a really lovely seafood restaurant, he drove me out to the Long Island Sound and we made out extensively. Much to my own surprise, I told him I wanted to take things slow. He said that was absolutely fine, and he would wait as long as I needed to feel comfortable.

Did this guy have a flaw?

Dating Hot Doorman was unlike dating any other man I'd met in New York City; he actually *tried*. Furthermore, he wasn't doing all these nice things because he was a narcissist or to "get in my pants." He seemed to genuinely care about *me*.

I want to tell you this story ends with Hot Doorman proposing in that apartment foyer and us honeymooning in Montenegro and having beautiful bilingual babies with great brains and butts. But it doesn't. Instead, I dumped him without ever sleeping with him, because I thought I didn't "like him enough" and started hooking up with Fuckboy Monster again.

Well, that's not entirely true. The night I dumped Hot Doorman, I met him for wine at another fancy apartment where he was dog sitting. After too many glasses of wine and sort of halfsies cutting things off, I asked if he wanted to have sex. He declined, because he is a respectable person with the sexual-activity discernment I was still trying to figure out.

I reconnected with FBM and, quelle surprise, it ended disappointingly, so I found myself texting Hot Doorman again, knowing I'd made a huge mistake. After a few weeks of me trying to rekindle things, he called me out. In person, at our old stompin' foyay no less.

"Your actions make no sense. You got drunk with me on our first sleepover, broke things off, and *then* you tried to sleep with me. I had a condom, but I wasn't going to sleep with you drunk and clearly so confused."

Hot Doorman was calling me out on something that was incredibly confusing—even to me—about my behavior.

I could meet a guy drunkenly for a one-night stand. Or I could fuck someone like Fuckboy Monster—who treated me like a total afterthought—faithfully for years. But then if there was an actual good-guy potential boyfriend prospect, I couldn't get (cl)it up.

I mentally cataloged the "good guys" I'd encountered during my time of exploration in New York City thus far.

- Mormon, someone I felt more understood and seen by than any dating prospect at that point: no sex.

- A really wonderful guy from Memphis who was a stagehand at *Les Miz* on Broadway and had asked me out after meeting me backstage with a friend who was running light operation on the show. We connected on our backgrounds and had a blast together. I ended things after date two and told him I wanted to just be friends: no sex.

- This total hottie hipster I met at a rooftop party through a mutual friend and thought was cool as hell. He was funny, smart, tatted up, bearded out, *and* a consistent communicator. For three months we went to loads of concerts together, had many late nights and long make-out sessions. I friend-zoned him *twice*: no sex.

- Oh, and remember First Tinder Date? Four months we dated and galivanted around the Lower East Side together: no sex.

- And now Hot Doorman, who was literally a rom-com dream come true: no sex.

What was my deal? Why was I so willing to jump into bed with guys who didn't care about or know me at all but not the guys who did? Why could I share myself physically OR personally but never both at the same time?

Clearly, I had a lot to figure out but, Colin, if you're reading this: I did not fuck the doorman.

PART FOUR
Rebuilding

31

SELF-HELPLESS

For whoever wants to save their life will lose it,
but whoever loses their life for me will save it.

— Luke 9:24

WHILE HOME IN MISSOURI for the holidays, over brunch I could actually afford, I spilled the truth about everything I'd gone through in New York during the last two years to my middle school bestie, Rachel. There is something about sharing you've been fingered on a street corner by a regular at the bar where you work to someone who used to know you as a devout purity-ring princess that really cleanses the soul. Rachel wasn't religious, so she didn't care about my getting fingered, but I do think she was still very shocked.

For as long as I'd known Rachel, she'd only had long-term relationships with really cool, genuinely great, *interesting* guys. She had traveled the world all while finishing college she'd paid for on her own, was bilingual, and had started her own jewelry-making business after moving to Portland. The point is, she was one of the few people from home I deemed cooler than me and who wasn't Evangelical-married but still maintained great relationships with men. I felt I could trust her opinion on dating in your early twenties as a normie.

"Why does this keep happening to me, Rachel?" I asked. "'This' meaning, I find these great guys but I am uninterested in any kind of intimacy with them. Especially not sexual intimacy, but also not relational? And don't say 'daddy issues' because I know I have those.

She laughed, trying not to spit out her Bloody Mary. Then gently, with just the right amount of spiritual sternness, she said, "This is not happening *to* you, Mattie Jo. You are *choosing* it."

Um, fuck you.

"What do you mean?" I asked, fully afraid to know the answer but asking anyway because I knew I needed to hear it.

"Perhaps this has nothing to do with men and everything to do with how you see yourself," Rachel suggested. "Know what I mean?"

"No, I don't." I truly didn't. How could what men do have anything to do with me?

Rachel continued, with the authority of a self-help guru I didn't know I needed, "Since you believe so many parts of yourself to be 'bad' you don't think you are worthy of good things, including good men. You're only really engaging guys who suck, because you believe you're only worthy of guys who suck. So it's not *really* about them, it's about you."

Oh good! So I just have to stop hating myself? Easy peasy.

The last two and a half years I had worked diligently to identify the harmful narratives in my life and find new liberating beliefs. But when I peeled back the Necessary Pendulum noise, there remained a subconscious but ever pervasive, fundamental belief that I was bad.

I was bad for allowing my unshakable faith to be shaken. I was bad for having sex. I was a *bad worldly whore.*

"So," I stuttered, holding back tears, realizing my incessant internal monologue was very, *very* mean. "If this is a *me* thing, and not a *men* thing, how do I fix ... me?"

She grabbed my hand and smiled. "You don't need fixing, MJ. You aren't broken; you just need some books!"

We finished brunch and headed to Barnes & Noble. We landed in the nonfiction/self-help/spirituality section, a book genre that became my new sanctuary and source for (un)devotional[1] content. Rachel bought me *The Untethered Soul* by Michael Alan Singer.

This book blew my fucking mind.

Though *The Untethered Soul* possesses a ton of lessons I still apply in my life today, its most memorable lesson to me at the time was the one that was in the most opposition to what I'd learned as a fundamental belief in my Evangelical upbringing:

Everything in our lives occurs as a result of our thoughts and beliefs. If we believe certain things, they will for sure play out in our lives. Therefore, if we want different results in our lives, we have to change our thoughts and beliefs.

In short, I wasn't at the whims of punishment or reward of God based on my behavior. I could create—even have some control over—my own life.

I'd dabbled in this idea previously, as I'd seen cool things happen in my life despite my sex-having and non-Christian being. But instead of just thinking, *huh, okay, maybe God doesn't hate me?* after good things happening, I could actively participate in pursuing different outcomes in my life. This was a tactical reframe.

Furthermore, there was a *biological* process to all this. Like, *sci-ence,* my dudes! Turns out, our repeated thoughts form neurological pathways that solidify themselves in our brains to become our beliefs. Once solidified, these pathways affect our actions. If you want new actions, you must work to form new pathways, which requires you to repeatedly tell yourself different messages.

Did you know that your brain actually does not objectively know the difference between a truth and a lie? It only knows what you believe to be a truth and what you believe to be a lie! So whatever you tell it is true, it will believe, and therefore, you will act upon that belief as truth.

Though I hadn't heard of this whole "change your thoughts; change your life" Jedi mind trick, the Evangelical church definitely had. This idea is exactly how they'd achieved control over me for so many years, even beyond my participating in religion! I got their bullshit in my damn neural synapses!

This institution works relentlessly to keep us scared, shamed, and severed from our own power in order to maintain their control. The concept of "original sin" alone is a perfect example of how self-helplessness = outsourced control. If people believe they are helplessly bad and the church contains the thing that will make them good, then the church maintains control and power over making lives good instead of individuals having self-empowerment to make their lives good.

In fact, the Evangelical church demonizes a life that is "your own." From worship songs to weaponizing Bible verses, we constantly repeated lyrics such as "Take my life, transform it to Yours, Oh Lord," or prayers saying, "Take my life, Jesus and do Your will through me," or applied Bible verses that said, "I will not do anything of 'selfish ambition' (Philippians 2:3)" to every thought, decision, and action. All of it must be outsourced to God, a small group leader, accountability partner, scripture etc., etc.

Nothing was ever up to me. Behaving or doing anything for or because of myself was selfish. And selfishness—especially for women—was a very bad sin.

There's also the whole Evangelical messaging around "God within you," which is a swirl of confusing contradictions. On the one hand, if God is on our side, who can be against us (Romans 8:31)? We are so powerful with God in our lives! We have the Holy Spirit, which, apparently, lives inside of us as our quiet internal guide.

God *is* within you, but He's also separate from you. A male being who influences you for the better. Because, once again, on your own:

You.

Are.

Bad.

This belief system had created the perfect storm of self-neglect, self-doubt, and self-hate in me. This powerful manipulation from the inside out kept me tethered to a system of outsourcing, without my knowing.

The good news is, the exact practice that had established in me such a strong faith, and the Evangelical belief system at large, was exactly what would get me out of it: subtle, repeated messages of "truth."

This new state of self-awareness, analyzing, and adjusting my neural pathways sounded very hard and time-consuming, but also ... *freeing.*

Based on this logic, I didn't have to wait on a God from above to bless me with good things and totally change my life. *I* could be the source of those good things and totally change my life. I could be that *powerful*.

The Untethered Soul offered what I had been seeking during this deconstruction phase of my life: a brain, body, and *being* that was all mine.

After a life robbed of self-love, self-trust, self- ... anything, of believing I needed to lay down my life, I was so very ready to pick up my life.

32

BLIZZARDS, BRANDON, AND BIBLIOTHERAPY

"While you're holding a grudge, others are out dancing."

— Jesus

(Just kidding. It's a Chinese proverb I read in a fortune cookie, but should definitely be in the Bible.)

BY MARCH OF 2016, I had fully settled into my normal New Yorker life in a tiny-ass Harlem apartment. My best friend, Candice (the one I handed the Plan B box to after I had sex for the first time and she cried lol), was visiting before moving to Hawaii, and thanks to a literal blizzard, we were cuddled inside marathoning movies, instead of out sightseeing.

While watching Anna Kendrick sing the song "See I'm Smiling" in the movie musical *The Last Five Years*, I experienced an unexpected tsunami of memories flow up from my belly button, through my chest, neck, and finally out of my eyeballs in the form of a grown woman sob sesh. I had no plans of having a breakdown listening to songs I'd heard hundreds of times before (#bfaproblems) but, art makes you feel shit or whatever.

Candice, kind of panicked but remaining grounded and available during my meltdown, paused the movie immediately and said, "Okay ... It's okay!" She held me close and rocked me back and forth on my tiny settee (since a couch could not fit in the "living room") we both barely fit on. After enough huffing and heaving, I finally caught my breath, looked up at her, and said, "Candice, I don't think I'm over Brandon."

"Um ..." Candice blinked, and then sweetly, reeling back from her surprise at the cause of my breakdown, said, "Why do you think that?"

It had been almost five years since Brandon and I had split, so I knew that wasn't exactly what Candice was expecting me to say. Externally it would appear that I had completely moved on from Brandon. After all, we hadn't spoken since my move to New York, and I'd dated plenty of other people since. I was *clearly* over Brandon. Right? *Right?*

In the months following my trip to Barnes & Noble with Rachel, I devoured countless self-help books. I was trying to become an untethered human, and these books offered specific advice on how to do this untethering. I had officially entered a phase of "bibliotherapy" in my deconstruction and was learning new shit all the time!

Concepts such as

- The stories we tell ourselves (that may or may not be true)

- Don't take anything personally

or the most simple

- Choosing suffering

were revealing all the ways in which I had been—for many years—projecting stories, taking things very personally, and therefore, choosing suffering.

I took Brandon's rejection very, *very* personally. Brandon's small statement about my personality being "too much" spun years of untrue narratives about my value and lovability. I internalized my "being too much" to mean my most honest self was forever unlovable and unattractive. *I will always be too much and never enough.*

This was all intermingled with the Evangelical narratives about a woman's value being attached to chosenness by a man. My breakup with Brandon was linked heavily to the most fundamentally flawed story in my head; God hated me for not taking the Godly, wifely, Evangelical Christian path. And therefore I was not worthy of good—especially in relationships and love —in my life. I held on to all those personally chosen, not-at-all-objective meanings with a clenched fist, determined to make myself suffer because of them.

I was the one who believed I was inherently bad. *I* was the one who believed my too-muchness was unattractive. *I* was the one who believed I would never be loved. *I* was the one who believed I was both too much and never enough. *I am the one who doesn't love me.*

That horrible view I thought God had of me? It was really just a projection of how I viewed myself.

Applying these self-help tools allowed me to release the "this is all about what an unlovable POS I am!" and embrace new narratives.

Our breakup had nothing to do with my being unlovably too much and everything to do with Brandon being (undiagnosed) depressed, cripplingly anxious, and understandably unprepared to make decisions that would affect the rest of his life, like going to medical school and getting married. Brandon was just trying to do what was best for him at that time in his life. Totally normal.

Furthermore, Brandon's comments about me were simply him poorly communicating that we had personality incompatibilities that already posed problems within our dynamic, and that might not bode well for lifelong matrimony. Although sort of cruel in his delivery, he was absolutely right. We needed to be apart for us to both live our fullest lives. I could stop holding a grudge. I could actually be grateful for him releasing us both to find our path and persons. And give him grace in that poor delivery.

After nearly a decade of not speaking to him, I drunkenly checked Brandon's LinkedIn without making myself incognito (oops). I guess this prompted him, after requesting I never talk to him again eight years prior, to reach out via my website. We agreed to a FaceTime date and caught up for four hours. Of the weirdo things Covid brought about in my life, this one was probably the weirdest.

Of the many topics we traversed in that conversation, he (naturally) inquired about my relationships since us.

"Have you had any actual good relationships in New York? Have you been in love?"

"Yes, I have," I answered. "But I couldn't experience love and partnership until I fully got over you, and I think that took me a solid five years. And not because I was waiting to get back together or something." *Please.* "I just harbored a lot of what happened between us—which was also mixed up with Evangelical-slash-patriarchal messaging about women that I've spent the last decade unpeeling off my skin and psyche—as Gospel truth for a long time after we split. I needed to *un*commit myself to those messages before I could really, fully 'move on' and allow love into my life."

"What?"

Never mind.

"Yes. I've fallen in love with wonderful men and had incredibly meaningful relationships since us. It just … took me a minute."

33

"Faith"

"For truly I tell you, if you have faith the size of a mustard seed, you will say to this mountain, 'Move from here to there,' and it will move; and nothing will be impossible for you."

— Jesus (Matthew 17:20–21)

LATER THAT WEEK, POST–BLIZZARD Brandon breakup breakthrough, Candice and I had plans to get dinner with Fuckboy Monster. As with most toxic relationships, what Candice had heard about FBM made her hate him (also made her annoyed at me), but she agreed to meet him because it meant a lot to me. I wanted to share all my New York life with my bestie! Including the man who, from my perspective, was the most substantial relationship I'd had post-Brandon. I think I also hoped that if she met him, she'd "get it."

She did not get it. Mostly because, instead of FBM showing up to dinner plans I'd made for him to meet the most important person in my life—*my best friend*—he stood us up.

We arrived for the reservation at an artisanal gluten-free pizzeria in the West Village, got seated, and waited for what felt like forever. After multiple repeat texts, making me feel like a crazy person because that's what unhealthy romantic dynamics do, I got the reply. "Caught up in the studio for a deadline. Not gonna make it."

I knew this was going to happen.

Embarrassed and sincerely sad, I apologized to Candice. Instead of being all "wake the fuck up, ya dummy!"—which was, of course, exactly what I was mentally shouting at myself—she said, "It's okay, Mattie. You're going to figure this out. You figured out the Brandon thing! All on your own!"

One thing Candice has always managed to do for me, that I could never quite figure out how to do for myself at this time, was be *so nice to me*. Even when my decision-making was straight-up idiotic, she always saw my heart. She could be encouraging, believe in my ability to do better, and see the best parts of my potential I couldn't see for myself.

Until that night, when it all finally became so clear: FBM was not some mysterious hottie who would always have my heart and nether regions in some hypnotic trance. I was not trapped in his unrelenting grip. *I was gripping him.*

FBM was all my internal confusion, self-loathing, and lack of self-respect personified. He was a 6′2″ drink of *every poison I am trying to bleed out of my internal goings-on!!!* So long as he was around, I would keep sending the message to my brain, nervous system, and the universe that how he treated me and our relationship status quo was *just fine* with me.

He was a perpetuation of my belief that having sex was bad. I'd externally rejected the idea that me having sex was bad, but I'd still only have sex with "bad" guys because I saw sex as my "bad" self. I wouldn't share my "bad" parts with the "good" guys because I didn't want them to see what I deemed as "bad." I was chaff-and-wheating myself, and it was manifesting in my sexual behavior. If I wanted to truly claim sex as a great thing in my life, I had to be more intentional about only sharing it with great people.

Furthermore, this guy was a real, actual, massive block to goodness in my life! Here I was with my best friend visiting before she moved halfway across the globe, and instead of enjoying an amazing meal to celebrate her and our time together, I was pouring tears into my cauliflower crust over a man to whom I constantly gave my time, energy, and adoration. The only things he ever gave me back was anxiety and UTIs.

He did not adore me. *He doesn't even respect me.*

What a colossal waste of my (now recognized) valuable time, energy, and adoration.

So right there, in that West Village pizzeria, I declared, "I am better than this, Candice. I am better than Fuckboy Monster." And for the first time, I actually believed myself.

I replied by telling FBM never to contact me again. *I* was done.

He never responded. Shocker.

After that night, because I am human, my scarcity-meany would pop up from time to time, plaguing me with scared questions like *Will I ever feel connected to someone the way I felt with him?! Will I ever have sex that good ever again?! Will anyone ever get me and make me laugh by sending me funny musical theater memes like him? Will I be single forever?!*

I did the *Untethered Soul* practice of allowing those feelings to arise, honoring them by politely answering, "Yes, you will find someone else. No, you won't be single forever. Also, he sucks," and moving on. But the thoughts continually popped up nonetheless.

I was learning a grueling part of this whole self-love thing. Taking action doesn't just mean one definitive choice. It means that definitive choice followed by days, hours, moments of living in alignment with that choice. I had to implement integrity with my actions, instead of just saying I wanted certain things without ever action-ally changing anything.

This taking actions in alignment with my words, the books said, was how I would learn to trust myself. I must consistently make decisions and, even if they are hard and the result is super uncertain, stick to them. Over time, I can prove to myself again and again that I will always have my best interest as top priority.

This very scary and precarious field study of trusting myself was *hard*. Especially after a life of being told I absolutely could not trust myself to make such personally empowered decisions toward a life I wanted and instead should make outsourced decisions based on what God wants for me.

Faith in myself? *That* was a faith that could move mountains.

Or, at the very least, could keep me from ever fucking a Fuckboy Monster again.

34

WORTHY OF PRAISE

*"Finally, brothers and sisters, whatever is true, whatever
is noble, whatever is right, whatever is pure, whatever is
lovely, whatever is admirable—if anything is excellent or
praiseworthy—think about such things."*

— Philippians 4:8–9

IN THE MONTHS FOLLOWING my "Fuck off, Fuckboy Monster!"
self-empowered proclamation, my life did genuinely get so much better.
Once so much of my emotional, mental, and physical real estate was no
longer occupied by a useless squatter, I had a lot of space to fill! And oh
fill I did.

In my Evangelical years, I was taught to fill my mind with and say only
words that were "worthy of praise." "Worthy of praise" meant Christian.
Only read Christian literature, listen to Christian music, have super
Christian close friends. I decided to reclaim this practice of mind-fill-
ing-word-saying. I read, said, and viewed only things that positively contributed to my new efforts at self-love, trust, and abundance.

I stopped reading Christian books altogether. I stopped going to
church. I stopped praying to Jesus. I allowed myself time away from
any kind of Godly figure. I honored my need to disconnect from the
God with whom I was raised so I could maybe one day redefine a better
relationship with God.

I allowed "place of worship" to mean something other than church. It could mean creating a space where I felt most connected to my purpose—in my own bedroom! So, within my babysitting-for-rich-people means, I started to uplevel my apartment. I turned my room into a place where a writer could write. I pushed two TV trays together, threw a blanket over them, and posted a view of the Manhattan skyline from the twentieth floor of a luxury apartment in Williamsburg on the wall in front of me. I didn't have a desk *yet*, but this was a good start. I didn't have a view of that skyline *yet*, but I would one day.

I cleared out my Instagram feed to only accounts that inspired encouragement instead of comparison and self-loathing. I listened to personal development podcasts and replaced Bible verses on my mirror with Glennon Doyle quotes. I surrounded myself with people who were examples of who I wanted to become.

I started a practice of verbal affirmations. I said things to myself for a long time that I didn't even believe, sort of wondering if I was doing the whole practice incorrectly. But the teaching of neural-pathway reconstruction suggested I just had to think it, even if I didn't fully believe it yet. "Fake it 'til you make it" and "act as if it's true" became my new commandments.

Which lead to thoughts like:

> *Am I allowed to feel this good about myself? Aren't I a sinful piece of shit who is not at all worthy of praise?*

Then I'd reply to myself, because neural pathways:

> *NO, MJ! You are a sinless pastry! You are delicious. You go, girl!*

I chose affirmations that helped me lean into loving me, that helped me reclaim my too-muchness as just-enoughness. Saying these things to myself felt *soul good.*

I even managed to successfully reclaim the idea of "dating to marry" as "dating for data." The practices of not taking things personally, staying aware of the stories I told myself, projection, how I loved and treated myself, etc., proved to be imperative in implementing the advice Katrin and Aneesha gave me years ago. I put less pressure on every single date to end in vows, and instead started to just like, take notes.

I still wanted to get married eventually, but I stopped believing all dates were a "failure" if they didn't end in a committed relationship. These dates—from my emotional accountability and regulation, to regular ole character trait awareness—were teaching me so much about the kind of person I wanted to be in a committed relationship, and the kind of person with whom I wanted a committed relationship. So that, IDK, I could actually have the relationship I deeply desired one day, instead of swiping blindly and hoping for the best?

And then, perhaps the most surprising transformation to result from my deconstruction, I started to heal the collection of eating disorders I'd developed thanks to the church's teachings on desirability, demonizing our bodies, and not adequately understanding anxiety.

In church I learned my body is a temple of the holy spirit (1 Corinthians 6:19), so we should take great care of it and not abuse it. Of course, what is considered "abuse" was determined by the pastor. For example, it's not okay to have premarital sex or take your body to a drag show, but it is totally okay to eat Taco Bell multiple times a week, be on countless medications, and drink Mountain Dew for breakfast.

And then there was this fun teaching: *Your body is not your own. You were bought at a price. Your body belongs to God.* (1 Corinthians 6:20)

The messages around my body were down right polarizing. It was presented as a thing to be objectified, sexualized, and demonized while also a sacred place to be cared for, but only because it's for God and men. My body was not for me.

In high school I was seriously anorexic. My hair fell out and I lost my period for years. By college, I'd started eating again but then developed another eating disorder—compulsive binging, followed by overdosing laxatives and running on the treadmill for hours.

Upon moving to New York, I quickly learned I was not going to be able to keep up with my overeating, exercising, and laxative-using because I simply didn't have the time. I had places to be and shit to do that couldn't involve shitting all day. I couldn't miss a full day of work and auditions to be near a toilet. I couldn't spend three hours at the gym because I bought a six pack of cupcakes and ate the whole thing in one sitting the night before. If I was going to be able to pay rent and prove I could do this whole actor thing, I could not maintain this life of excess and abuse.

So while I stopped overexercising and executing laxative bulimia, I continued to compulsively overeat. I'd wake up in the middle of the night and, half-asleep, consume a sleeve of crackers, a bag of chips, leftover mozzarella sticks. Sometimes, these food items weren't even *mine*.

My rock bottom came when Colin confronted me in the kitchen one morning. Holding his jar of peanut butter I had definitely binge-eaten a decent amount from the night before, he stared into it and said, "It appears there is a peanut butter elf in the apartment."

Oh my God.

By the time I got to the *"way more attuned to what was going on with me internally"* chapter of life, I was able to confront the source of my compulsive eating habits: the terrible, horrible, no good, very bad thoughts about my body that had become a regular part of me + anxiety.

So, years after Colin calling me out in our kitchen, I tried something new. In the moments of my overwhelming feelings of anxiety, sadness, varying degrees of panic, I would sit still with the feeling, name the feeling, and then allow whatever the experience was offering to do its offering. Instead of covering *all that* up with food.

I learned to listen to my body's guidance. She sends me messages constantly that keep me safe, healthy, and happy! When to drink water, sleep, when to get the heck away from the creepy dude on the train. When to spend time alone and when to hang with some valued company.

It wasn't until I got quiet and started to listen to my body that I uncovered yet another effective manipulation tool by the Evangelical

Church: severance from our bodies. My body was not there to guide me to good, only to take me to the depths of fleshly sin.

But that was all a lie. My body is so smart, and should be listened to intently. She's also really great! She gives me so much that helps me live a great life—running, seeing Broadway shows, sweet relief in the heavenly hilarious gift of flatulence—that has absolutely nothing to do with being sexually sinful or staying small.

After nearly a lifetime of being at war with my body, I wanted to make peace with her. So every time I found myself on the edge of a body beratement bash, I committed to stopping, breathing, and saying audibly (even if it made the muscly meatheads at the gym or randos on the train look at me weird):

> *Trust your body to guide you. Be your own friend.*
> *My body is good.*
> *I love you so fucking much, Mattie Jo.*

Throwing a curse word in the finale really helped the transformative catharsis.

Little by little, I started to ... like myself. I was not in full-blown, self-love, I am-a-total-baddy-watch-me-twerk status, but I *liked* myself! And that was more than I could say in ... my entire life at that point.

On my journey, I couldn't achieve full spirit–mind–flesh integration—the antidote to Evangelical/purity culture severance—until I healed my relationship with food, exercise, and learned to honor my feelings, while rewiring my thoughts.

It didn't happen overnight, but my mind was slowly emptying the lies and filling with things that were *true, noble, and worthy of praise.*

35

ABUNDANT LIFE

*"The thief comes only to steal and kill and destroy;
I have come that they may have life,
and have it to the full."*

— John 10:10

As MOST FUCKBOYS DO when they're bored, Fuckboy Monster did eventually reach out to me again. He was going on a summer contract and wanted to see me before he went. AKA, he wanted to get it in before he left for months and didn't know if any girls on that contract would want to fuck him.

I thought I was self-loving enough at that point to not "give in" and fall into my physical-MANifestation-of-self-hating-beliefs spiral, so I agreed to get together. We briefly caught up, and despite learning in this reunion that he had no recollection of me setting the boundary of him not talking to me, or of him standing up Candice and me—"I got caught up in the studio that night. And I just assumed you've been busy."—I still fucked him. One last time.

I didn't have sex with FBM because I needed his affirmation and love and was hopeful he would "maybe be different this time." I literally had sex with him for the most carnal reason ever. I hadn't had sex since our wintery half-assed farewell, and I wanted to have great sex. (PS: Did you know that women are fully capable of choosing to have sex not based on

259

emotional manipulation or feeling terrible about themselves? But just like, wanting to get laid? Now you do!) I knew I was acting in scarcity, as if no other dude out there could satisfy my lusts, but baby steps okay.

Anyway, something happened in that final fuck that I was not at all expecting.

The sex was actually ... not great.

But it wasn't that FBM's sex skills had changed, *I* had changed. All the work I'd done on myself in the previous months was enough to alter my sexual experience entirely. In other words, my Fuckboy Monster goggles fell off!

Upon my FBM goggle removal, I could actually pay attention to FBM for who he actually was, not as the romanticized fantasy I'd created him to be. I noticed how he touched me, spoke to me, kissed (didn't kiss) me. How he wasn't even really paying attention to my experience.

Did you know that when you are actually aware and alert in an underwhelming sexual experience, your mind wanders like crazy? Being penetrated and fully present caused internal panic.

> *Why am I even here? I'm basically his masturbation hole. Okay, he did say a nice thing about my butt. I do have a great butt. No, kiss my neck. Why are your eyes always closed and/or just looking at your dick? Can you actually acknowledge I am here, please?!*

Fuckboy Monster left, and I wouldn't see him again for another two years. (He was the music director for a close friend's show. We awkwardly said hi and that was it.)

I'd finally fucked this guy out of my system.

Because God works in mysterious ways, beauty from ashes[1] and all that, I believe this not-so-great experience was essential in showing me something really integral for my continued healing: clarity.

I had once been moving through life in a fog. I had no idea why certain things were "happening to me" and why they couldn't seem to get better. As I became more present, aware, tuned in to other aspects of my life, so too was I in my sex life. The clearing of my identity fog percolated into my *fucking* fog. I was paying attention during sex, having thoughts and opinions and feelings in the matter instead of just blacking out for the whole thing—which is so problematic and all too common for most women, not just purity culture survivors—and/or going along with whatever he wanted.

Oh my God. Why was I blacking out?! Why was I going along with whatever he wanted?

I hit the books and did some more research. Turns out, it was more purity culture shit to bust through!

Purity culture trauma manifests itself in myriad ways from person to person. In my earliest years of sexual activity, I learned, mine was mostly in the form of dissociation or, as mentioned with FBM, a compliance method.

Trauma Related Dissociation is defined by the *Journal of Trauma & Dissociation* as:

1. A "mental escape" when physical escape is not possible, or when a person is so emotionally overwhelmed that they cannot cope any longer. Sometimes dissociation is like "switching off." Some survivors describe it as a way of saying "this isn't happening to me."

2. Dissociation is a process in which a person disconnects from their thoughts, feelings, memories, behaviors, physical sensations, or sense of identity. Dissociation is common among people seeking mental health treatment.[2]

In learning this term, I realized I did not have clear memories of most of my first two to three years of sexual experiences. I know I was there, and I know who it was with, but I don't really remember what happened. Sometimes it was because of alcohol, which I used unconsciously to make myself less present in the situation. Other times I was completely sober and still have no idea what happened.

I reflected back on my experiences since Pop Singer. I often gave enthusiastic consent for the sex, but was not an enthusiastic participant. Though I'd "agree" to the sex, I was not fully engaged; I wasn't even fully *there*. I wanted to be there, but my brain and body were too scared to be there. I was completely disconnected.

This time with FBM was the first occasion in all my sex-having when I was an alert, aware, and analytical participant. What I saw during that last FBM ride—what I felt in my heart and in my body—I did not like. Perhaps that's why I'd made myself unavailable to the full experience in the past. This feeling—a person inside of me but not *with* me—was awful.

And then there's the whole compliance-method thing.

I think my sexual relationship with FBM seemed great because I was excellent at making *him* feel great. Which, based on purity culture teachings, was the measure of a quality sexual dynamic. The more you make him feel desired, the more he'll desire you.

I was in a wedding back home—well into my slinging sex and shots in the city fog—and we were doing the night-before-the-wedding thing of swapping "juicy sex advice." One of the bridesmaids told the bride that sometimes you won't want to do it, but you have to. "It's not always about you. It won't be enjoyable every time, but you just do it."

. . . . .

I *think* this woman was trying to do the bride a solid, telling her to keep her expectations realistic since purity culture lied to us about sex being this life-altering event of orgasmic pleasure if you waited. I think she was also trying to suggest this is a way to "show up" for your partner?

While I believe this advice was well intentioned, I think it was *horrible* advice. What this actually communicates to wives is: don't prioritize your needs, sex isn't that great so don't expect it to be, and normalize getting sexually assaulted by your husband.

I tried to speak up. I wasn't even having great sex at that time, but I knew *that* was problematic advice. I was shut down pretty quickly by the marrieds. *"You* don't understand, Mattie Jo. Having a real partner is different from Tinder hookups!"

The point is, obviously FBM loved fucking me. I never expected/required orgasms, and I certainly wasn't going to interrupt his experience to have a say in mine. I was a low-maintenance, amply giving lover. (Also worth noting, however, I think I liked fucking FBM because he was novel. We rarely had sex in the same place, and it was always spontaneous. He fulfilled a fun fantasy fuckbuddy role in my life. If I had been more mature and had a healthier understanding at that time of what I needed in a sexual partner, we probably could have been just fine as that: fuck-buddies about town. But neither of us were that evolved or self-aware or good at communicating yet so instead it was just … a mess.)

Ultimately, what I discovered in that final fuck revelation was this: There was no way to avoid finding clarity in my sexual identity when I was finding so much clarity in my everything-else identity. There is no such thing as my everything-else-but-sexual identity.

Evangelical systems taught me to dismember so many parts of myself; the key to healing a lifetime of severance was to pursue full-ass integration. Emotional, physical, mental, spiritual, even—and especially!—*sexual* integration.

I finally had my life-changing sexperience.

Then I moved to New Hampshire.

36

NO MORE OBLIGATORY BLOW JOBS

ANOTHER GREAT BYPRODUCT OF my deconstruction glow-up was getting so much better at auditions. As I became more attuned to what I enjoyed, I got more specific on what I auditioned for, and as a result, started getting way more callbacks. Anyway, I booked a musical theater contract that would relocate me to the White Mountains of New Hampshire for six months.

When I was plucked out of the City for this contract in the middle of nowhere North Conway, I truly was so grateful. I knew this contract was going to give me peace in consistency I was deeply lacking in New York City, as well as confidence in my #craft.

Maybe I'll finally finish the Harry Potter *series! Watch "Friends!" Become vegan!* (I did all three.)

But I was also admittedly a little bummed.

I'd been on enough musical theater contracts to know what this working actor thing meant—a six-month cockblock 'cause no straight boys + lots of jazz squares.

I had been single for five years. I felt like I was *finally* in a place to date with clarity, get to the fog-free fucking, *and maybe get a boyfriend dammit.* How was I supposed to do any of that *here?*

I really tried to accept yet another season of singlehood, believing that maybe the Universe was working on me in some way I couldn't quite understand. But when another castmate's hot boyfriend showed up for the week, I had reached my threshold of higher-selfing. Watching them be all pretty and perfect made my inner Veruca Salt surface to another castmate in full-blown tears, being all "Where's *myyyy* boyfriend? Why don't *I* have a hot sweet boyfriend??"

"Umm ..." Castmate rightfully reacted. "Well, maybe you won't find a boyfriend, but you could at least get laid. You're a New Hampshire 'Ten.' Download Tinder and have some fun."

I guess I'd forgotten there were men outside the theme park cast in the greater White Mountain area I could have been fog-free fucking.

I downloaded Tinder.

New Hampshire Tinder was a bit bleak compared to the variety of hot, interesting bullshit to sift through on New York dating apps. But once I swiped past enough men holding fish, I finally came upon a man holding a guitar. *Okay. I can work with this.*

Long story short, the start of the date went fine, but it hit a quick and unexpected decline.

I guess he was having more than a "fine" time, because after beer flights and okay conversation, he asked if I wanted to go stargazing at the top of the nearest mountain.

I agreed to go stargazing because it did sound romantic and *Maybe a little more time with this guy will give him a chance to increase my interest?*

The stars were stunning, but everything else was still very average. He kissed me, we made out a little bit, and with my new sense of alertness in these matters, I found myself wishing I was in bed with a heating pad for my period cramps, watching *Friends* in my retainer and a face mask. Basically, I was not interested, and I needed to go home.

In similar situations in my past, I'd start kissing a dude and think, "Oh, he wants to have sex now," without even considering what *I* wanted. I told myself this time would be different, so after a little kissy-kissy, I spoke up. "I really need to get home and go to bed," I finally said, afraid I might hurt his ego but doing it anyway. "I have a twelve-hour day of performing for children and I simply cannot do that on less than eight hours of sleep."

"No problem, I totally understand," he responded, to my surprise, without throwing a grown-man tantrum.

Phew!

He dropped me off and I was *Friends*/retainer/face mask/heating pad bound!

After I was already in bed and ready for the real fun to start, I got a text message.

> **New Hampshire Tinder Date (NHTD):** Hey, so, I hate to do this but it's so late. I'm like, falling asleep at the wheel. Do you think I could maybe stay over?

Um, what the fuck? I just sent you away, dude. And you have the audacity to ask if you can come back for a sleepover? No way! I'm in my jammies and retainer, ready to laugh myself to sleep, and also, I have period cramps.

So much for him not throwing a grown-man tantrum. This was absolutely a rejection tantrum masquerading as "I might die if you don't let me sleep in your bed!" manipulation. So naturally . . .

> **Me:** Oh man! Yeah, driving late is no bueno. Can you get a coffee?

> **NHTD:** I did, and it's not doing much. I won't be a bother! I can even sleep on the couch.

You cannot sleep on the couch, dude. I have seven other roommates in this house, and that would be so inconsiderate! I have the ability to promptly consider my roommates when you can't even consider my already telling you multiple times I need to get sleep ... grr.

So then ...

Me: No you can't. I have roommates and that would be weird.

Good job, Mattie Jo! Be Direct!

NHTD: Could I sleep with you
then? I promise we can go right
to sleep and I'll leave ASAP in the
morning.

*Oh my Gawd! No! I do not want you in my bed tonight! How are
you so fucking shameless? I can barely hit on a dude without working up
the courage for weeks! And you're repeatedly inviting yourself over for a
sleepover after every no?*
I was so mad. *Why is he putting me in this position?!*

Me: Um. Okay. But we need to
go right to sleep. Don't keep me
up. I'm serious. I have a very long
day tomorrow and you need to
leave by 7:30.

Bad idea, MJ. This will not go well.

NHTD: Oh yes, of course! I
promise I'll let you get your
beauty rest ;)

And then he absolutely did not let me get my beauty rest.
What occurred for the rest of the night was him badgering and badgering me for kisses, cuddles, fondling, fooling around. What was frus-

trating is that I wasn't, like, repulsed by the guy. I did enjoy kissing him and it was nice to cuddle. But I wanted to go to sleep!

He'd try to put his hand down my pants, and I'd say no. He'd start to go up my shirt, and I'd ask if we could just roll over and go to sleep now. Then he'd spoon me and start kissing my ear, unyielding in his pursuit of pussy.

I was so confused. Was I not being super clear that I did not want to have sex or fool around? Also, what kind of shameless imbecile invites themselves into another person's bed, gets a "Sure but we must go directly to sleep," and then tries to keep them up all night until they get what they want??

Why is he doing this?

I knew why he was doing this. He was doing this for the same reason so many men do: *Because they can.*

Before the #MeToo movement really gave clout to women's stories about the subtleties of sexual misconduct in men, men had no reason to think they couldn't get away with this level of relentless cajoling. It would eventually get him what he wanted, and because I—a woman—let him into my bed, the fault would be mine.

Regardless of how many times I said no, the letting him into my bed—even though lots of things happen in beds all the time that aren't sex, like farting, stretching, SLEEPING—would be translated as a "yes." He would get dismissed for his behavior and I would get demonized.

I knew this, and yet, exhausted by his interminable pestering, I did what I am ashamed to admit I had done way too often in the past: just to get this dude to leave me alone, I gave him a blow job and made him cum.

And guess what? Smooth sleepy-time sailing! For him at least. He fell asleep immediately, and I proceeded to get absolutely no sleep. Alertly participating in sex had, once again, left me feeling appalled.

As I sat in the dressing room the next day, adjusting my wig for the fifty-seventh time and trying to pretend to be okay, my stomach turned. I felt just like after my last fuckround with FBM—absolutely awful.

I used some of Aneesha's lawyer investigation questions to examine this sexual experience. Why did I feel awful?

In the past I would have chalked it up to just doing sex things outside of marriage. He was not my committed partner, so that's why I felt "guilty" or "convicted." But I was learning the nuance of my gut feelings, my body's messages. This wasn't conviction or me feeling guilty. This was anger and I felt disrespected.

He hadn't listened to me when I said no.

I had done something I was not comfortable with just to appease *him*, a stranger!

My "yes" to him was a "no" to myself.

My "yes" was really an "okay, fine." Why would he even want to sleep with me if it wasn't an emphatic "yes!"??

It took *me* putting his dick in *my* mouth to get *him* to shut up.

I was also sincerely sad that something so not okay had happened, and I wouldn't be able to talk to anyone about it because I was afraid their answer would be exactly what repeated within me:

"MJ, you let him sleep over. What did you expect?"

I dunno, for him not to badger me incessantly until I exasperatedly agreed to blow him off?! Is that just a totally *wild* expectation?

The truth is, him badgering me until I got him off *is* what I expected. This kind of disrespectful dumb-dumb behavior is what I had been taught to expect from men. They can invent the lightbulb and run entire countries, but a man with a boner is a mindless monster with no accountability for his actions. And whatever woman aroused him and put him in such a reckless state is to blame!

The ickiness I'd felt in years past from sexual experiences started to resurface. I recalled many situations in New York where (when I was actually "present" for them) I tried to show that I wasn't interested in getting sexual beyond kissing, but that seemed to be disregarded entirely. Once the man was erect, I was doomed. *Why would I even try speaking up for myself? He won't listen.*

I was right. I was always right.

Despite what I had learned about dudes and their unaccountable boner behavior, I knew what NHTD did that night was not okay; but it was *normal*.

This, more than anything, is what devastated me. Why was this abhorrent, abusive conduct in men deemed normal? And why does something being "normal" mean it's acceptable?

This amazing year of rebuilding myself to a better me from my deconstruction rubble was also, very conveniently, 2016: the year Evangelicals were supporting Donald Trump—a proud and self-proclaiming misogynist neanderthal—as America's next president.

What looked so unimaginably hypocritical to much of America made perfect sense to me. I knew exactly how a group claiming to follow Jesus—a man who welcomed the helpless, destitute, refugee, and outcasts—could also proudly support a man who bragged about sexually assaulting women, building a wall to keep out desperate refugees, and establishing totalitarian rule. Because I knew firsthand the power and nuance of their true beliefs.

Before 2016, "Evangelical" was not a term or culture people outside of the Bible Belt could really conceptualize. Explaining the specifics of the world in which I grew up to people outside of that world was like explaining the brushstroke method (or lack thereof) of a Jackson Pollock painting to my mother. *Who cares and why though?*

But now, lots of people cared about Evangelicals and wanted to genuinely know "why though?"

The (white) Evangelicals, largely, were not a group committed to the Golden Rule. They had successfully built an institution of toxic masculinity, female suppression, mental and emotional manipulation, abuse, racism, ethnocentrism, and a love for capitalism that kept their organizations untaxed while the poor grew poorer. All the messy, dark shit I had been discovering about my previous faith and identity over the last three years was now on everyone's daily news brief.

During this time in American history, I experienced another strange mix of feelings. As a person who had been on the inside of that system, but now was on the outside, I felt compassion and empathy combined

271

with rage and pain. *I had been there.* I lived within the head and heart of this belief system. I knew exactly how *this = that.* So while I understood my friends and family who supported Trump, I was still *so fucking mad.*

I was angry because, now having thrashed through a very difficult unlearning of that system, I had earned my assuredness of just how harmful, abusive, and poisonous that belief system is. I was passionate about calling out the insidious social control of this group and freeing people from being mired in a lifetime of manipulation. I still am! See: this book.

Despite my not-super-left-leaning political views at the time, watching Hillary Clinton be above-and-beyond qualified to become president of the United States, while Donald Trump was arguably less qualified than a drunk baby goat and he STILL got elected was infuriating. The lengths that America was willing to go to in order to justify not electing a woman as president built on my already-festering anger toward the misogyny I had experienced for all of my life.

That was the background noise for me finally trying to have guilt-free, empowered, fun, orgasmic, fully alert sex. I thought I had left all the Madonna-whore slut-shaming behind with my preference for "Godly guys," but turns out, this misogyny poison knows no bounds in a culture that dismisses misogynistic behavior, therefore upholding and perpetuating it. Being met with situations that showed me non-Evangelical men in America like NHTD were abiding by this misogyny thing was infuriating, disappointing, and deeply disheartening

After my experience with NHTD and amid the 2016 Trump trauma, I experienced my "Oh *now* I get it! Men have been able to use their being men to control, belittle, and shame me for ... forever" aha moment.

How did I live in a world where kissing meant I wanted to have sex? Where "no" required endless repetition and reasons, and even then, it didn't matter? Where getting your dick sucked by a woman you clearly don't respect enough to listen to was expected, normalized behavior? How was I supposed to move forward being single, being 100 percent honest with my boundaries, and having enriching sexual experiences in *this* world?

I started to beat myself up. This was not the empowered, sexually liberated experience I'd hoped for post–fuck fog clearing. It was just the opposite. *What kind of strong, independent woman sucks a dude's dick just so he'll let her sleep?*

So many strong, independent women.

As I shared this story months later with my cast and other friends, I was met with so many *me toos*.

You mean, I'm not a dirty, gross person, fully alone in this obligatory blow-job giving?

Apparently, it was an epidemic among women. "MJ, I think every straight woman in America has given an obligatory blow job," one friend offered in solidarity. "They don't listen. That's just how guys are."

Why are women doing this?! And how can we make it stop?!

Maybe I couldn't stop this abhorrent, socially acceptable abuse in American culture all on my own. But I did have the power as an individual to never condone this level of dipshit behavior in men ever again.

I will not give up control of my body because a man cannot control his own. I told myself.

I didn't want to believe that all men were barbaric, carnal, predatory monsters slinging their boners in my face when I really just wanted to watch *Friends*. But alas, culturally ingrained misogyny had set them up to succeed swimmingly at being just that.

Though I knew this whole ordeal with NHTD was not "my fault," I knew that moving forward, I would not succumb to what a dude wanted if it was so clearly not what I wanted. I didn't want to relive the shame and anger from that experience. I was angry at his behavior, ashamed at following suit despite my own desires and better judgment, and also angry that I was making game plans to change *my* behavior when, really, men just need to practice the fucking Golden Rule.

I would never be physically intimate with someone out of obligation or frustration. Ever. Again. Either it was an emphatic "Hell yes!" or it was a "go fuck yourself quite literally, sir/no." Engaging in obligatory sex stuff would just be reinforcing the belief that I'm not worthy of being listened to or given basic respect, and that it's okay for men to disregard me entirely when they're ready to fuck. I was not going to partake in this shithead standard for an entire gender.

Despite it feeling awkward or uncomfortable, I committed to always stand firm in my boundaries. I would not say yes to be nice, kind, or palatable. My noes would always be noes.

That night left me both really relieved and really sad.

Relieved at not having to deal with straight men for another five months if I didn't want to, but sad at going on five years totally single with no potential of meeting the kind of man with integrity and character worthy of my time and energy, because America is full of disappointing dick-havers. And unfortunately, unlike what the Evangelicals will tell you, you can't choose to be gay.

37

GODLY GUYS

As soon as I fully let go of the idea that I'd meet anyone —no more app dates, no more attempted fog-free-sex, *just finish your Brené Brown book and try not to listen to the news too much, MJ*—and leaned into #Godsplan for another season of singlehood, an unexpected group of employees showed up at the theme park.

The park manager had mentioned international employees were arriving later in the summer, but I guess I'd forgotten during my misogyny lightbulb crisis. I quickly remembered and was elated when a dark-haired European boy who sort of resembled Zorro smiled at me in passing. I got butterflies in my stomach, then later devised a plan of how I would talk to him. But then I decided against this because *Remember, men are disappointing, so maybe I'll just let this little foreign-affair fantasy live on in my brain and not ruin it with reality.*

We passed by each other a few more times before not saying hello would be considered plain rude, so, ready for my entire summer crush to implode, I introduced myself. He greeted me with that adorable accent "I am [dramatic pause] Zorro!" (His name is, unfortunately, not actually Zorro.)

I could hardly contain myself.

His introduction was so regal, I thought he might actually bow and kiss my hand. He didn't, but sometimes I still imagine this happening. I think he just smiled super big and told me he was from Romania. I didn't know where Romania was but didn't want to seem like the geographical American idiot I was/am so I googled it later.

Turns out, Romania is not Rome's neighbor (and Rome is not a country—okay, I did know *that*); it's in Eastern Europe, there are lots of castles, and Romanian is a Romance language.

I suggested we (the cast) get together at some point and hang with Zorro and his fellow foreign hotties. I knew I was supposed to be accepting of this divinely imposed dick desert, but *come on. A Romance language? He looks like Zorro? What do you want from me, Universe?* I was about to find out.

Zorro said some form of "absolutely," and I was on my way, ready to spearhead enduring whatever language barrier for the sake of attempted flirting.

The cast gathered with coworkers from Turkey, Romania, China, Taiwan, Azerbaijan, Nigeria, Poland, Ukraine, and Slovakia to play an icebreaker game involving high fives. After all of our hands got bruised from that nonverbal, actually-really-fun hand-hitting game, a lot of questions about Trump and an argument about gay rights with a Nigerian later, Zorro asked if he could walk me back to my house.

I was honestly shocked he wanted to continue hanging out with me after my expressing impassioned verbal distaste for America's Republican presidential candidate in a "light and fun!" setting. But he seemed unbothered at my inability to do small talk, and that seemed like a good sign. *Or maybe he just doesn't understand what I said ...*

Either way, I had someone to protect me from New Hampshire bears on my walk home. *Sweep me away, Zorro!*

My excitement was short-lived, as I quickly remembered my less-than-ideal encounter with NHTD. Then I was just stressed.

What if he tries to kiss me? I don't want to kiss him yet! We just met! What if he doesn't listen and then I'm sad about men all over again and ugh.

He didn't try to kiss me. He walked me to my door, told me he looked forward to seeing me the next day, thanked me for coming to meet everyone, and "to be so patient with ours English." Who knew jumbled possessive determiners could be so poetic?

Unlike with NHTD, I went to bed that night so little-girl giddy. He didn't even ask to come in?! Didn't assume I would sleep with him because we sat next to each other on a couch for twenty minutes?! He wasn't scared away by my loud expressions and strong opinions? *Can I marry this guy now or what?*

For the next few weeks, I reveled in the anticipation of wanting to see him the next day, the next break, the next meet-and-greet where he would wink at me.

I felt like I was on an episode of *Bug Juice* falling for some dude at summer camp when Zorro asked if I'd like to go on a walk one evening. I agreed, despite my very real fear of bears, plus he assured me I'd be protected. Which of course was very sweet, but he wasn't actually Zorro and he didn't actually have a sword. He was just an Eastern European in skinny jeans, and that bear would eat us both.

The conversation on that walk was the last conversation I ever expected to have as a recently deconstructed purity-culture-adherer Evangelical. Let alone with a European crush in the woods while on a musical theater contract in New Hampshire.

For the next twenty minutes, he would say some version of, "Um... it is like... um... you understand?" Then I would respond back, explaining what I thought he meant and asking if that was correct. So basically, it was a really long, language-barriered game of telephone between two people translating to this:

Zorro opened very directly, as someone without the ability to unnecessarily elaborate in their third language could: "To me, my religion is very important."

Oh no.

"Oh, um," I started, trying not to seem too worried/bummed about this information curveball. "What religion is that?"

"Romanian Orthodox."

Okay I can work with this.

"Orthodox, nice! The OG Christians! The Catholics think they're the originals, but really y'all came first. Yay Byzantine art!"

He chuckled a chuckle I hoped meant he was impressed with my Christian/art history knowledge. "Haha. Yeah." Then continued, "So it is this thing about me, that I am not having sex. And I want you to know because I know I am the weird one here, not you. And I just want to make sure you're okay with this part before we continue . . . to like each other more."

No, no, no, no, no, no, no.

I knew it! *No regular guys are this nice! Just like Mormon, they always come with fucking religious baggage. How do they find me?! Am I, like, doing Law of Attraction wrong, where I'm focusing so much on what I DON'T want, I'm attracting that instead of what I do?*

I burst into laughter.

"Sorry. I'm not laughing *at* you! It's ... it's a long story but, let just say I toooooootally understand." He exhaled a sigh of relief, and then, just to make sure I wasn't misunderstanding this incredibly ironic situation, I asked, "Just to clarify, did you just tell me you've never had sex, you're not planning to have sex with me, and you want to make sure that's cool before we continue spending time together?"

His eyes brightened, I assume, at my ability to translate his simplicity in explaining something that's very personal and kind of a big deal. "Yes, that's it. So, it's okay?"

You mean is it okay that I was prepared to set all the boundaries with you and instead you beat me to it, and now I have to decide if I want to go on crushing on someone I can't practice sex with?

"Is it okay if we keep 'liking each others more'?"

"Da! I mean, yes."

I looked up at Zorro's irresistibly endearing, hopeful stare with zero hesitation and answered, "Da."

Zorro leaned in, and with the swagger I didn't know someone who just told me they don't have sex *because God* could, gave me a kiss so sexy, I almost forgot we were still at risk of getting eaten by a bear.

"You are nervous?" he asked.

"Yes. Very." *And not because I could get eaten by a bear.*

38

"Summer" Lovin'

Spoiler: I fell totally in love with a devout Orthodox Christian who was saving himself until marriage, because God has a sense of humor and/or I hadn't quite figured out the Law of Attraction. Jury's still out.

By the time Zorro and I had that quasi–purity talk/walk in the woods, I had fully accepted I was not an Evangelical "Godly girl." In fact, I was sort of repulsed by the kinds of dudes who wanted a Godly girl. Once I no longer shared values of putting Jesus first, being led spiritually by my spouse, saving my "hymen-busting" for post I-do's, and, like, general woman-hating that is synonymous with purity culture, I didn't want a "Godly guy." Which was good news, because they definitely did not want me.

Until I met a Romanian Orthodox man of God apparently.

I was genuinely confused by why this Godly guy would be into me, but Zorro was nothing like the Godly guys of my yesteryear.

Starting with his very grown-up, honest communication, amid language barriers, about dating intentions, Zorro blew me away with his character. He didn't initiate the talk to address marriage and make sure our "dating relationship honored his future wife, whomever she may be." He did not have this conversation to decide if *I* was pure enough for *him*.

He never even inquired about my sexual history! When I asked him later in our relationship if he cared to know he said, "No, why would I? You are a woman with a life before and it has nothing to do with me."

I hadn't done manifesting wrong! As I was starting to judge myself less negatively for my sexual behavior, so too were the men I was attracting. Law of Attraction gold star, Mattie Jo!

His character didn't stop there.

Even though he was already working 7 a.m. to 6 p.m. at the theme park, he took on an evening restaurant job so he'd have plenty of money to take back to his family in Romania. He never got more than five hours of sleep a night all summer.

He brought me back French fries every night from this restaurant because he knew my love of French fries runs deep.

I learned that he had gotten sober from alcohol in his early twenties. When I asked why, he said it was because alcohol made him a totally different person. "I want to fight everyone. I am not like this in my real life. It's not good." He attended meetings and counseling for his sobriety. He was barely old enough to drink in America and he was already self-aware enough to get sober and seek help.

One time, after a conflict we were unable to resolve right away because we were at work, he pulled me aside to say, "I know you are upset at me. But we cannot have time to talk now, so we will talk later. I know you're upset and I care." *Did you just acknowledge my feelings, validate them, and assure we'd talk about it ASAP? K, it's cool. I don't think I'm mad anymore.* Even as he was learning to improve his English, he could adequately communicate. Which then made me realize, men everywhere have zero excuse for their lack of effort in healthy communication.

He did really thoughtful things totally unprompted, like line up all his breaks with mine. Every time he did this, I was still surprised. (One time I literally gasped when I saw him come through the break room door. How embarrassing.) We each only got one day off per week, so he asked the park manager if he could have the same day off as me.

One time he even asked how to say "ass" nicely to your companion because he didn't want to say, "I like your ass." "It sounds rude to say that to someone you love, right?" What a gem.

He called me his "American Dream Girl," which is so corny to write, but at the time I not-so-secretly adored his cheesy term of endearment.

I loved that he recognized my genuine interest in people. "You are the only American who is really friends with the foreigners. You care so much about our experience here in the States." Turns out, Americans are mostly asshats to people who look and sound different from them, so I felt very protective over the international employees. Especially in the year of developing Trump fury.

In the fall, Zorro visited New York City with me for my birthday. I was getting a haircut and didn't want him to leave the salon because he didn't have cell service and I was afraid he'd get lost in Zabar's or something. After we argued a little too publicly, he finally said, "I am a man! Let me go!" After I tipped my stylist and frantically walked upstairs, hoping he hadn't died on the streets of the Upper West Side, there he was, punctually arriving with a giant bouquet of flowers.

Oh.

Later, on the top of the Empire State Building, he convinced everyone up there to sing me "Happy Birthday." Though I am no stranger to an audience, I was still very surprised and embarrassed. He comforted me with a cinematic birthday kiss once everyone had looked away.

The point is, he was really great.

Let me be clear, this isn't me saying, "Look! I did all this work on myself and God finally gifted me a boyfriend!" If I haven't said it before, here it is again loud and clear for all the single Recovering Evangelical women who really need this reminder, like, every day:

God does not provide purity collateral in the form of straight men. In her infinite majesty, God is not out here giving *straight men* as the ultimate life-on-Earth prize.

This is also not me saying, "Stay the path, Recovering Evangelical women! One day you'll fall in love and kiss on top of the Empire State Building!! Look at that self-love–turned-boyfriend!"

What it is me saying is that I think, if I hadn't done a decent amount of the personal undoing and redoing, I wouldn't have been in a place to experience the fullness of our relationship.

I could have met his remarks about his faith and morality with triggered reactions and said "Hell no" to falling in love if it didn't involve sex. Instead, I was able to acknowledge how he communicated, see his character, and also communicate back that I was cool with the boundaries (*as long as we can, like, do other stuff right?*).

I was no longer in a place where my entire value was contingent on my relationship status, where the relationship *had* to end in a longer-term future together in order to be "valid." I was able to have way more fun and learn from love without feeling so damn fragile, to experience the exceptionally honest, joyful, romantic, life-enhancing relationship Zorro was offering.

Our relationship showed me I could actually *have* a successful relationship. I needed to know I could fall in love and be in a healthy relationship with an amazing person. I also needed to validate and accept that as a totally normal thing to want to know! It didn't make me weak or less of a self-loving feminist to want to see myself in a quality, adult relationship outside my Evangelical yester-bonds.

Additionally—and incredibly ironically—falling in love with someone who chose not to engage in penetrative straight-people sex helped me further explore my personal sexual ethic.

Our season of not sex-ing gave me a clearer timeline for when I was comfortable getting physically intimate with a partner. This wasn't a hardline must-be-together-at-least-three-months kind of rule. But it helped me take time to realize how I wanted to feel with someone before getting intimate.

It helped me learn how to communicate maturely about sex, not making it awkward or weird but just matter-of-fact. And then also learning what kind of responses I was and was not okay with receiving from a potential partner once I'd communicated clearly.

I also learned a truly shocking concept, given how drilled "equally yoked" had been into my DNA: You actually don't have to hold yourself to your partner's sexual ethic. Whatever I did before I met Zorro was my business, and I absolutely did not have to report it to him or feel shame about it! I felt comfortable with Zorro because he agreed with me that my body was my business—because it was and always will be! He did not feel ownership over my body in the way the "saving yourself for your future spouse" messaging encouraged in American Evangelical men.

Also, as I had hoped, Zorro was indeed an "everything except" sex guy. Meaning, I had a lot of orgasms that summer.

Our penetration-free dynamic made me better at sex because we actually took our time through the best part! It was all about the process, not the must-get-penis-into-vagina-soon pressure.

And then it confronted me with how often I felt that pressure. I learned how different it feels to actually be on the receiving end of someone who is totally stoked to be making me feel good, not just thinking about themselves.

Our time together also confronted how much importance I put on penetrative sex as being "the thing." There are loads of other sex things besides P in the V and he was really excellent at all those other things! After that Summer, I wished Zorro could maybe tell American straight men about this foreplay-as-sex phenomenon. Then maybe culturally we could stop putting dicks on a pedestal and diminish the Orgasm Gap?[1] A girl can dream.

In other words, waiting a hot second to have a hot second with Zorro helped me further integrate and embrace my sexual identity along with my everything-else identity.

Being with Zorro taught me how to speak up for myself beyond the bedroom as well. We had discussed the religious world from which I hailed and had no desire to return. I shared how purity practices were super harmful to me in my life and in my previous relationship, so I wasn't going to allow that same mess to permeate ours.

I was so proud of myself anytime I said something that meant a lot to me but would potentially upset him. The Evangelical-ingrained "must be lovable at all costs, woman!" message still reared its ugly head in those moments. But I remembered to tell myself that being lovable to another is not nearly as important as honoring and loving myself, so up I spoke, dammit.

And of course, because Zorro was a man of emotional intelligence and character, I was always met with tenderness and understanding in these vulnerable moments.

Zorro stayed in the States for as long as he possibly could without risking deportation, but eventually we had to accept the reality that he'd have to go back to Romania. Though it broke both of us, we decided that "breaking up" was the only choice at that time.

We stayed up all night before his early-morning departure, galivanting around New York City, watching movies, eating Nathan's hot dogs, getting ticketed for jumping MTA turnstiles ...

We spent the cab ride in silence, partially because we were pissed about the tickets, partially because, what do you say right before the goodbye you really do not want to say?

We got out of the cab and stood in the Turkish Airlines terminal at JFK staring at "each others" awkwardly before I broke the silence. "Zorro, come on. Say *something*." And then, he burst into tears I didn't know grown men were capable of shedding. Especially in public.

I dug my face into his shoulder, and he held the back of my head, crying until our faces were sore.

"I love you, my American Dream Girl," he finally managed to say.

"I love you too, Zorro. So much." I really did. *So much.* "Thank you for being the angel I didn't know I needed."

And with that, we peeled ourselves apart, shared one last iconically sexy kiss, and went back to our separate lives.

Sort of.

Four months later, I found myself crying in his arms in another airport. This time, in Bucharest, Romania.

Despite having said goodbye, Zorro and I continued to speak every day. In that time apart, I did see a few other guys. And yet, I couldn't shake that I missed Zorro more and more every day. We knew our story was not over yet, so I planned a month-long Eurotrip, spending most of it with him, roaming the countryside of Romania, Slovakia, Austria, and Hungary. We had castles in the countryside of romantic Romania to visit! Polenta to try! Nine of his siblings to meet! (Yes. *Nine.*)

On the first leg of our trip, in Romania, Zorro and I stayed with another theme-park friend, Maria, in Bucharest. While making out in her parents' bed (because Romanians are incredibly hospitable despite having one-to-two-bedroom homes, so they gave us their bed and slept at the grandparents'), Zorro started to—I don't know how else to say it—prepare for penetrative sex. I stopped him, a bit panicked and very surprised, to say the least.

"What are you doing?"

"I want this, with you."

"Now?! Zorro, we are in Maria's parents' bed!"

"Oh. That's true. So, you want to wait?"

His level of casualness, given what a big decision this usually is, would have been laughable if I wasn't totally caught off guard and also ... confused.

All this time waiting, and you're just gonna strip your boxer briefs to have an official virginity-giving ceremony in your friend's parents' bed, bro?!

Then I had a quick moment to reflect on how very *not* thought out my "first time" was and decided not to judge him.

But I did need some context! Zorro had not, in all our FaceTime dates leading up to this trip, mentioned a potential loosening of the reins on this commitment that had meant so much to him in the months we'd spent basically living together in the States. Now we reside continents apart, and he wanted to start having sex? I just wanted to know where his head was. The one on his shoulders.

"I just think we should at least talk about it," I answered. "And yes, preferably not 'do it' for the first time in Maria's parents' bed."

"Okay," he replied. Again, so casual and matter-of-fact. "You are right. Let's talk on the train tomorrow."

The next day, on a long train ride from Bucharest to Cluj-Napoca, Zorro brought up the penetration in the room. "Here's what I am thinking," he began. "I love you and you are meaning everything to me. I want to share this with you. It is not less special because we are not married. And I think, who I do marry, if she is not you, will understand that."

Okay, I obviously agree but "And what about ... God?" I asked.

"What this is between us, it's so beautiful. In our time together, you are showing me that God cannot be mad at something so beautiful. So... all of love."

God cannot be mad at something so ... all of love.

Was I getting a *doing-it*-over for my previous self?

Everything I wish I would have known and implemented in my relationship with Brandon I got to bring to my relationship with Zorro. I was getting to take part in a *mutually* informed decision about loving expression based not in fear but fully in love. Look at me using my purity trauma to do the Lord's work grassroots style!

This is how it's supposed to be.

"MJ?"

"Sorry, yes. That makes total sense. But like, you're not afraid? I don't want you to live with regret and shame because of this. I only want to do it if you're very, very sure it's ... all of love."

"I am sure. For sure."

But then, after we got my feelsy feels and clear communication about his readiness out of the way, sexual-health logistics kicked in.

In the months between Zorro leaving the States and me visiting him in Europe, when we were not officially "bf/gf," I'd had sex with other dudes. Plagued by how this would turn out in my Godly guy yesterdates, I started to panic again thinking, *I don't even have any plans to actually have a future with Casual Dating Guys and now Zorro is going to hate me and think I'm a ho and I've just ruined our romantic month in Europe! Gah!*

But being honest about my activity and letting him make an informed choice was worth the risk of him hating me, so I spilled the beans about my goings-on.

"I didn't expect us to rekindle like this and I've seen other guys and we have had sex and—"

He cut me off. "MJ, I don't care about them."

Oh?

He went on. "And neither do you."

GOD, SEX, AND RICH PEOPLE

Once again, I was shocked at how unlike "godly guys" Zorro was. I use this example whenever women tell me about men who judge their sexual behavior as something that makes them "less desirable." *Ugh. Barf. Go away.* Because here is this dude who was holding himself to a level of sexual abstinence many grown men do not, and *even he* did not respond from a place of *his* insecurities and projected misogyny—because he didn't possess either of those!

He was also very confident that nothing I'd done with someone else—especially some dudes I saw improv and ate sushi with a few times—would be better than what we had. Me having sex with someone else didn't make sex between us less special. We were in love, and his decision was made. *Period.*

All the tension in my body escaped in a belly laugh. Zorro was absolutely right. I leaned in, kissed him, and rested my head on his chest for the remainder of that train ride. Excited and very nervous for what was to come (cum pun!).

Our first time together was not life changing and didn't make everything between us immediately more intense. It was just like Zorro—connected, thoughtful, romantic, and so very sweet. It was another beautiful way we got to share ourselves intimately. Also, love-making around Eastern Europe with your Eastern European–made love? How *fun.*

From Zorro telling me he wouldn't have sex with me in the woods of New Hampshire to deciding he'd like to have sex with me on his home turf in Romania and everything in between, we knew what we had was truly so ... *all of love.*

39

THE LOVE OF MY LIFE

OUR ALL-OF-LOVE LOVE WAS not minimized by distance. Zorro and I decided to stay together, officially, and make this relationship happen. Which meant, of course, we'd probably need to be on the same continent at some point in the near future.

Nearly every FaceTime was some version of troubleshooting this whole long-distance thing. I suggested him moving to New York, because, at least to me, that was the most obvious and logical move if there was one to be made. After some contemplation, he declined my suggestion. Apparently, I'd found the only Romanian in the world uninterested in a "better life" in America. By Zorro's standards, life in the States was actually not better.

"Everyone is obsessed with work," he told me. "And what about my culture? My friends and family? Where will I go to church and eat Romanian food?"

"Queens, duh." I replied. He didn't think that was funny.

"MJ, can you imagine having to leave everything you love—your home, family, language, friends—just to make money? I want to be a professional in my country, instead of a poor immigrant in another." *Fuck. I knew I shouldn't have taken him to the Ellis Island museum.*

But seriously, Zorro and I had discussed these issues at length. While he was growing up, his parents swapped months of working in Germany, Spain, and Italy to provide for him and his siblings. His two older brothers were currently working in England for as long as it took to save for a property purchase in Romania.

Many non-Americans grow up knowing they will eventually have to leave their home to make a legitimate living in a country with a better economy. Zorro did not want this for himself.

"I know I will be poorer than most Americans if I stay in Romania." He looked down, and then back to me. "But at least I will be *home*."

My heart said, "But do this very big thing for me!" but my heart also said, "*Not* doing this very big thing for me is exactly why I fell in love with you." Being so damn mature and genuinely caring more about his culture, familial relationships, and general non-capitalist values was *hawt*.

Though Zorro was able to clearly see why he wouldn't want to make this life-altering choice for himself, he still returned the request. "MJ, do you think you could come here? We can stay together while I finish my master's degree. You can teach English, and then we decide where we will live?"

My internal response was immediately: *Absolutely not*. Me going to Romania was not the same as Zorro moving to New York. At least if Zorro came to America, there would be other Romanians! We could legit move to Queens, and he could speak Romanian to other Romanians all of his days! What would there be for me in Romania? Other than castles. Lots and lots of pretty castles.

I did, however, mull over his request for quite some time, because, for starters, I really, *really* want my love story to be big and romantic and show-offy. Moving to Eastern Europe to be with the man of my dreams was more than sufficiently grandiose. And, yes, I loved him a lot or whatever.

Also, and probably more importantly, I am a midwestern, "steeped in traditional gender roles" woman, raised by two teens who were pregnant before marriage while attending a private General Baptist college. *Bring on the adversity, Universe! I will overcome for a husband!* Everything from my Evangelical path was singing praises of *Hallelujah, you'll finally be someone's—an incredible someone's!—wife! Maybe you can get married in Peleş Castle like that dumb Hallmark Christmas movie!* (You know the one.) *You did it, MJ!*

You did *it*? *Did what, exactly?*

I thought about the logistics of actually moving to Romania.

First of all, I didn't know the language. Yes, I could learn, so that wasn't *the* dealbreaker (even though it would be hard, and I'd probably be grumpy about it), so, moving on to other, bigger issues ...

I was just going to move to another country for the rest of my life to start a *marriage*? Adjusting to being a married person while also adjusting to the culture shock of another country after I had finally adjusted to the culture shock of New York City?

The only person I would really know in that country would be my husband, so I wouldn't have any life outside of him and his friends/family. Yes, I wanted a partner who was my best friend, but I didn't want them to be my *only* friend. As I was learning in my developed sense of autonomy, I didn't want a partner who was my entire world.

While Romania is a beautiful, incredibly underrated country, I would not have the acting or financial earning opportunities I had in the States. In New York, I could work for billionaires while speaking on podcasts about sexual ethics post–purity culture and audition for *Oklahoma!* all in a day.

His family is hella religious! Though I respected Zorro's faith, I didn't want to be a Christian again. I write publicly about sex and the church and how demented it all is. I knew I'd be a fish out of fucking water in Zorro's world.

Where would we live? *How* would we live? He'd be in grad school while I twiddled my thumbs in his dorm or went out to make us money tutoring English?

Then there were our conflicting timelines. Despite Zorro not being subtly woman-hatey with his religious values, he did still very much desire a traditional life. He wanted to be a dad in his twenties and raise a family close to his family, while I'd spent the last five years realizing I was not at all designed with desires for young-wife-mommydom. Yes, I did want kids at *some* point. But I wanted to act, write, frolic about New York, and enjoy overpriced cocktails for at least the next decade. Furthermore, the last adjective I could think of to describe the partnership or, idk, *life* I wanted was "traditional."

Plus, my acting and writing career were just starting to go well. My dreams so big and ambition so robust were slowly coalescing into an ever-so-faint, visible reality. What once felt like I was chasing myself in the dark, going nowhere but feeling very tired, was starting to feel *real*.

This whole moving-to-Romania-for-the-love-of-my-life thing got less romantic as I dissected the realities of what that would entail. Just as I was beginning to build a life of my own that I loved, the love of my life asked me to start building with him. Giving up your entire life to be in someone else's? Not at all romantic.

In processing this to-move-or-not-to-move-for-love decision, I started to see just how much I'd grown in those last five years in New York.

I had grown into a new woman. I had become and continued becoming a version of me with whom I really truly was enamored.

I liked my life. I *loved* my life.

So I did a thing I never in my "please love me, men!" wildest dreams thought I'd do. I told this incredible "Godly guy" that I couldn't go on being with him if it meant giving up my life.

I knew my metaphorical slab of concrete and some structural bones didn't seem like much, not yet at all impressive on the outside. But it was my home.

I was my home. And I wasn't done building her.

Despite agreeing to no longer be together officially, Zorro and I did stay in touch. Not every day, but there was still plenty of love between us.

He eventually met someone else, which I obviously knew was inevitable, but I was still devastated. He moved on from us while I danced in a chicken costume all over Florida to earn my Equity Card[1] in a musical version of *Click Clack Moo*. At the time, hopping from Motel 6 to Motel 6 on the side of highways throughout the American South just to achieve a big career milestone hardly felt worth "giving up this amazing man" for.

In time, however, I did know. I'd made the right choice. *We'd* made the right choice.

In the time since Zorro and I parted ways, I learned to integrate all my creative passions—storytelling in writing, acting, and directing—finding lots of joy, actual happiness, and personal fulfillment in my creative work. I learned my path was telling stories as an on-camera actor, as well as a writer, so I eventually left musical theater altogether.

I started saying *out loud* I would write a book. And here I am.

I got best-actress nominations at film festivals, found bicoastal and midwestern agents, met with producers all over LA and New York to work the pitch for the *God, Sex, and Rich People* series. I got publishing offers, wrote, directed, and starred in multiple short films, as well as the proof of concept for *God, Sex, and Rich People.* I starred in movies you can stream and see in theaters. I expanded my network of authors and actors, and now have a huge community of creatives I get to collaborate with all the time.

I spent months in Japan, Taiwan, the Philippines, the American Southwest, Portugal, Spain, Italy ... I moved into better, bigger, beautifully spacious apartments. I made massive strides in healing my purity culture sexual trauma by getting into sexual-trauma therapy. I started dating only really amazing, quality men.

Zorro sent me photos of his wedding day and I sent him a wedding gift. I cried tears of so many feelings, but mostly gratitude. How sweet that all these years later, this incredible human is sharing his life with me.

A few years after that, he sent me videos of his brand-new baby girl. I received those photos on the tail end of a trip I gave myself to Spain and Portugal.

Later that year, I shot a movie with Lionsgate and met my now partner while drunk swiping on Hinge in Italy.

My life was weird, wild, and wonderful.

Zorro got the life he wanted, and so did I.

Unlike how it is portrayed in Evangelical culture, the relationship I shared with Zorro taught me that falling deeply in love does not require rushing to the bullshit finish line of marriage. Furthermore, a relationship ending at all is not a failure. Love—in all its pain, vulnerability, risk, pure joy—is simply one more tactic life uses to mold us into a beautifully and continually alchemized version of ourselves.

All the pendulum swinging, from purity rings to fucking pop stars, asking hard questions about my faith, discussing those questions with my Jewish roommate, challenging my beliefs about myself and my worldview, continuing the grind of pursuing my dreams of being a professional actor (even if I didn't really know what I was doing or where I was going, only that I'd figure it out eventually), learning the City inside and out so I could creatively and resourcefully find a place to live, working for and living in the homes of rich people, relating to my body differently, changing my neural pathways from being a dick to myself to being my greatest cheerleader, so many shitty dates, auditions, nights spent alone wondering if I'd be alone forever and then shamefully eating spoonfuls of peanut butter for dinner (again) ... metaphorically belly flopping onto the pavement of this concrete jungle ... to falling very in love, God assisted me in gaining something so much greater than the Evangelical reward of a husband;

The love of *my* life.

40

RECOVERING

"A painting is never finished.
It simply stops in interesting places."

— Paul Gardner

I READ THAT QUOTE in *The Artist's Way* as I looked out over Katama Bay on Martha's Vineyard. I liked the quote, because for the last month of residing on Martha's Vineyard—babysitting for billionaires, living in their guest home, writing in the morning, auditioning, and watching beach sunsets in the evenings—I've been telling people "I think I finished my book." I say "I think" because I truly do not know.

The end of this book is really only the beginning of my story.

It is true that by the end of this book's stories, I was genuinely in a better place. I was no longer just *reacting to* life; I was engaging, reflecting, and consciously *acting in* life. My life throes didn't stop; I was just better equipped to weather them with self-assuredness, clarity, and confidence. So, while my life did get exceptionally brighter and clearer as I learned to love myself and that God didn't hate me for defining me on my own terms, things didn't necessarily get *easier*.

There is so much more that has happened within that story of Zorro and post-Zorro that radically highlighted the ongoing, minute effects of Evangelical purity culture on how I navigated life, particularly when life involved men.

In the time following my split from Zorro split, I:

- Started dating again, and was immediately date-raped

- Withstood the 2016 demise of America when Evangelicals helped elect Donald Trump as president

- Participated in the #MeToo movement

- Marched in Women's Marches

- Called Planned Parenthood to get tested after my rape, and was instead connected with a social worker, doctor, and sexual trauma therapist provided by nonprofits (This, above all, changed everything for me. I still see this therapist.)

And on that note ...

- Learned how to feel my body's twenty-plus years of held trauma

- Embraced female rage

- Figured out how to not hate men after all that, so I could get back to my IRL fucking field study and have sexual experiences that were wonderful and rewarding

- Dated for a lot of quality data

- Learned terms like "trauma responding"

- Entered my thirties

Needless to say, that's a lot of ground to cover, and I don't want to brush over the details, so I am committing another book entirely to this (s)exploration. Look out for this on your bestsellers list: *A Blueprint for*

Boning: How to Unfuck Yourself from Purity Culture and Finally Get Fucked. Or something like that.

As I've been writing this book, mentally and spiritually reentering my beginning chapter in New York, I am amazed at my resilience in those years. I marvel at my courageous curiosity that led to some answers, and my ability to feel okay about leaving some questions unanswered. I'm both proud and astonished that when I felt the weakest, I was actually so strong. And, crazily enough, I am blown away at God's goodness through it all.

I knew moving to New York would bring about a lot of change in my life—like not owning a car, the value of grocery delivery, and making way more money than I'd ever made in order to still be poor. I knew moving to New York would require unrelenting hard work, financial strain, and eating quality bagels. (Sayonara, Sara Lee!)

What I did not know was that moving to New York would force me to trailblaze new definitions of my faith, my world, my sexuality, *myself.*

I did not know that living among and working for the 1 percent, going on shitty Tinder dates, and having lots of one-night stands I can't really remember, would lead me to excavate my Evangelicalism in order to finally find my fullest, weirdo, outspoken, sexually excited, adventurous, open-to-always-learning-and-growing, untethered-by-fear, most-abundant, self. And that in doing so, I had only just begun recovering.

I call it "Recovering" Evangelical and not "Recovered" Evangelical because, much like addiction, this stuff never really goes away. I am now in my early thirties, and though I am happy to be through the murkiest trudging of my deconstruction days, I still happen upon behaviors and beliefs that stem from my Evangelical yester-ways and require self-assessing and correcting.

I have spent a decade acquiring skills that help me relate to my Jesus and purity culture trauma differently. I can identify and then navigate when a trauma response occurs. Most importantly, I've learned to not beat myself up when I still sometimes act from a place based on information I acquired in Wednesday-night youth group.

Beautifully recovering, but never fully recovered.

Our testimonies are supposed to include how we found God, but I think my testimony is how God helped me find me.

God, Sex, and Rich People: What a testimony.

FURTHER READING

I'M INCLUDING SOME SOURCES I've read and sources I've heard about on podcasts. These are from atheists, Muslims, Jewish folks, and Christians.

God: A Human History, by Reza Aslan

On Her Knees: Memoir of a Prayerful Jezebel, by Brenda Marie Davies (of God is Grey, a great YouTube channel as well!)

Jesus and John Wayne: How White Evangelicals Corrupted a Faith and Fractured a Nation, by Kristin Kobes Du Mez

A Brief Introduction to the New Testament, by Bart D. Ehrman (or anything by Bart D. Ehrman)

How The Bible Actually Works: In Which I Explain How an Ancient, Ambiguous, and Diverse Book Leads Us to Wisdom Rather Than Answers—and Why That's Great News, by Pete Enns (or anything by Pete Enns)

Searching for Sunday: Love, Leaving, and Finding the Church, by Rachel Held Evans (or anything by Rachel Held Evans)

You Are Your Own: A Reckoning with the Religious Trauma of Evangelical Christianity, by Jamie Lee Finch

Pure: Inside the Evangelical Movement That Shamed a Generation of Young Women and How I Broke Free, by Linda Kay Klein

Come As You Are by Emily Nagoski

ENDNOTES

In the Beginning

1. **The Call** is the voice of God you cannot ignore. This voice usually requests you become a full-time pastor or, worse, a full-time missionary in Africa. Every Christian dreads The Call, because it means your life will be hard and you will probably be poor. But they also love The Call, because it makes them feel spiritually superior to everyone else who claims to "love Jesus" but keeps their reliable and easy career as an accountant. *Pffft*

2. **Small Group:** A group, usually organized by age and gender, that meets weekly in a church to foster friendships within the faith, otherwise known as "fellowship." It's kind of like a Christian book club, except these people are meant to be more than just a book discussion once a week. They are meant to become your closest friends, so that if you ever start to "backslide" you will find yourself many layers of "accountability" deep in friendships that will make sure that doesn't happen. Anyway, lots of sleepovers and talking about all the sex stuff we weren't supposed to be doing with boys.

3. **Counterculture:** Doing the opposite of what the world accepts as normal or "okay." Driven by the belief that we as Christians are at war constantly with the fallen, sinful world and our own human flesh, we must live in a way that is totally different from what the culture around us deems "normal" or "okay." It is not "normal" or "okay;" it is sin.

4. **Spiritual Leading:** Must be done by a man because they are so much better at spiritualing than you, woman! They'll encourage you to get up earlier for your devotionals, start a women's small group when life is really hectic, and be better at holding sexual boundaries than you are, ya horny harlot (despite also being the gender that simply cannot control themselves and are not expected to control themselves). Spiritual leaders will make you a better Christ follower because they know better than you do. Did I mention they must be a man?

5. **Modest is Hottest:** A phrase we heard *a lot* in youth group. There were shirts, beach towels, even school binders that contained this phrase to constantly remind young women the importance of keeping our shit covered. It was always framed as us helping keep our "Christian brothers from sinning." By not accidentally looking at their Christian sisters' titties? Ok.

EVERYONE IS GOING TO HELL

1. **Left Behind:** A multimedia project about the Biblical rapture, written by Tim LaHaye and Jerry B. Jenkins. Movies produced by and starring Kirk Cameron, because obviously the only choice for an apocalyptic Christian movie hunk is the *Growing Pains* son.

2. **Kanakuk Institute:** A Biblical-studies institute offering various degrees that will equip men and women for a lifetime of ministry and Biblical knowledge. As defined by me, a really sad excuse for Biblical education based on the belief that the Bible is without error and spoken straight from God's mouth. Breeds great stars for those TLC shows we can't stop watching, mommy bloggers, and pastors who perpetuate trauma in the name of the Trinity. Give Pete Newman a Google. Not a good look.

Biblical Marriage

1. **Proverbs 31**: A passage in the Hebrew Bible Book of Proverbs with advice given by King Lemuel's mother about what makes a good king/leader, where he describes the ideal woman. As an Evangelical, the good king/leader thing was often overlooked, and we were immediately directed to obsess over the attributes that make an ideal woman in the eyes of God and man. Although these attributes include being a shrewd businesswoman, hard worker, respectful, trustworthy, compassionate, wise, worthy of celebration for being a total badass ... in Evangelical circles she was often minimized to "not focused on outward beauty but being as Godly as possible by being sexually pure, leading multiple Bible Studies, being a Christian camp counselor, and engaged by twenty-one."

2. **Equally yoked**: Based on (a single passage in the Bible) 2 Corinthians 6:14–18. The passage states that Believers should not be unequally yoked with Unbelievers. The metaphor is based on oxen pulling a plow and how they're hooked up to said plow. If the oxen are two different strengths, sizes, or if there's an ox and a donkey, they won't be able to pull the plow effectively. The Evangelical teaching is that if you and your significant other do not see God exactly the same way and pursue a relationship with God exactly the same way, you will not have a successful journey together. It will be unstable and messy, like a ram and a donkey trying to guide a plow lopsided.

3. **Chris Tomlin:** A Christian Singer-Songwriter who wrote most of the worship songs every Evangelical kid from the 1990s/2000s grew up singing. He has sold over 7 million records and *TIME* magazine claimed he may be the "most often sung artist anywhere." His songs are meant to be sung in a dimly lit room, hands in the air, eliciting a very strong emotional connection between you and Jesus, or you're probably not doing it right.

4. **Job:** A book in the Old Testament/Hebrew Bible where a man named Job, who has immense loyalty and faith in God, is used as an example of such faith by God to the Devil. But the Devil is all "Of course he's faithful; his life is easy as fuck." So, God's all "Okay then, go ahead. Test him. You'll see! He is a loyal follower!" This is all happening, I guess, without Job's knowledge. So then, with God's permission, the Devil just starts making Job's life suck. He kills everything, from his crops to his kids. I think the story ends with Job crying out, "WTF, God?" And God being all "Sometimes hard stuff happens. But look how you've persevered because you know I never left you." Then Job gets all his wealth back + more, has a bunch more children, and lives another century or something. So, I guess God and Job win the bet against the Devil. PS: I want you all to know I recalled that entire thing from memory, then looked it up, and my summary is very accurate. I told you this shit is cellular.

Pure Love

1. **Jesuits:** Of the priestly orders, the Jesuits are my favorite, followed closely by the Franciscans. I'm down with the Jesuits because of their heavy focus on being "contemplatives in action." Basically, they're hella educated and aren't "just priests." They're doctors, lawyers, teachers, scientists ... The Jesuits start schools, write loads of educational texts, and generally bring positivity into the world with all their scholarly goodness. Basically, I like the Jesuits because they're educated *and* active. It's hard to be a closed-minded asshole when you're so damn educated. The Franciscans are my second favorite because they brew beer in Brooklyn and have fun beards.

2. **Backdoor virgin:** Because of the ridiculous focus on P in the V intercourse being sex, some devout purity ring wearers would let dudes fuck them in the asshole. Of all the patriarchal benefits to purity culture, this has to be the greatest, most unfortunate one. Anyway, no one put anything in my asshole until my thirtieth birthday. But that's another book.

3. **Stumbling block:** A term based on Romans 13:14 used to describe anything that causes Christians to sin. Women are often used as examples of stumbling blocks to men in their efforts at purity. You know, if we wore a bathing suit where our navel was exposed and whatnot. That lack of belly fabric is a stumbling block. The woman wearing the lack of fabric is the stumbling block.

Curfews, Chastity, and the Great Commission

1. **Beauty is fleeting:** A reference to that Proverbs 31 bullshit. Based on verse 10, "Charm is deceptive and beauty is fleeting, but a woman who fears the Lord is to be praised." Fun fact, if you google "Beauty is fleeting verse," the first hit is a Magic Johnson tweet of the verse + photos of him and his wife. LOL! That is some strong SEO.

Missionary Position

1. https://www.bbc.com/news/world-asia-63869078#

2. **Log in your own eye:** References one of my personal favorite Jesus quotes, where he essentially tells the disciples to STFU, don't be judgy assholes, and mind your business. Matthew 7:2–4 (NIV): *For with the same judgment you pronounce, you will be judged; and with the measure you use, it will be measured to you. How can you say to your brother, 'Let me take the speck out of your eye,' while there is still a beam in your own eye?*

Spiritually Gaslit

1. **Jesus in the Garden of Gethsemane:** Matthew 26:37–39 The part of the crucifixion after the Last Supper but before Judas's betrayal where Jesus is all "This blows, God. Don't make me go through with this! But also, anything for you, Dad." Cuz daddy issues. Here's the actual quote, *"My Father, if it is possible, may this cup be taken from me. Yet not as I will, but as you will."*

Biblical Marriage, Part 2

1. **One Flesh:** Based on Genesis 2:22–24, a very specific term only used in Christian circles for sex, to make penetrative sex sound like a super-big deal. You are becoming *one body* with *one person*. Except kings be fuckin concubines like crazy in the Bible. Anyway, some friends of mine jokingly used this as the unofficial hashtag for their wedding, and I might steal it as the official hashtag for my own wedding.

New York Is My Boyfriend/Wild Love Affair

1. **BYX:** "Brothers Under Christ," a Christian fraternity on college campuses. I once went to a BYX New Year's Eve party where we drank sparkling grape juice in a bathtub. Like, we all crawled into the bathtub, fully clothed, no water, and popped open the sparkling grape juice to drink from the bottles. Totally badass.

2. **Blaspheming the Holy Spirit:** I was taught this meant rejecting God's guidance. But actually, when it's used in the Biblical context, it's the Pharisees suggesting Jesus was healing with demonic powers, not holy powers—essentially calling Jesus a liar. As in, they were literally saying the Holy Spirit isn't real and cannot heal demons, which has nothing to do with God's guidance...

V Day

1. **Bounce Your Thoughts:** A skill that Evangelical men are encouraged to implement any time they randomly (and uncontrollably!) find themselves thinking about boobs in the lighting aisle at Home Depot or something. At my church, the boys were taught to have a specific Bible verse and/or Christlike image ready to combat that lustful thought immediately by replacing it with a thought that honors the Lord. Evangelical women were not taught this skill explicitly, because obviously we would never think about boobs at Home Depot! Dicks in Midtown Manhattan (the suits!) however? Hi. Anyway, I was a horny thought-bouncer.

Baptism by *Tinder Flame*

1. **The Case For Christ:** A book investigating the factuality of Jesus as the Messiah. Even though lots of other historians, textual criticism experts, archeologists, etc. ... have done this, Christians like this particular story because it's written by an atheist skeptic who, through his investigation, becomes a Christian. Sorry to ruin the ending.

Fucking Rich People

1. ***Just Like Jesus:*** A book written by minister Max Lucado that outlines the principles Jesus lived out that we should all be implementing in our lives.

(Fuck)Boy Monsters

1. **See You at the Pole:** An event held every year (still! I thought for sure it was done away with at some point cuz it's so dumb) at schools where Christian students "profess their faith publicly" by praying around flag poles on school property. In 5th grade I went around from class to class handing out flyers and speaking about the event. Why did these teachers allow quality class time for me to do that? Google it to get the full scope of its weirdness.

Too Soon?

1. **Shame Spiral:** I recognize that, especially if you're from a purity culture centered religious background, men have shame spirals too. I'm just saying that society doesn't constantly sexualize men, and then demonize them for being sexual.

Self-Helpless

1. **(un)devotional:** If devotionals are daily connections with the Evangelical God, undevotionals are daily practices that connect you to a God and self that helps undo the view and belief of that very limited experience. For example, if devotionals are reading ***Captivating*** in the morning, an undevotional practice could be reading *The Ethical Slut*.

   Captivating: Essential reading for every Evangelical Woman. It claims to understand the desire of "every woman's heart." It's basically a very atrociously gendered, hetero perspective on what all women want—to be pursued by men. And then I think it says we have that ultimate pursuit in Jesus, who gave the greatest gift—*his life*—to show His love and commitment to us. Which, like, let's just break *that* down for a second. First of all, here's the perfect example of conflating Jesus's Godlike love with romantic love, and it's fucking weird. Didn't He die for, like, all of humanity? So, what? Are we not exclusive, *Jesus*? Secondly, I didn't ask Jesus to die for me. If a real potential human partner did this and called it "the ultimate pursuit" we'd call him a psychopath. Anyway, don't read the book; it's trash.

Abundant Life

1. **Beauty from Ashes:** Based on Isaiah 61:3, and also a famous song by Christian artist duo Shane and Shane. Translated to mean God will make something beautiful from the hard stuff. It's a beautiful concept (and song).

2. International Society for the Study of Trauma & Dissociation. Public Resources. Fact Sheet III—Trauma Related Dissociation: An Introduction

"Summer" Lovin'

1. Heterosexual women are the demographic *having the least orgasms during sex*. D. A. Frederick, H. K. S. John, J. R. Garcia, *et al.* "Differences in Orgasm Frequency Among Gay, Lesbian, Bisexual, and Heterosexual Men and Women in a U.S. National Sample." *Archives of Sexual Behavior* 47, (2018): 273–288.

The Love of My Life

1. **Theatre Actors Union.** Just means your jobs legally protect you and you sometimes (not always) get paid more than non-union work. It sort of legitimizes you as a stage actor.

To contact Mattie Jo Cowsert
for speaking engagements,
please visit mattiejocowsert.com.

Many Voices. One Message.

quoir.com.